TAMYARA BROWN

Fat Girl Vigilante

Insanity at its Finest!

Insanity at its Finest!

Tamyara Brown

Tamluestto Write

Writing my way
into your hearts & minds

INSANITY AT ITS FINEST!

For information contact;

www.tamluvs2write.com

Please Sign Up for My Email list

http://eepurl.com/buo-xH

Book and Cover design by Tamyara Brown & Pixel Studio

ISBN: 13: 978-0692525401

Library of Congress: 2015915323

First Edition: October 2015

10 9 8 7 6 5 4 3 2 1

INSANITY AT ITS FINEST!

Tamyara Brown

This book is dedicated to every woman who has been teased, broken and belittled because of the way you look. Love will never have a waist size. If you haven't heard it today, "I love you."
For those women whose innocence has been stolen and was told to keep it a secret just know someone will listen. I hear you! I believe you!

A BIRTHDAY CELEBRATION & MURDER
"I watch my mother murder my father and I didn't stop her."-

Ooh! I watch my mommy do something bad. We are supposed to be celebrating Daddy's birthday. It turns into something totally different. I'll never forget it as long as I live. We are driving for a long time. I saw a lot of different colored trees and mountains. The sky is blue, the sun is shining on my face and for some reason the air smelt like honey dew melons. In a fairytale, it's a perfect day to pick strawberries, eat lunch and fish at the lake. Daddy love to fish and I love to pick strawberries. We pass a sign that read, "Welcome to Devil's Hop yard State Park".

On the radio playing is Oran Juice Jones song, "I saw you and him walking in the rain. You were holding hands and I will never be the same."

Mama is singing the song, popping her fingers and bobbing her head. She looks at my daddy and tries to kiss him on the cheek.

Daddy jerks away from her and taps his fingers on the dashboard. He looks back at me and he starts smiling. He says, "My princess Bunny looks beautiful today."

I wore my favorite pink sundress, my pink jelly sandals, and my hair is in three long ponytails. "Thank you, Daddy." I pull at my barrette and twirl my hair around my finger.

"This is the best birthday gift, spending time with my favorite girl. I love you, Bunny."

"I love you too, Daddy. It was all Mama's idea to come out here."

"I love you, Steven and nothing is too good for you."

Daddy clenches his teeth. Mama attempts to hold his hand and he snatches it away from her. "I told you before I don't want shit to do with your ugly, fat ass. I am only here to celebrate my birthday with my daughter. That's the only way I get to see her if you tag along." He folds his arms, stares out the window and mumbles under his

INSANITY AT ITS FINEST!

breath. A black crow lands on the hood of the car. Auntie Miyama told me it meant somebody was going to die.

Mama lowers her head, smooths her hand over her dress and sucks in her lips. "Why do you continue to disrespect me in front of our daughter? I just want to love you, Steven besides it is your birthday. For once, just try to be nice to me, please."

New Edition was on the radio and Mama starts singing to Daddy,

"If you want to make things right
Love can make a way
If you want to take the time
Act like what you say, yeah

A little bit of love is all it takes
A little bit of love goes a long, long way
A little bit of love is all it takes."

She sounds so good I clap and Daddy starts laughing. His eyes go up and he says, "I can't respect you, because you don't respect yourself. Look at you, in that raggedy ass dress. Fat spilling all over the place and looking like a big bag of shit."

Mama's cheeks became red, she stops the car and parks by an old farm. She lowers her head, wipes the corner of her eyes and fidgets in her seat. Daddy continues talking. "What the hell was on my mind marrying you? It must have been because of the way you sing. It damn sure ain't your looks!"

"I'm just trying to make you happy, Steven. I'm trying to get you to love me again, but you keep insulting me in front of our daughter." She holds on to the steering wheel and starts shaking.

"You give me a reason to insult your ugly ass. I told you from the get-go, I only want to spend time with my daughter anyways. I don't want anything to do with you so stop singing and talking to me."

He spits out the window. Mama pulls this long knife from the side of the seat then she raises her hand high. Daddy turns his head and looks at her. My eyes got big. My heart is beating fast, she stuck the knife in his shoulder. She starts cutting and hitting him in the face. Daddy's blood started squirting out all over the seats, the dashboard

INSANITY AT ITS FINEST!

and even in my face, His body fell over and he lets out a loud scream.
I look at daddy. He was all bloody and his nose is crooked. Mama
got out of the car and open the door on daddy's side. I scream and
cover my face. Mama screams,
"Shut up, Michelle or you will be next."
I put my hands over my mouth. The whole time Daddy is looking at
me. I wanted to help him, but I'm scared. Mama didn't look like
mama. Her green eyes changed shape like a cat. Her skin is almost
red and hair is sticking up everywhere. Mommy pulls down her
panties and then she pees all over him.
"Now see what you made me do? You have awakened the beast, I
pleaded with you to treat me with respect and treat me like a wife.
I'm sorry, I didn't want to hurt you. I just wanted to have a nice time
and celebrate your day, with our daughter. She laughs and said, "a,
isn't this what an ugly, fat ass beast does? Pees wherever they want to
and mark their territory? You are mine. It's just sad I had to take a
piss, for you to realize it."
She pulls up her panties. She stares at him for a minute, then started
rocking side to side singing, "Is this the End?"

*"Is this the end? It seems to me you want to be free. You use to be mine when the
chips were down."*
I follow her as she drags daddy by his feet. His body is covered in
animal poop, hay, and dirt. I hung my head down and he looks at
me. The barn is like the ones you see on T.V. It was hay all over the
place. It was a mess and it had a whole in the roof. Mama told me to
open the door, it squeaks.
A rusty folding chair sat in the middle of the barn and she throws
him into it. She wraps the yellow rope around his body, she giggles as
he screams for help. Daddy is too weak to run to save his own life,
his left eye is swollen shut, his bone sticking out of his shoulder and
blood running down his body. He is breathing loud, gasping for air
and he finds the strength to say,
"Help, daddy please get someone."
I stood there, I couldn't move if I wanted to. I was froze.
"I love you, Bunny. It's okay, I know you're scared!"
Sweat drips from my forehead, my clothes damp from tears, urine
and the smell of animal poop in the air burns my nose. Daddy's
INSANITY AT ITS FINEST!

blood falls in my mouth and in my eyes. Mama's green eyes glow in the sun and she runs her tongue across her teeth. She took the red gas can and pours it all over him. She didn't speak, her green eyes turn red and she keeps singing the Happy Birthday song.

My face covered in tears and blood. Mommy stood there and asks him,

"Do you love me?"

"It's been over for us a long time. You know why, Pat. You are an evil fat Bitch. I love my daughter, but I will never love you for doing this to my baby. So you going to just kill me in front of her and mess her up?"

She laughs and looks over at me.

"Yes, I'm teaching her something important. You made a conscious decision to not love me. I deserve to be treated like a wife should. This is your choice, not mine to be killed by me in front of our daughter."

"No, you know why. You did some foul shit." He's still breathing hard, sweat, blood, and poop drops off of him.

She cuts him off. "You fucked my best friend and made a baby with her. Just admit it. I promise I'm not going to be mad anymore. I just want the truth." She put her hand behind her back. She starting going around the chair every so often looking at me and then him.

"I did it, okay. I made a mistake and I did a lot of things to hurt you. I am guilty of messing with Camilla. Yes, Nya is my daughter. Please, don't kill me in front of our daughter, I'm begging you."

She lowers her head, her hand trembles, she digs her feet into the dirt, and begins singing,

"Mama told me one day it was going to happen, but she never told me when. You told me it would happen when I was much older I wish it would have happened then."

"You have secrets, you lied and no matter what you say she will always be my daughter. You fucked my.... Ugh."

She kicks him in the face, smacks him with the gas can and then kisses him in the mouth. I look at Mama and then she looks at me. A single tear runs down her face. I'm trembling, my teeth chattering.

INSANITY AT ITS FINEST!

It's so hot but I am freezing. I am watching a scary movie starring my Mama and Daddy. She took the back of her hand and wipes her tear. She picks up the gasoline can and pours the rest all over him. I want to stop her, at least say,

"Mommy don't hurt my Daddy, no more."

I just cried like a baby. I try to cover my eyes, but she smacks my hand from my face. She makes me watch. I can't believe what I've seen. "Don't you dare cover your eyes I'm teaching you something, Chile."

She bent down in front of my Daddy holding his ding-a-ling in her hand. She smiles at him and said,

"All I ever wanted you to do was love me the way I love you. Happy Birthday, Honey and rest in peace".

Mama cuts off a piece of his ding-dinge screams. The cows surrounding the barn to moo. I watch as she picks it up, kisses it and put it in her pocket.

I cover my mouth so I won't scream again. Mommy is scary and I don't want to be next.

She said to me, "As long you're fat no man will ever love you. It's why after today I will work hard to lose the weight, take back my control. I vow no man or woman will ever again get away with hurting me." Her eyes got big, and she says,

"Michelle, don't you ever let anyone get away with making you feel worthless and let them live to see another day. You hear me, Chile? If you do, I will kill you myself? If anyone asks about your daddy you better say you haven't seen or heard from him. I'll roast you like the pig you are."

"Yes, Ma'am" I whimper.

"Now tell your Daddy Happy Birthday, goodbye and I love you. After I kill your father, I'll clean you up, take you to dinner and have a nice ice cream sundae for dessert."

I shook my head. He was dying.

Mommy told me to leave the barn. I walk to the door and turn around. I see daddy whole body in orange and flames. He is screaming so loud. Mommy walks toward me and takes my hand. We walk out the barn and to the car. "Don't look back. It is over the old me. Everyone who ever hurt me will feel the wrath of Fat Girl Vigilante."

INSANITY AT ITS FINEST!

Tamyara Brown

INSANITY AT ITS FINEST!

SPLIT DECISIONS OF MURDER

Listening to Rihanna's song "Take a Bow" while staring at my ex Markel King's picture. I sling his picture in the fireplace and watch it burn like he let our love. I stand up, look in the mirror and I admire my new body. My thighs are thinner and I can wear skinny jeans. My stomach is flatter and I can wear a tight dress. A hundred pounds lighter from my once three hundred and twenty-five-pound frame. The men who wouldn't give me a second look are trying to get with me. I am not interested until I put my ex to sleep by death. I've been so eager to watch this smug muthafucka die all the pain he cause now it is time to pay back. I've woke up in a full orgasm from seeing his dead body burned to a crisp. It will be my honor to serve his nuts to his wife on a platter. Tonight, after I murder him I will kneel and ask God to forgive me for my sins. I let his indiscretions steal my sleep, nestle in my memory and his harsh words eat at my heart. He has to be punished.

When I was twelve years old my Mama said, "Never let a man get away with hurting you and live to tell about it."

I never took it to heart until today. I sniff his shirt and inhale the scent of Armani Blue cologne. I slide it on my body and for the first time in a year it fits me. I take it off cut it up in shreds like he did our heart. Michelle still loves him and I despise him. She wants him breathing and I want him dead. I lay on my back and do fifty sits up and side crunches. Sweat drips in my eyes, my belly burns from the muscles being overworked. I stand up stretch each part of my body. I walk to the bathroom, strip off my clothing and jump in the shower. The cold water hits my skin. I pour a handful of sea salt in my hand rub it all over our skin and try to scrub Ms. Goody Two shoes Michelle away so I can rule. I hear her voice in my head calling my name begging me to give Mr. Markel another chance.

INSANITY AT ITS FINEST!

"Shut the fuck up, Michelle. It is over and we agreed he dies on his birthday."

"Just give him one more chance, please." I bang the palm of my hands against my head to silence her but she becomes louder.

"He does love us, remember he gave a place to stay and bought a lot of food."

"So I am supposed to forgive a nigger who kept us fat and unhappy. He never loved us and all we were was his whores. He is going to die end of discussion."

I step out of the shower, the air from the vent causing small goose bumps to rise as I dry off. I rub organic coconut oil on my skin. I brush my teeth with baking soda and peroxide. Spray on my pulse, my neck and in between my legs with Mama's special perfume. Everything I put on is the color green from my panties to my green timberland boots. Mommy always said big girls should at least dress nice. I lick my lips laced with raspberry seduction. My skin is cinnamon brown; my eyes the color of money and my micro braids are fire engine red. I stare in the mirror and I feel powerful. Tonight justice is going to be served. I can end the nightmares he caused in my life. The reflection of me in the mirror is a woman with two souls mine and Michelle. She is weak and afraid and me I feel like I am the most powerful Bitch in Buffalo.

For days, I stalked and followed him like the hunter's does their prey. I watch his coming and goings. I ate at the same restaurants, switched up my voice and made sure I could talk to him. I pretended to be potential buyers, realtors and even had sex chats with him as Laura on the chat line. His silly ass wife even hired me to be their housekeeper and clean their house. He didn't remember me and all the moments we shared. How could he forget me? Even with the weight lost he should remember me, right?

I tied up Michelle, threw her in the back of my mind because nobody fucks with us. Nobody! The ultimate payback on this day of his birth would also mark the day of his death. This is also the same day he kicked us out in the dead of night in the freezing cold. After hours of sexing and sucking his toddler dick he would discard us like a dirty tampon. This smug mutherfucka beat our unborn child out of us.

INSANITY AT ITS FINEST!

He stole someone to love us- our baby. I treated him like a King and he treated me like a crack whore. The days he beat on us and then sexed us until our body ached. How could that meek Bitch Michelle let him get away with that? How could she be so stupid? Every dog has his day and Markel has earned his. I promise before he dies he will suffer.

I pack my tools of the trade pink dildo, duct tape, lighter, hunter's knife and gasoline tin. I put it in the backseat of my car. I pull my hood down and scrape the snow off the car. I jump in my car and set the mood for killing. I throw on some inspiration music 8ball and MJG, *"You don't want Drama."*

I drive down East Delavan until I reach Olympic Avenue. I make a sharp left, rows of houses, piles of snow pushed to curb while the wind blows it into the streets. I've set up an appointment to view one of his apartments. Markel became inspired to personally show me the apartment. When I sent him an email with a picture of myself in a green thong and green heels. His weakness for a curvaceous and plus size women showed when he emailed me back with a date and a time to meet him. He owns over 50 rental properties on the East and West Side of Buffalo, N.Y. His life is all about the money, pussy, power, and respect.

He believes that a black man with college degrees, no prison record and being a multi-millionaire made him invincible at least in his mind. He lives, breathes and drinks having his dick sucked while counting his money. It is his breakfast for champions and his aphrodisiac.

His prime tenants are the ones who were are homeless and in need of a place to stay. He sends his managers to local shelters to scout out tenants. He does this for two reasons, one he looks like a hero saving the day for the less fortunate and two, he's guaranteed to receive his rent from the Department of Social Services and Section Eight. He makes sure each apartment is met up to code and half ass decent to live in. He is considered to be the pillar of the community, a real humanitarian that saves the lives of the poor and needy. Awarded for being a savior and a womanizing philanthropist.

Yet, in reality he only cares about himself and the paper with dead presidents. You fuck around and not have his rent he's throwing you in the streets. If you get flip with your lips he'll hire his goons to

INSANITY AT ITS FINEST!

whup your ass. Everything Markel ever did was about business and satisfying his desires. He has fat women secrets and desires. For over two years, Michelle and I have been his biggest one. We did as he commanded and nothing we did could ever make him love us.

We fell for every lie, every game and became so damn drunk off his toddler magic stick. He reminded Michelle and me every day of all our shortcomings and our failure for being fat. That's all we ever had going for us was the good sex we gave to him. We turned him on, but as soon as he released his cum he became turned off. The feeling was immediately gone. We became his lust factor and in the same token his personal downfall.

Our foolish heart was playing tricks on our mind that he could, in fact, love us. We never saw the truth until he put our asses out in the cold. We were so overfilled with illusions we never took the chance to listen to the truth. Some men can make a lie so beautiful, make it so real that you soak it up and absorb it. The truth is ugly especially when it comes to love. We cried about it, we ate until we were a size twenty-six and almost killed ourselves over this smug muthafucka. We were the victim but no more.

That's the past and opportunity has presented itself to end a chapter to this story of being his whore. Markel steps out of his Mercedes Benz wearing a long black Cashmere coat, a Grey Armani Suit, shirt to match and the scent of Gucci Black cologne. His tall frame of six feet four inches, his deep chocolate skin and long wavy hair pulled into a ponytail. Markel chisel jaw. The cleft in his chin and dark complexion makes him an attractive man. I step out of my car, a small smile appears, and he licks his lips and rubs his hands together. "You look good. You must not be from Buffalo. I have never seen you around here before. Where you from New York City?"

I pinch my lips together, I feel a tightness in my stomach and bare my teeth in my lips.

"I'm from Brooklyn." I rub the back of my neck and poke my tongue in my cheek. He doesn't remember me at all. Am I that unforgettable? I think.

"What brings you to Buffalo?"

INSANITY AT ITS FINEST!

"A fresh start on life, find a good man to help me get over the old one."

"I might be able to help you if you suck my dick right. I could give you this apartment for free and take real good care of you. Just as long as you let me beat the pussy up whenever and however I want." He adjusted his watch, blows air into his hands and pulls the scarf up to his face. He takes the shovel and clears the doorway of snow that has piled up.

"Fucking stupid worker I have to stop hiring crackheads to work for me." He puts the shovel on the side of the house. He fiddles with the ring of keys until he finds the right one. He opens the door, and I follow him in the apartment. He closes the door behind me. I sit down my duffel bag next to the rusted pipe. The apartment has the same tacky beige rugs, the drab yellow paint and light fixtures he gets wholesale. The scent of fresh paint lingers in the air. He has Venetian blinds in the windows the color of beige. I extend my hand to him and softly speak.

"Mr. King, I am so glad you took the time out of your busy schedule to let me view the apartment. My, you are one handsome man." He grins showing the gap in his teeth.

"Of course I am. I've never fallen short of being the finest man in Buffalo. I don't like small talk my time is valuable. Do you want to look around or let me fuck the shit out of you? I rather do both because you are one pretty bitch." I wink at him and pull my hand away.

"I like a take charge kind of man." He leans against the wall, folds his arms and crosses his legs.

"I don't have to chase pussy it comes running after me. I'm the man you've dreamed about all your life. Be grateful that you are in my presence."

He walks close to me and pushes his full erection on my butt. I slide my hand down his chest and grab his bulge, squeeze it enough that it causes a mixture of pain and pleasure. I put my mouth near his ear and whisper softly,

"Take off your clothes, Big Daddy!"

"Bitch, I don't follow orders I give them. You strip me naked and bow before me I'm the King and you're the peasant."

I wink at him, take a bow and reply,

INSANITY AT ITS FINEST!

"You're wish is my command."

I trace small kisses down his back, wrap my hands around his waist and unfasten his buckle. I grab the heavy metal pipe place it in my hand and hide it behind my back. I take my other hand begin to massage his erection and squeeze it until he lets out a yelp. I continue until I feel the sticky film of his pre-cum drips down on my hands. His eyes are close, his lips in an O formation.

"Bitch, come around here and suck my dick and you better not use your teeth.

"Okay, Daddy."

I grab the pipe and hit him in the back of the head three times until blood soaks his hair. He falls to the floor tripping over his clothes, I kick him, lick his lips and pull his head back. I shove the pipe up his ass. He howls like a wolf to the moon blood. As I pull it out shit shoots out his ass. I hit him in the back of his neck multiple times. He is semi- conscious as I duct tape him to the chair. He gathers the strength to say, "What do you want?"

"I want revenge, Markel."

"For what I have done nothing to you, Bitch."

He spits at me and I kick him in the face. I backhand him until his nose is bleeding. I bend down and pull out the dildo stuff it down his throat. He gags and tries to spit it out so I shove it farther down his throat. He spits it out again. His eyes widen. Markel muscles and veins straining through his skin. He gags, spittle building up at the corners of his mouth. He breathing is labored and he coughs to clear the blood out of his throat.

"Markel, do you know who am I?"

"I don't know who you are. I've never met you and if you think you're getting my money you might as well kill me now."

"That's exactly is the plan to murder your smug ass. Take my knife plunge in and out your ass until I feel satisfied. After that set you on fire and smell your flesh burn."

His skin loses it color, the tendons in his neck are standing out and his pulse is visible. He stutters and lowers his voice,

"Lady, I will do whatever the fuck you want. Let's be rational about this I don't even know you. We can settle this in a rational manner."

INSANITY AT ITS FINEST!

I pick up the canister and pour the gasoline all over his body. He shivers and he whimpers.

"You know all of this is out of love and hate. Silly man, forever we could have been together but you opted to be killed. It is all so simple just to love Michelle and me."

"Who is Michelle? I don't know who you are talking about?"

I pick up the dildo smack the shit out of him with it and stuff it in his mouth again. I move it in out of his mouth. Come on now you have to remember me? Look, I'll make a deal if you remember me I won't cut your dick off and feed it to the pit bull across the street? I promise a crazy Bitch scout's honor."

I sound like an eight-year-old girl. For a moment I think he's enjoying this as much as I am until I see the tears in his eyes. Snot is running down his face and his eyes are bloodshot red. I remove the dildo he vomits on the floor.

"Lady, I'm not the man you're looking for. You are one crazy..."

I cut him off by running my knife across his dick detaching the head of it. I giggle at his screams, the blood splatters on the floor and the ceiling. Oh, what a beautiful waterfall of blood pour from his dick.

"A promise is a promise, Markel. Do you remember saying that to me?"

His eyes are open wide, He is squealing in agony to the point his body is trembling.

"Let me refresh your memory of who the fuck I am. I'm the woman you put out in sub -below zero weather naked. The woman you beat the fuck out of and humiliated. I'm that bitch that wasn't good enough to have your baby. Is your memory refreshed now? In fact, I'm glad you don't remember me because it will be easier to fry your ass like a piece of chicken. Happy Birthday and Rest in Peace with our baby."

I pull the lighter out click it twice and turn his body into an inferno. I walk away without looking back. His screams are deafening. I look at the head of his dick in my hand roll it in between my fingers as blood drips between my fingers. Who said revenge isn't better served warm? Mine is anyway.

INSANITY AT ITS FINEST!

FLASHBACK- MEMORIES LAST FOREVER.
November 14, 2007

Markel is in the bathroom washing his dick off again after we had sex. He makes me feel like I am nasty and dirty. I look at my body in the full-length mirror it is disgusting. I want to vomit the way my stomach protrudes, the stress marks and love handles. My fat thighs, my double chin, and my complexion. He walks out and then smacks me in the mouth and then spits on me. He screams,

"Didn't I tell you to cover up your nasty ass body?"

He removes his belt and runs towards me and begins beating me with the belt. The beep of the fire detector, the sound of heat coming on and Ms. Velma playing old Motown songs drown out my screams.

After he is finished I put on my clothes. I try not to look at him as I dress. I don't want to anger him again. He fixes his pants, puts on his coat and hat.

"Your run of living here and sucking my dick is over. You're terminated and so is your lease. You have twenty-four hours to remove your shit from my home. If I come back and you're here I will throw your fat ass in the street." I swallow hard as the tears are running down my face.

"Markel, where am I going to live? I'll do anything please don't put me in the street."

"You fat disgusting bitch what can you do for me? You don't have shit and you're weak. You're worthless to yourself and society. I mean you truly got jokes. Does something for me? Fat Bitch, please." He laughs.

Hours of crying, I finally fall asleep and I hear a banging on the door. Two men, the size of wrestlers grab me my feet, and to the floor. Markel stands over me and folds his arms.

"A promise is a promise."

INSANITY AT ITS FINEST!

Is all I hear him say as he rips off my nightgown? His hire goons all point and laughs at how fat I am.

"Throw this Bitch in the street like the trash she is."

They drag me down the porch stairs. Snow is covering me body. I am trembling. My fingers, feet, and body are numb. He stands by me kicks me in the stomach over and over again.

"Willie and Jack kick her right in the gut. I want to make sure the baby she is carrying. I want it dead."

"Oh yeah, great job sucking my dick. I told your fat ass to get on birth control you didn't do it. I hope I beat the baby out of it. I don't want any ugly ass baby from you."

I laid on the cold concrete hoping I froze to death. The cramps rip through my stomach, the sound of sirens and there I know I lost my baby.

In losing sometimes, there's a win. I lost our baby and my soul. I lost my soul that was hidden under the layers of fat. I have been the outcast and the butt of fat jokes. The frozen pavement on my naked body reminded me that I would never be loved by a man. I was never going to have the privilege of being a wife if I held on to the weight. Out of all that Markel taught me a valuable lesson that I would never measure up as long as I am a three hundred pound woman.

INSANITY AT ITS FINEST!

WHEN A WOMEN'S FED UP

I watch as the house is engulfed in flames. I am fed up with these dudes. I sit while the police cars and the fire truck surround the house with yellow tape blocking off the street. The sirens, the sound of water and glass breaking as they contain the blaze. R. Kelly's "When a woman's fed up" is playing.

The night air is frigid and full of smoke, people standing in the street and watching from their windows. I see Markel's wife Tucker run up to the building wearing a full-length mink coat. She screams, "My husband is missing. He might be in there I've been calling his cell and he isn't answering. "

She is distraught her beloved money machine is missing. She is so full of shit falling to the ground. This bitch is fake pretending to be concerned about her husband. I'm laughing hysterically at how she's performing. This skank is happier than a faggot in boys' town. She has a lot to inherit all of his money and properties.

He has one son by another woman who lives in California who he has paid well to stay away. Her prenuptial agreement would leave her a millionaire and a home paid for. She has the body, the beauty and damn near white complexion his perfect trophy wife. She is all in her feelings about a man she never loved. She was paid well for being pretty and making him look good.

I'm still holding the head of his dick, his blood on my hand which reminds me I need to keep a promise. I step out of my car and walk over to the pit bull and feed it to him. The dog licks the blood off it and then chews on it. I step back in startup my engine and pull off. I pull into my driveway. I walk in and strip naked throw all of my clothes into a bag. I step in the shower and find myself weeping. My tears are running like the water in the shower. I'm not crying about the crime I committed. Shit, in actually a motherfucker like him, deserves to die. Too many men get away with being a liar, cheating, and disgraceful individuals.

INSANITY AT ITS FINEST!

Millions of men cheat, misuse and fuck over women especially us fat girls. They walk on this earth getting millions of other victims. They fuck us without lube emotionally and physically. They go home to their wives, their girlfriends and in some cases boyfriends. What gets me the most is in today's society it is okay. No guilt, no conscience or care for us fat girls. It is a society of men plotting to destroy the next big woman.

Some of us big girls are filled with his cum and empty promises. They run game on how much they love us to death. We all sitting gullible like Michelle believing in fairy tales only designed for Disney. After all the years of paying their bills and putting them through college, promoting his career or sending him commissary while he does his bid.

Now this Negro is brand-new and Mr. Hotshot. He's no longer the pitiful unpaid ass Negro he was while eating the food you bought. Sleeping in the bed you made and wearing the clothes you bought his sorry ass. Now that he is brand new, rich and famous. He is now successful, but you no longer fit in his equation. All of sudden you're not skinny enough, you're not pretty enough or light enough. So he leaves you with a "Dear Janet" letter and the bad feeling you're not qualified to have the man you was riding and dying for. He terminates his love and moves on to the next one.

You gave up your hopes and dreams just so he could achieve his, now you feel stupid. The feeling of knowing that you're playing yourself and now he's evaporated into thin air. So you turn to food, to drugs and whatever else just so you can self-destruct. You don't care how you look or how you feel. In fact, you're numb because you've given him your feelings a long time ago.

You go by his house screaming and yelling ready to fight the trick he chose over you. You're pleading for the man you love to just stay. He can't hear you over the moans of the woman who let's just keep it real is much prettier, smarter and sexier than you are. Even if she is uglier than you are. Now you feel worse because he chose her over you. Some of us allow history to repeat itself falling into the same pattern. Loving all the wrong men because in this field of weeds there's not one rare flower willing to love a big girl.

Some of us work, have beauty and brains, but now we are angry at the world because still they don't accept our bodies. We're bitter and

INSANITY AT ITS FINEST!

mistreat the good men because of the dirt all the bad men have done to us. C.S.I don't have shit on how we investigate our men we are searching his drawers down to his socks, smelling his dick, checking for pussy hairs and female's secretions. Our distrust will eventually run him away into the arms of another woman. All because our self - esteem is low and the next man has damaged our souls.

Oh, some of us have babies just to keep him. Even though he has made it clear he doesn't want nothing to do with you. He denies he's the father. Now Child Support Enforcement steps in or Maury Povich and proves that what he called fiction is now a fact. He is the father. So after he's tired of "being raped" by the weekly support payments. He decides to quit his job so he doesn't have to hold up to his legal obligations. He has once again took a big shit on you and your babies.

He runs your heart through the shredder. So now you're not supposed to be angry. You're supposed to just forgive and forget. Write his disrespect and get over it.

No man wants a woman with a house full of another man's babies. He doesn't want any of your baggage and the extra weight of your body you carry. So your spirit is no longer just wounded it's dead. Some of you take it out on the kids beating and cursing at them like it is their fault you chose the wrong man. We preach to our daughters there aren't no good men around. We teach our sons to be players and pimps. The cycle is a rotation of a family dynamics broken. You're so miserable you can't even love. You watch him walk by taking care of children that aren't his while you struggle to make ends meet. It is another arrow in the heart because it a constant reminder of how you could have done better.

Some of them beat on you and when you get the courage to tell your nothing but the lying bitch. Tell Myspace and the world you're lying on them just so you can get a welfare check. Tell me sisters how many of you been there? Are there or right around the corner from it?

 Mama's right when she said enough is enough. When she said it's time to wipe our tears and take back our lives. We make them pay for

INSANITY AT ITS FINEST!

not marrying us. For treating us like the scum of the earth. Ladies, it times to get back our lives. That's why I lost the weight that's why I got rid of Michelle for the night. She'd never had the heart to kill Markel King. Once I step out of the shower she will reappear until it is time for me to kill again!

INSANITY AT ITS FINEST!

PAYBACK FOR BREAKING CODE 0071

"Camilla, girl you still can cook your ass off. This peach pie is off the chain." I dip my fingers in the whipped cream and lick it off.

She is soaking wet from the gasoline I pour all over her. Her chubby face swollen from me dishing out a major whooping to her ass for breaking code 0071. She has put on a lot of weight and looks quite pitiful to me. Camilla used to have a beautiful body like Beyoncé. She was mixed with Black and Korean. That could be my just desserts that I am a perfect size six and look better than her. I came here on a mission to get justification for the indiscretion against me. She duct tape and tied like a hog to the chair.

"Why are you doing this to me? I have jewelry and money upstairs just please don't kill me."

Her home is exquisitely decorated with the finest appliances. Her kitchen is red and black with appliances to match. Clean, photos of her cooking in the kitchen.

I finish the last bite of the pie and lick the back of the fork, walk up to her and smack her in the face with the plate.

"Boo, I don't want your possessions and money. All I want is the sweet satisfaction of seeing you die. That's it, sweetie."

I cut another slice of pie so way against my diet, but I have to admit this is some damn good pie. I eat slowly and savor the flavor, close my eyes and let the fat girl taste buds come alive. I get up and put in the video I recorded two weeks earlier.

"Who are you?"

I press play and it is Nicholas performing oral sex on me in their bed.

"You still don't know who I am, booby cat? That's sweet and sucks the hell for you. If you had the courtesy to remember me I might have been merciful on your soul. I mean you really don't remember me? Well, for one in the video playing I'm the bitch fucking your husband. Don't I look good, girl? I'm in total awe of how he uses his tongue and how good I look. Did he ever do that to you? Of course

INSANITY AT ITS FINEST!

he has but anyway, sweetie. Watch how I cum in his mouth. Damn, now that dude right there can drink my pussy juice anytime. His tongue action is phenomenal. Good choice in marrying him."

I taunt her and poke out my lips.

"Are you mad, Camilla?"

"You trifling whore you come in my house and fuck my husband. How dare you?"

"How dare I? Let me tell you how dare I, Bitch? Payback's a motherfucker isn't it?"

"I don't remember you at all. You want my husband you can have him. I'm not dying over no man"

"I know you don't remember me. I was hundred and seventy- five pounds heavier. My spirit broken and I look like shit. It's me, Sweetie Patricia Sargent. Or as you call me a fat green eyed beast. The one who had your back? The one who helped you through college and wrote your papers. I was there for you."

"I let you stay in my house when Steven put you out. I did a lot for you too, Michelle. Why kill me over your ex-husband?"

She did help me but I helped her too. I did shit for her, babysat her sons, and cleaned her house from top to bottom. I stuck by her when she had surgery. When none of those bullshit friends wasn't there I was. I was there when Vicki tried to beat her ass and I beat her ass.

"You did including fucking my husband and talking about me behind my back. You know the one you foolishly keep saying is Nicholas. Now wait before I go any further look how your husband is fucking me good. Did you see how he was stroking my pussy from the window to the floor? Just beautiful how he shot cum on my ass."

I flip off the video and throw the remote at her. I take a deep breath to finish my conversation.

"I was your friend even when no one wanted to be around your crazy stink ass. You have always been jealous of me."

You know what I love about this conceited Bitch she always wrote a check with her mouth she couldn't cash.

"Jealousy. That word is a dangerous word to say to a Psychotic Bitch like me. Today isn't about your feelings. It is about justification."

INSANITY AT ITS FINEST!

"Like I said, you hate that you could never be me. You are fat, you are ugly and ain't nobody like you but me. Yeah, you might have lost the weight but I fucked your man in your bed. And you still ugly."

"It is time to clear the air but before I do let me wash this plate out." I go to the kitchen sink and wash out her plate. I take the fork and stab her in the face and rip out her eye. Blood runs down her throat and her eye dangles on her cheek. She screams.

"Aww, poor baby you just lost your eyeball. You're right back then I might have stunk. I might have been obese but jealous of you never." She screams,

"Please, just listen to me. Please, hear me out."

She exhales and sniffles. She groans and blood runs from the sides of her lips, her eye bobs up and down on her face. I spread my legs, place my face on my hands.

"I'm listening." She sobs and clears her throat.

"I messed up and you know Steven never loved you. How many times did he wish you dead? I'm sorry but let this go and move on. I'm pleading for you to forgive me."

I stand up and walk close push the chair and it topples over.

"Forgive you let bygones be bygones. Bitch, are you serious or delirious? You fucked my husband, you take everything away from me that meant something and you want me to forgive you. Now who's the lunatic?"

Flashbacks of every nasty word he said to me playback. My anger is mixed with adrenaline. His words penetrated me in the ass every time he spoke of how I would never measure up to Ms. Camilla Wright in his eyes. I continue my speech,

"Before I lullaby your ass and send you to hell. I need to get this pain off my chest. Steven, reminded me for five years how you are prettier than me, that I should be more like you, have a cleaner house like you and most of all be thin like you. I was the dummy fat bitch. I was the underdog. I was so lost and you played on that like everyone else. All I wanted is a best friend and I loved you. Do you know how that feels to be last on everyone's list? Do you know what it is to love a man and he doesn't love you back? Huh? Of course not because you are Ms. Perfect. You remember behind my back you talked about me

INSANITY AT ITS FINEST!

but in my face you were my friend. I was the butt of your fat jokes. I heard you laughing with Lyric about how I look like a green eye gorilla. It is okay now. I'm no longer that Fat ass woman you talked about. The joke is on you."

I pull her down the stairs by her hair making sure her face hits each step. The sound of her bones breaking is sweet music to my ears. All of the anger I held in for years is erupting like lava. My hands cover in black latex gloves I reach for the bat in the corner and begin to beat her in the head.

"I hate you, Bitch. This is for taking my husband away from me. This is for humiliating me. This is for making me cry and betraying me."

The bat cracks in half her blood splashed all over my face.

Her brain matter oozing out of her ears. Her eye out of her socket and her nose smashed in her face. I take my pink dildo and stick it in her mouth. I shove it down her throat. I swear that isn't enough for me so I pour more gasoline on the stairs of the basement all the way to the Gas stove. I take the videotape out of the VCR. Turn on the stove knowing the flames, the slam of the door and the gas valve I broke would turn her happy home into an inferno. Tick! Tick! Tick and as soon as the door closes and I take seventeen steps. BOOM! I see the door I painted my name Fat Girl Vigilante fly in the middle of the street and flames are illuminating the sky.

I begin to sing, "Happy Birthday Camilla, Happy Birthday Camilla. Happy Birthday to you! Happy Birthday to you!"

I skip down Olean Street and I get into my car. The night air is filled with smoke and the sounds of sirens. I time everything perfectly. The freight train that is a block way comes at 3:45 a.m. is blocking them from saving the house and Camilla.

I am a scorned woman seeking revenge on all those who have hurt me. I am angry, bitter and derange which may qualify me as a sociopath. The anger has lived within me since I was nine years old. It's like poisonous cancer that has ravaged my body and now my soul. What motives me is the fact when I was fat, my heart stuck on stupid and believing folks was my friend they chopped and screwed me. Something in me broke and it was that day I had no issues with murdering someone. I truly don't give a fuck anymore. I kill without a conscious. I killed my own Mama to get my point across.

INSANITY AT ITS FINEST!

Shit, I want to be caught because then I can recruit and train more female warriors to stop a MOFO from ever placing her in the position to be the underdog.

My motives are not all bad though. I want to save our Black women from being what I once was. My goal is to help women come back to what they have always been beautiful Queens. We who live in the city ghettos are committing genocide on ourselves.

We're overeating, we are on drugs and we're depressed. More and more of our women are living in this culture called "riding and dying for their men. The sad shit is while we riding and dying our men are leaving us for the one that's thinner. It's a sad ass fairy tale because along the way we forgot to take care of ourselves. We forgot what class and beauty is. I'm tired of seeing women stuffed in jeans too small. Shirts showing their bloated guts and nappy ass hair weaves. What the fuck is with these fake eyelashes that look like bats? We forgot about how good it feels to be proud of our beauty and our culture. It scares me because we let these horrible men eat our souls. The men, who molest you, take your panties down and tell you they're saving your souls. They don't think of the damage it will cause for years to come. Why? They don't care. He rips you open take away the one thing you can't ever get back your virginity.

They train you to be whores dress like they want you to, act like they want and forget your identity. The brainwashing of our black women to be what society wants us to become the weaker inferior sex.

I'm walking in the land of the living dead zombies. Women are giving all their power to their men and children. Women breaking code 0071 never ever sleep with your friend's man.

It is why I started the Revolution Gym and Restoration of Souls. I've tried for three years to get funding for this and every bank in Buffalo has turned me down. One banker said, "Black women don't exercise and eat right. A gym will never work in a poor community."

Yet, it is so sad and true a large amount of minorities don't work out. How sad we neglect ourselves?

I started the revolution gym with the money my father left, my husband insurance and death benefits. In my basement is where I started my own personal gym. I have bachelors in Nutrition and

Health and certified as a group instructor. I teach weekly boot camp classes at Buffalo Athletic Club as well as private sessions. My body is a perfect size six with only six- percent body fat. I've rebuilt my body with eating clean, no red meat, and no swine. I eat only organic fruits and vegetables. I work out five times a week. I turned a three-hundred body without fad diets, surgery into a perfect body.

I went around to the thrift stores buying used exercise equipment and DVDS. I handed out fliers of my before and after pictures. I offer free gift cards to every woman who attends the full twelve weeks. At first it was slow but after those first five women came out losing weight women from the community starting coming in.

My groups aren't just about losing weight, but a changed a mindset. It's about nutrition; it's about self-esteem, a clean living and most of all never taking any one's shit. Not everyone understands the method to my madness. I really don't give a fuck because it's our people who are suffering. Our people who are stuck in front of TV living with diabetes, cancer, high blood pressure and every other ailment that exist. More African-American women are dying from these diseases than being cured. The medications further hinder their health when it is all about eating right and exercise.

Yes, I walk in the room with my face painted in war paint and in full military gear. We women are at war with animals called men and a society who hates fat women. We are treated less than equal to human beings. In their mind women will always be superior. It does not matter if we make more money, run a household, go to school, and raise their asses because some of their Mamas taught them nothing.

What I teach will save their lives. I teach that if a man hits you once you kill his ass so he won't do it again. Fuck calling the police or getting restraining orders that shit don't count. At the end of the day if you gain an ounce or fall off what they consider to be beautiful .He will dismiss your ass. The reality is a bitch and then you die. So a woman has to always be ahead of the game and never ever give the man you love the power.

The sirens are loud, I smell the smoke and all I can think about now is how I should have cut off her tits and ran my car over them. I let my fingers slide down my belly, I feel my nipples get hard at the images of her battered body. I sit back and all of a sudden I feel a fire

INSANITY AT ITS FINEST!

that burning in my loins as I rub my clit. My pussy is hot and a rush of warmth and pleasure bubbles in my pussy. I cum as I playback images of Camilla dying. I moan out, "Damn, that felt so good."

Detective Bishop

TO CATCH A FAT CHICK.

It's twelve degrees out here but feels like zero below. The wind cuts my face like a Ginsu knife. The snow blowing sideways and the woman known as Fat Girl Vigilante has struck again. We'd recently caught the bike path rapist and sent him to prison for 75 years to life. Yet, we still couldn't catch up to the woman who has been terrorizing Buffalo for the past two years. Sanchez was caught January 15, 2007. His D.N.A and a confession solved a case. Chief Wilder told me he lived, breathed and drank catching him. The day he caught him he broke down in his office and cried.

Mine was catching Fat Girl Vigilante, she is slick and it said that it's harder to catch a female serial killer. She left her victims without a dick and burned to a crisp. Tonight she leaves another victim with his blood on her hands.

Markel King, a fifty-six-year-old male found burned and the head of his penis cut off. The same pattern this time it's affecting the community. He was one of the city's philanthropists and real estate tycoons. How in the hell did he come in contact with her? What is their connection? For the past two years, several men have turned up dead by fire and their penises cut off.

The Mayor, the Governor, the Chief and the community are on my ass to solve this case. His wife is sobbing uncontrollably I walk up to her and touch her shoulder. She pushes my hand away.

"Mrs. King, I know this is an awkward time, but I would just like to ask you a few questions. My name is Detective Jones and I'm…"

She looks at me and rolls her eyes, blows her nose in a monogrammed handkerchief and drops it on my boot.

"My husband is dead and you Officer Friendly think I killed my husband. Are you serious?"

"Well, as stated before my name is Detective Bishop Jones. You are not a suspect, yet. I need your cooperation to answer some questions." She wipes her eyes, shivers and pulls her coat close.

INSANITY AT ITS FINEST!

"Follow me to my car, please. It is freezing out here."

I open the door for her and she slides into the seat. I sit next to her.

"Go ahead with your questions so you can leave me alone."

"Was your husband having an affair?" She sucks her teeth.

"Look at me, Officer Friendly. Why in the hell would he cheat on me with a fat girl?"

I look at her and think to myself maybe because her attitude sucks to hell. I throw on my fake smile. She is indeed beautiful, her fair complexion, her hazel eyes, her sandy brown hair, toned body all that beauty and the personality of a bitch.

"You're right, Mrs. King. I apologize. Does your husband have any disgruntled tenants or enemies?

"Of course he does. That's a dumb question, of course, he has disgruntled tenants. He's a landlord. He had to throw tenants to the curb for failure to pay their rent, Officer Friendly."

"Any of them overweight? Anyone so angry they wanted to take his life?"

"Half of Buffalo is overweight. Only the men he usually had issues with but not where they wanted to kill him." I hand her my card.

"When was the last time you seen your husband?"

"Two days ago, I was on a business trip in Atlanta. You can check with the airlines, the hotel, and my driver will verify my whereabouts."

"Again my condolences, Mrs. King. If you have any further information give me a call."

I walk over to Hernandez who resembled Marc Anthony dark slick hair, sunglasses in the dead of winter. Average height and thin frame. He responds before I even ask,

"No one has seen a thing. One old lady said she saw King pull up in the Driveway and go upstairs but never saw him again. She said he was alone. So you think the wife may have hired someone to murder him?"

"I'm still investigating she was quick to confess her innocence. Defensive and jittery."

INSANITY AT ITS FINEST!

"So we keep our eye on her I mean she had the motive. His money is real long. I'll check out some background info on her. I'll see if she had any lovers on the side."

"Cool."

I pull out my cigarette and light it. I listen as the fire Marshall and his staff are talking. They said they found a burnt up gas tin and a dildo stuck in his mouth. The medical examiner explained the majority of the burns were on his head, face and upper torso. The head of his dick was missing so most likely she took it as a consolation prize like most serial killers they needed to keep a souvenir.

Markel is the sixth victim to be murdered in two years all the same Mo. Her name branding she committed the murders in the person's blood, no fingerprints, and no D.N.A. Lester Jones, Raheem Grant, Leon Saxton aka Black Money, Jerome Johnson and Nickel. All of them died on their birthdays and none of this shit is connecting the dots.

The day I started the job was the day he murders began Raheem Grant found dead in his bed with his dick stuffed in his mouth, glass shoved in his ass and his body burned on his birthday. The next victim Leon Saxton was just a petty drug dealer found with his head decapitated with a pink dildo stuff in it and dick cut off and body burnt. Lester Jones, taxicab owner of Buffalo Eveready cab service was found stab in the face, dick split like a banana and his upper torso. She hasn't broken her pattern with the killings.

When I was offered the position of lead Homicide detective I never thought I have to find a serial killer in Buffalo, I came here to get away from my past. I walk in the door to the death of Raheem Grant. I've gone through our files no one fits the profile. The ones that do has a tight alibi. I'm looking at every angle and plus size woman hard to figure out who she is. All in the same token understanding the Queen City area.

Living and breathing the life of a detective in a strange city. I've become accustomed to death. It has circled around me like buzzards and black crows waiting to eat my flesh. I left Los Angeles because I accidentally killed a little girl. When a drug lord used her as a personal shield. I never saw her in the dark house. The sick bastard took a child who was sleeping, covered her head with a blanket to protect his life. Thoughts and nightmares chase me, why and what ifs where

INSANITY AT ITS FINEST!

my buzzards eating at my conscience. The black crows ate at me making a stupid move. Not the media, my family or the community could help me to believe it wasn't my fault.

My father who spent his entire career chasing the bad guys of L.A. bred me to be a cop. My grandmother said my calling was to minister the community and work for the Lord. It was the pride I felt seeing my father step out his patrol car in his full uniform not listening to some Pastor preach. It is what I knew I wanted to be at six years old a detective.

My grandmother hated cops because one killed her brother for being black and on the wrong side of the street. My father chose to be a cop to stop white cops beating our people. I became a detective to satisfy my thirst of catching the bad guy or girl. Her prevention plan was stay prayed up.

Sadly, my journey was different from what she expected. The day I graduated from the academy she stop speaking to me. I knew I had broken her heart, but I had to follow my life's calling.

I live to serve and protect. Living by the motto has some setbacks of losing what counts like a family. It has always been my belief a detective should never get married because your work life will take over your personal life or is it just me? I worked my way through the ranks. I walk the beat, earned every accolade base on my own merit versus this life being handed down to me. I am a man after my father's own heart.

On the other hand, my brother despises cops. It was him who took on a different path of becoming a social worker trying to keep the gang bangers from dudes like me. He wanted to steer them in the right direction of life.

In the same year of 2005. A woman who I messed with dumped me and aborted our unborn child. I'll admit I didn't know how to separate career and family. She told me to choose her or my career when it became clear to her I was unsure of what I wanted she made the choice for me and bounced. Now that I look back at it leaving me was the best thing she could have ever done. I knew the departure was for the best. I never gave myself time to grieve or accept it hurt me. I was consumed with the chase of the bad guy.

INSANITY AT ITS FINEST!

My grandma died in that same month. Again, I saw the black buzzards and crows over my head. I see death more than I see life. My nights were restless, her cries, seeing her lifeless body. So when the position became available in Buffalo, N.Y. to assist in tracking down Fat Girl Vigilante. I accepted it and took the next flight out. I needed a change of scenery and a slower pace.

When I stepped off the plane two years ago, the way I was welcome was being called to duty and another victim of Fat Girl Vigilante. Yet, one woman has me questioning my ability as a detective. She is the pursuit I've been chasing and until she is locked up I will not sleep.

The agony of being five steps behind her every move. To know that I have missed every clue. She could live right across the street from me and I wouldn't know it. I'm fucked up and the unrest is I haven't a clue or inkling who she is. I drive and every big girl is a suspect. I am obsessed with her and all I dream about is putting the cuffs on her.

As I drive from the scene of the crime. I realize I'm homesick and have huge craving for Roscoe's Chicken and Waffles. My family and friends are in LA. The Watts and the East Side of Buffalo are the same with new gangs forming every day. I take the scenic route as I hit East Delevan and turn right on Jefferson Avenue. I look at the neighborhood I see potential here and hope.

I see prosperity despite what the media and what other folks say. I pull into the TOPS Plaza and notice that the supermarket is open twenty-four hours now.

I go in and walk to the back, grab a whole cooked chicken, some macaroni and cheese, a Pepsi and some cornbread. I walk up to the register and ask for a pack of Newport 100s. The woman looks at me and said,

"Is that your real eye color or is contacts?"

I can't tell you how many times I get that question asked about my eyes. My eyes are baby blue against my dark brown complexion. I answer,

"My eye color is real."

"So which one of your parents is white?"

"Neither one of them. They're both African- American."

She laughs and whisper to her friend, "Mama was creeping for sure."

INSANITY AT ITS FINEST!

Tamyara Brown

They give one another a high five. I pay for my groceries and walk
out. I see this beautiful woman with bags she drops her purse. I tap
her on the shoulder. She turns around and said, "Yes."
I pick up her purse and hand it to her.
"You dropped your purse."
 Fire red braids flow from her hat,

Bishop

A DATE WITH CRAZY!

As soon as I walk into the office the phone is ringing. I answer,
"Homicide."

"I know of the Satan who has used men for sacrificial offering. I know who she is." I clear my throat and rub my temples because the day has just started and already bullshit is calling me up.

"Really. So who is she? I throw my hands up in the air and blow out air.

"She is the daughter of Satan and Serpent of Arms."

"God told me to call you because you are the Messiah who would deliver us from evil. Can you do this Bishop Ezekiel Jones?"

The phone clicks and the dial tone returns. My gut instinct tells me to research this. How did she know I was investigating this case? I called the number listed 716-555-4614. I let it ring and the third ring she answers,

"Praise the Lord, Bishop. I knew God lead me in the direction of you for a reason."

"What?"

"She has gospel music playing in the background.

"Yes, the Lord and Savior ask me to contact you so that you may stop the evil that floats in this woman's life. I live at 508 Monroe Street come so I can inform you of what the Lord has asked me to reveal to you." I rub my lips and think for a minute.

"What is your name, Ma'am?"

"Miyama Grant."

I plug her name in the database and her picture appears she was arrested for burning a cat in 2005. I realize I need to have Hernandez come with me.

"I'll be there in fifteen minutes,"

I call Hernandez

"Hernandez, I need you to take a ride with me to this spot.

. I have another car follow me and park at the corner. I walk up and in her yard are rows of crosses covering her yard. She is standing in

INSANITY AT ITS FINEST!

the yard, bare feet, hair wrap in a white scarf. She is a woman of about three hundred pounds, her face has a tattoo of a cross. I think to myself that maybe I got in way over my head. I walk in the gate I introduce myself and show my badge.

"I'm detective, Bishop Jones. Are you Miyama Grant?" Her clothes are wet. Her face is full of tears. She walks down the snow-covered steps barefoot; I reach for my gun. She raises her hand to reveal she has no weapon.

"Bishop, you have hair just like wool from the lamb. Skin beautiful like Jesus. You are a handsome man. I will not hurt you for I need you to save the world from Satan's daughter. Please if you want we can talk on the steps but I prefer in my house. It's holy in there I dare not taint my home with sin."

I follow my instincts and walk in the first thing that hits my nostrils is the stench of urine and rotten meat. A hundred pictures of Jesus covering the wall. On the left side are bible verses written in dried blood. I stand and I hear Hernandez dispatch my radio.

"You cool, Bishop? I'm coming in now."

"I'm good."

Hernandez walks in, he looks around, covers his face with his hat and gags. She screams and begins to speak in tongue. I pull out my gun.

"I love Jesus more than I love myself. Yes, I do, I need, and I need to set my soul free. I'm bound by Satan's hold on me."

"So Miyama let me help you talk to me." She wipes her nose with her hand. She speaks slowly,

"I know who commits the sin murder. She leadeth me the way the serpent led Eve to the forbidden tree. She gave me the forbidden apple and I bit it and now I am filled with sin."

"Who?"

"She is Serpent of Arms. Her eyes are colored with greed and money. She does not love the Lord as I do."

I pull out my pad and write down the name. She is as crazy as a bedbug but crazy sometimes solve cases. I hold my breath because the stench of piss, rotten meat and blood is choking me. I inhale and then exhale.

INSANITY AT ITS FINEST!

"I need her name, Miyama. I feel like you are wasting my time. "
"Listen to me Bishop she runneth to Satan instead of the Lord. She taught me death and destruction of men. I took the Lord's will and put it in my hands. She told me to kill Raheem, my husband. She told me to drench him in gasoline I would purify his soul and take away the sin. I castrated him for performing perverted sex on my daughter. He was kissing her Nancy and doing nasty stuff to her. She was special Bishop and he put his mouth on her vagina. She was just a baby. Not the police, not society or no one else believed me because he used just his mouth on her. They let him free. I waited and waited for justice to serve my baby and me. I fought and I lost…."

She is sobbing. She opens the drawer and pulls out a picture of her daughter and hands it to me. From the picture, you can tell she has Down syndrome. She kisses it. I feel that salty taste in my throat and tear forms in the corner of my eye. I wipe my face. I ask,
"Where is your daughter?"
"She is home with the heavenly father where her soul belongs. This cruel world took her from me. I woke up one day and went to her bed her eyes was close, in a deep sleep. They say she had a heart attack, but I know it was Jesus who felt she belonged to him." She rocks back and forth speaking in tongue. I let her calm down and I speak,
"So you kill Raheem for hurting your little girl." She looked up now her eyes red and cold.
"Yes and that bastard of sin deserved to die. Yet, I knew better than to act out of haste I should of letting my Lord handle him. I have sinned and now no matter what I will dwell with Satan because Jesus he hates murderers. There's no forgiveness for that."

The sound of her water hits the floor again, I look down and I see it run down the carpet touching my boot. She sits back and she looks in the sky, folds her hands and tells her story.
"Bishop, I waited and plotted the way I would destroy that bastard. I let Serpent of Arms coax me into becoming a murderer. His birthday May 18 was the day he died. I follow him and waited till he was good and sleepy. I watched him shower, defecate and shave. I hid in his closet the way he did my precious baby. I let him take his sleeping pills and a drink his forty-ounce of beer." She stops and picks up his picture looks at it and throws it back down. She continues her story.

INSANITY AT ITS FINEST!

Tamyara Brown

"He fell asleep at 12:35 a.m. Thirty-five minutes after his birthday began. I grabbed a butcher knife and cut off his penis and stuff it in his mouth. I pour gasoline all over him. Satan took over me and told me to beat him until I could see blood pouring from every orifice. I broke the glass and turned him over. I shoved it up his ass. Once he was bleeding out the sin, he committed I set him on fire. I was enraged in anger and possessed. Sweet Jesus. I'm sorry father for I have sinned." She rocks and shakes. She lets her eyes roll to the back of her head. I call back up,

"She is having a seizure. I need an ambulance at 508 Monroe street also she needs to be sent directly to psyche for evaluation." She is defecating all over herself. The ambulance, my back up and the fire department rush in.

"Listen she just confessed to murdering her husband, get forensics in here to pull whatever you can. Miyama you are under arrest for the murder of Raheem Grant... Hernandez Don't notify the media yet until we got 100 percent proof of this murder." I read her rights as the paramedics work on her.

Hernandez said,

"Bishop, would you check out this here." I look at the jar.

"Is that what I think it is?"

"Exactly my words. She has a dick in the jar. Get the fuck out of here she persevere his dick."

"What the hell is going on? Is she the serial killer?" Hernandez shakes his head.

"Maybe she is the Serpent of Arms. Maybe she is the Fat Girl Vigilante."

"I don't know. I have a feeling she isn't."

"Bishop, the bloody scriptures on the wall, the motive and that man's penis in the jar. Once you take this to the Captain he going to the press. Every city official has been on our ass. Man, she admitted to cutting her husband dick off and setting him on fire."

"True, but if she had enough balls to call me up to tell me she murder one man then she has enough balls to say she did the other dudes in."

INSANITY AT ITS FINEST!

I look at the scriptures written on the wall. I keep staring and its smeared blood. Maybe my gut is wrong. She admitted to killing Raheem. She trusts me depending on this whole ordeal and whether she lives. This case is more complex than it seems she keeps speaking of this Sergeant of Arms. Is she the leader and why is she setting out to kill all these men?

"Hernandez investigate Raheem Grant and the sexual molestation allegations. Whatever information you can find on Miyama, relatives living and dead."

"I'll get on it"

The paramedic, the firemen, forensics is combing the apartment with a fine-tooth comb. I look over at the picture of Miyama smaller and that woman I saw her before. I pick up the picture with a paper towel and it's the woman I saw at TOPS supermarket. Wrap it in more hand towel. What if these two have a connection? I feel my gut contract. This story isn't over.

INSANITY AT ITS FINEST!

Tamyara Brown

Michelle

SARGE DID IT!

I woke up naked as the day I was born. My head throbbing, I hear the shower water running and the T.V is blaring. I get up out of the bed and go to the bathroom. The tub scent of ammonia, streaks of blood running through, my bloody fingerprints on the tile. I cover my mouth, I look around and I realize this is not a dream. She did it. She killed Markel.

Oh my God Sarge made me turn into Mama. What is wrong with me? I promise I'd never do it again, promise I live differently. I look over at the picture of my Daddy. I look over at Markel's picture and Sarge voice appears in my ear,

"That mutherfucka deserved it."

I keep hearing her voice telling me to do the things my mama's been doing. I never wanted to kill Markel. Or did I? Was this deranged thought in my mind? I hated Markel for what he did to me.

I have no control of Sarge once she takes over me. She is her own woman even though she lives in my body. She is opposite of me. She is wild, she is violent and without a thought she will kill first and no need for a rhyme or a reason.

I fear her because she is the woman what I want to be. My mother beats me because I remind of her of my Daddy. I fear allowing Sarge to kill her but she won't stop hurting me. I'm weaker than she is but my desire to be like her is strong. The alter ego that people fear and respect normally is the person they want to release.

I've battle this voice in my head since the day my daddy died. Sarge takes over me; she makes me more dangerous than my Mama. I wash the blood down the drain. I pour bleach in the tub. I look in the full-length mirror and I am at my smallest I've ever been. I am still a plus size woman in Mama and society eyes.

I use to wear a size twenty-six but now I wear a size sixteen. I look at me and even I don't recognize myself. At last I'm not obese anymore. I no longer feel embarrassed to walk outside. I can wear almost anything I want.

I've changed physically yet I am still broken inside. I battle myself every day. I battle not to hurt Mama for taking my Daddy away. He took care of me, he love me with everything inside of him.

Being thinner I thought I find a real man but here in Buffalo there isn't any. Every woman who comes to group has the same sad story some brother who has play them, their man in jail or their man beating on them. The good ones are either dead or married.

Mama educates us to self-love; self-protect and stay in shape. I joined the Revolution because quite frankly I got tired of being everybody's joke. I got tired of being winded and tired of being lonely. The sad part is after all the weight is gone I am still lonely. I go to work every day at the St. John's Home as an administrative assistant but I'm invisible in many eyes while the nurses and staff hang out everyone just ignores me. Sarge has begged me so often to just kill but I refuse because I am not a murderer.

I turn on the Television and YNN is broadcasting the arrest of Miyama Grant. I cover my mouth. She is being the name as a suspect for all the men dead including Markel King. I hear Mama's voice, "Do you see this shit, Michelle? Mama yells. Mama dressed in all black with keys in her hand. I don't reply. She hits me in the back of the head.

"Miyama, gain back the weight I helped her lose. All my hard work gone to waste. She done set us back again her hair isn't done. She looks god-awful? How are you, Baby Girl? Why are you naked cleaning the bathroom? Look, let mommy cook you some breakfast." I look at her and nothing has register to her that Miyama is in jail for something she and Sarge has done. I wash up at the sink. I choose a color and it's brown. I put on my brown lace bra and panties set. I put on a brown sweat suit, brown thermal and Uggs boots.

Mama is sitting at the table drinking her FIGI water. The table is set with bowl of steel oatmeal, sliced bananas and strawberries. A glass of Almond milk sat beside it. I pop a strawberry in my mouth and savor it for the moment.

"Mama this is wrong letting her stay in jail? She stills eating never looking at me. I call her name again.

INSANITY AT ITS FINEST!

Tamyara Brown

"Mama, you can't do this? How can we help her? She swallows and wipes her mouth.

"Her Lord will get her out of this? He always does?" she said sarcastically. I lose my appetite. I get up from the table.

I need to go see her and make sure she is all right. I remove my bowl and Mama said,

"Don't go down to see her. You hear me, Michelle?'

"Why? Are you afraid she told about you? Afraid of going to jail?" Before I can put on my coat mama grabs me by the throat and pushes me against the door.

"Listen to me if I find out you went down to that jail I will kill you. Do you understand me? I know she's your aunt but don't betray your mother, never betray me." I pull her hand from my throat so I can breathe.

"I'm going to the gym. Is that alright with you?"

"It's alright but I frown upon disloyalty, Michelle. I hate to have your tits hanging up on a wire. You know me and how dangerous I am." I grab my bag and slam the door. All my life she has told me how to think and how to feel. I've lived under rule and thumb. Even Sarge has control of me she bullies me in my head and tortures me with thoughts to kill. I get in my car and drive off. I pull up to the garage and grab a ticket. I walked over to the holding center and go through the verification process of being allowed to see her. It's bitter cold in the visiting room, the heat turned down intentionally and the inmates shivering. She walks in her orange jumpsuit looks too small, her hair is almost gone and snot crust formed around her nose. I want to hug her but instead ask,

"Are you okay? She shakes her no.

"I know you are innocent." She said

"My God, Michelle I'm the one who killed my husband. I may not have killed all the others but I killed him. I went against God's will. I know the battles you have endure but you have to promise me you'll break away from Satan's hold. She is against you in every possible way and she will have you burning in hell."

I wipe the tears falling from my eyes.

INSANITY AT ITS FINEST!

I speak softly, "Mama won't let me go. She has hold of me for no unknown reason. I've tried to get away."

"Look at me and listen. They think I'm crazy but God got my back and as long as God has got me he got you. Yes, my Lord is angry with me now and I am aware of the sin I committed. I have to pay for my sin."

"Yes, but not Mama's too. They'll have you in prison for life." She is touching my hand now. The fat guard with a tattoo of an eagle walks past us.

"I know but I won't suffer anymore with the sin that weighs heavy in my heart. I will rest more. I'll be closer to Lisa she is crying now.

"I know you didn't murder your husband."

I raise my eyebrow, look her in the eyes and she turns her head.

"Does your Mama know you're here, Michelle?"

"No, I won't tell her I was here. She didn't want me to come here to see you." She chuckles.

"I allowed it to happen. I wanted him dead so I was accessory." I hold her hand tighter.

"You can't spend the rest of your life in jail for a crime you didn't commit."

She leans in closer and holds my hand."

"We are the Gatekeeper of her secrets and eventually all truth will surface including mine."

"I know."

"I love you and be safe."

I walk out and the guards escort her through the metal door. I bump into the man I met at the market. I look up at him and he stares at me. His blue eyes piercing through me. His face is handsome, a rough beard and his nappy curly hair. I can tell he has a muscular built. I turned away and slide past him. He smiles at me and I return the smile. I move away quickly.

INSANITY AT ITS FINEST!

Bishop

CRAZY IS AS CRAZY DOES

I greet the officer at the window. "Hey, McGuire what's cooking? "Shit, nothing but these damn animals in here." I chuckle. "Hey, the woman with the red braids do you know who she visited." I point to her. "Oh yeah, she visited that crazy bitch that keeps urinating on herself. Miyama Grant. Yeah, she listed herself as her niece."

I feel my stomach contract.

"Can I have a copy of her ID and address? He makes a copy of the I.D. I listen as the guard speaks German to the dog. He sniffs around the lockers and everyone else.

"Thanks, man. I'm going in to visit Miyama." My cell rings and I open the phone.

"Hey, Hernandez tell me what you got good for me."

"Well, first off I have a lot of good for you. She is telling the truth about the fact her husband was accused of molesting the daughter, but the bullshit ass former DA and child protection service listed this as "unfounded".

He wouldn't prosecute because it was no evidence of penetration and the little girl could not talk which makes this hearsay. Yet, the little girl would try to perform the acts of oral sex on other students but because of her disability it went ignored." Hernandez coughs and clears his throat continuing with details of Miyama Grant.

"The case was dismissed and the father was allowed visitation because he paid child support. Also, Miyama has a history of epilepsy and her parents are dead she has a sister named Patricia Sargent-Dickens and her niece, Michelle they both live on Empire Street. "The block on the East side where all of the houses is burned down. Where old man Arthur lives?""

INSANITY AT ITS FINEST!

"Yep. Miyama has been attending New Deaconess Baptist church since she was a little girl. She is on the choir and one of the Pastor and Deacon favorite member. I spoke with the members of the church they say about ten years ago after she married Raheem Grant she started acting weird. After the birth of her daughter who was diagnosed with Down syndrome. She would start walking around barefoot and claiming to be a prophet. The pastor who I spoke to said, 'She was anointed and with the gift of voice. She starting hanging around this lady who was her sister?' She began losing weight. When her husband left her something changed." Hernandez coughs and sneeze he continues,

"She has also been diagnosed with Bipolar disorder she was put away at ECMC four times in 1997 and 1998. Each time for trying to commit suicide after each miscarriage." I breathe out and say,

"Damn. I want you to research the niece and her sister.'

"Already done, Bishop."

"No record on the niece Michelle she clean as a whistle. The mother Patricia she clean too but check this out her husband died in 1986 in Hartford, Connecticut of…." I cut him off.

"By fire and castration. So was the mother a suspect?"

"Yes, but her alibi was as tight as a virgin's pussy. Her mother and step-father vouched for her. The rest of the hours were accounted for by her job at a local supermarket.'

"So was Miyama under investigation for the murder of her sister's husband?"

"No, because Miyama at the time was here in Buffalo. Patricia Sargent Dickens is the love child of the father's affair with her mother. She too is deceased. "

"I have a gut feeling Miyama not in on this alone check out that Patricia chick more. I want you to find out her birth date, the men she fucked and anything that can get us closer to solving this case.'"

"Boss, I still in my heart believe the loco Miyama committed the crimes. She had a motive and the man's dick floating in vinegar. The bloody scriptures I'm telling your boss she did it."

"I know she had a part, but I'm riding on everything I own she was not alone. Take care of your cold you sound horrible. I've got to go in and talk to Miyama. Thanks, Hernandez, I'll meet up with you later."

INSANITY AT ITS FINEST!

Tamyara Brown

I walk through the gates and Miyama is handcuffed. I sit next to her she smells horrible. I shake my head and inhale to ignore the smell. "Miyama what's going on?' She looks at me with a blank stare.

"I have given you all you need to stop Satan's daughter."

I rub my face and lean forward with my hands clasp and twirling my thumbs,

"Miyama actually you haven't you see I don't believe you committed all those crimes even up to last night. I believe you. For the record, that bastard was molesting your daughter. I believe you. I read the reports and it was as clear as today is Monday this sorry piece of shit was touching and sucking on your baby girl. Yet, you didn't kill your husband the Serpent of Arms did. Let me help you get out of this hellhole and to your holy home.

She begins to laugh aloud to the point she has tears rolling down her eyes. She speaks finally,

"You men are all alike. Now you believe me about my baby girl. What took you so long? Huh? Now you need answers. I told you everything you need to hear Bishop. You just haven't listened at all to what I'm saying because then you would have found your answer."

I listen to as she sings Mahalia Jackson's, "I will move up a little higher." The song my grandma would sing to me on our Sunday trips to church and this restaurant called the Serving Spoon. She singing and the guard wants to tell her hush, but she sounds so good. The inmates, visitors, and officers applaud her. Her voice sounded as if the angels marched out. She clears her throat and said,

"Your grandma use to sing that to you. She would drive you out to Inglewood and take you to the Serving Spoon to have chicken and waffles. She sings it every Sunday in the choir and on the way to church. She'd tell you she name you Bishop because God knew your calling was to be a man who led many not a detective. Your grandma's angry because you chose a different calling, but that didn't stop her from loving her favorite Grandchild. She up there in heaven and she told me to tell you that she loves and is protecting you."

I want to speak but can't. I get up and walk out. Bewildered I know nothing of this woman. How did she know of my grandmother, know of the song she sang to me? I jump in my truck and pull out a

INSANITY AT ITS FINEST!

Newport and light it. I take a puff and try to figure Miyama's angle. Is she playing mind games with me? I drown out her voice by turning up the music. I pull off, put my Bluetooth in my ear and call my brother,

"What's up, Bro?"

"Nothing but the gas prices and the rent. Shit being realistic the price of good pussy than quadruple." we laugh he continues,

"Man, I'm still trying to figure out what possess you to go out to cold ass Buffalo, NY. I mean snow and cold don't mix for an L.A. boy. I could see you hitting up the N.Y.C but Buffalo."

"I'm starting to question that too. I needed a change and…"

My brother interrupts, "Running from that accidental shooting of that little girl. Bishop that wasn't your fault, Man, you didn't know that she was in there."

The memory of me trying to revive her and carrying her lifeless body out of the house plagues my dreams. What the hell was her mother doing have her in a crack house? All I remember seeing was the dude with ak-47 in one hand; it was dark in there. She didn't cry or make noise. When he shot at me, I fired back at him hitting the little girl in the head.

"I don't want to talk about the past right now. Listen, I have a question did grandma know anyone in Buffalo?"

"You know the answer to that Nana never left Inglewood unless to go to Vegas to hit the slots. Once in a while. Shit, grandma hated being cold. Why"

"Nothing this woman I arrested as part of this serial killer shit going down here. She spoke about the restaurant and the song she sang to us. It's crazy-forget I brought it up. How's the wife and my niece?"

"They are doing well. My question have you slid into some good coochie out in the B-low?"

I think damn it's been months since I've had sex or any type of female companionship being so wrapped up in this case nothing has crossed my path.

"No, I've been on hiatus. It is all about more work and work."

"Yeah, come on back home the women must be sorry if you on hiatus from the sweet good good."

"No, I'm trying to solve this case."

INSANITY AT ITS FINEST!

"Like I said bro, the pussy must not be like them here in LA. Bishop just a word of advice don't get so wrapped up, in this case, you lose yourself again. You just like pops living and breathing the motto of serving and protecting. Take care of yourself, get some pussy and enjoy life please" I look at the white chick with blond hair smiling at me. Not my cup of tea and I turn my head.

"Yeah, I hear you, Bro. Well, I'm out and off in this cruel world of Buffalo Be Breezy and stay up."

"I'm trying, Bro. And I'm serious don't drown yourself in your work."

As I pulled up to Spot Coffee on Elmwood Avenue. I park on the side street. I go inside and there goes the lady with the red hair and green eyes. I take a good look at her and she is beautiful. She has on no makeup any fake nails and she is reading the immortal life of Henrietta Lacks. She is drinking from the key colored mug. She hasn't taken her eyes off the book and I can't seem to take my eyes off her.

They say the only way to get to know a person is to say "Hello.

INSANITY AT ITS FINEST!

Michelle

BLUES EYES!

I see him staring at me his blue eyes seem like an ocean of questions. As long as I've lived I never saw a man with skin so dark with blues eyes. He sits across from me, cigarette behind his ear and a lion ring on his pinky. I sip my cappuccino and take a bite of my banana walnut muffin.

He speaks and his voice is deep like Barry White.

"Hello."

I look at him and he is sitting across from me. My heart is beating fast. I look up and reply,

"Hello".

"How are you today?"

"Fine and yourself."

"I'm good. My name is Bishop Jones and it seems we have been running into one another for the past couple of days. So it has been said when two people keep meeting one another they are destined to meet. Do you agree?"

I don't know why but I smile at him. I push my hair out of my eye and take another sip of my drink.

"Maybe. My name is Michelle Sargent. It could just mean Buffalo is a small place."

He scratches his beard and licks his thick lips

"That may be true, but I'm not from Buffalo."

"Really, where are you from?"

"California. Grew up in Englewood all my life. "

He pulls at his ear, his blue eyes against his dark skin makes him look strange, he has clean fingernails, no wedding band and the diamond in his earring is real.

"So the cold weather must be a culture shock for you?"

"Hell yes! I mean damn I'm used to 80-degree weather in November but I've been here for about two years so I'm used to it now. Have you been in Buffalo all your life?

INSANITY AT ITS FINEST!

"No. I move here when I was thirteen. Wait, I'm answering all your questions like I know you. You could be a mass murderer or a rapist." My eyebrow rises up and I look at him.

"Yes, you're right. I'm all up in your business and you don't even know me." He scribbles his number on the back of a spot coffee business card and hand it to me he continues speaking and I notice the LA accent.

"I have to admit I find you quite beautiful. Take my numbers give me a call. I'd love to get to know you." He extends his hands and I reach my hand out he shakes mine.

"It was nice to meet you, Bishop Jones."

"The pleasure is the same." I watch him walk up to counter and he orders a large coffee. He walks out pulls out a cigarette.

My face is all red from him calling me beautiful. I eat the rest of my muffin and I'm floating on air until Mama Calls.

"Hello, Mama!"

"Where are you, child?" I roll my eyes.

"I'm at Spot Coffee. Why Mama?"

"Did you disobey me?

"No, Mama. Why would I do that?"

The lie slides off my tongue easily. I half listen as she talks about the Revolution and being more active in recruiting women to create a nationwide organization. After minutes of her ranting, I disconnect the call. I don't want to go home. I don't feel comfortable. I don't want to sleep I fear of Sarge taking over me. I get up and walk to my car.

It is now dark and I am driving aimlessly as if I have nowhere to go. The truth is I do not want to be alone tonight. No one is calling my cell. No one to talk to. I look at Bishop's number I should call him. What if I seem lonely and desperate?

Patricia
Recruitment

"Ladies, you sit before me pathetic losers. You are lost puppies and I am the top bitch that has scooped you from the pound. I am going to shed that fat off your guts your thighs and ass. You ladies are undisciplined and now is the time to get it together."

INSANITY AT ITS FINEST!

I walk around them all five of the ladies at my meeting. I am dressed in army fatigues and a white tee shirt. I have on combat boots and my face painted half black and the other half white.

"If any of you mutts have a problem with my rules then that's your business. I promise you'll thank me later and be kissing my ass because of the end results." I give each of the ladies a box of garbage bags.

"First thing first I want you to clean out all the processed foods out of your cabinets. No pork, no dips, no junk, no cakes, neither cookies nor ice cream should enter into your mouths. You will be here every morning at 4:30 am. You will put in two hours of exercise. You will drink a gallon of water a day. Last, but not least no sex with anyone except yourself if any of you mutts doesn't agree then step to the door."

Shayla stands and up put on her coat and hat. She walks to the door and I block her way.

"I'm sorry this isn't for me."

I step up towards and look her into her eyes.

"Is my fucking language too harsh? Are you afraid you might actually survive? Shayla, I know your story. Hmm, let's see you're the mutt who never completes what she starts because you are afraid of the outcome. So you run around in circle chasing your tale crying woe is me stories all damn day. You're not going no fucking where. You are going to complete this. Sit your ass down, Mutt!" She looks startled. She sits back down and lowers her head."

Shayla is a two hundred and seventy-pound woman who has lost her children due to drug abuse and neglect. Shayla was found in a filthy house piled with food and overdosed on heroin. Her husband gained custody of her children. She stop using the drugs but went from one addiction to the next addiction of binge eating her problems away. My job is to help her rebuild her body and get her mind.

Her sister who lost ninety pounds in a year referred Shayla; she felt I could help her. I know with this approach she could turn out to be one of my strongest soldiers, I look in her eyes she's hungry for all the things she lacks, love, a sense of self-worth and a hate for her husband. She feels as if he holds the power and control.

She reminds me of Michelle who was so against my program until she saw what the revolution could do. My Daughter looks absolutely

INSANITY AT ITS FINEST!

beautiful today. She is what society accepts. I still believe she needs to lose fifty more pounds, but right now she is not three hundred pounds.

"Shayla, what do you want out of your life?" I walk close to her rub her matted ponytail. I rub my hand on her face.

"I just want my children back and to lose the weight. I shake my head put my foot on the coffee table.

"Shayla, do you want a body like mines? I run my hands along the side of my body.

"Yes."

"How are you going to get a body like mine?" She looks up and sighs.

"Hard work.

"Yes, and though I'm one tough Bitch. My plan has worked foolproof. Now I can't let you run from your opportunity to change. I can't let you fail out of fear." I look at the rest of the women sitting there.

I continue and point my fingers at each of them,

"None of you. I'm going to piss you off. You're going to hate me a lot of times, but I'm not giving up on you unless you choose to give up on yourself."

I walk to Ray Lexus and she has on a dirty sweat suit and smelling like tuna fish. I spray Febreeze all over her. I spit at her and she wobbles.

"Who are you spitting at I'm not Shayla over there. I will bust you in the head." I chuckle and cover my nose.

"When you to come to my home don't come smelling like rotten tuna and dog shit. You need soap I got over a hundred bars. All that garbage you eating you need a colon cleanse and Chlorafresh...You need to have your clothes washed. I'll wash them but if you ever disrespect yourself or anyone else with that stench. I will put your fat funky ass over my knee and whip your ass like a little ass kid. Now get in the bathroom turn the shower on hot and scrub from your dingy ass neck to your funky ass pussy. Now get the in there, Mutt."

INSANITY AT ITS FINEST!

She hangs her head low and puts her hand on her face. She allows the tears to run down her face. The other women in the room chuckle and whisper among themselves about Ray Lexus

"You are crazy. I'm came here for help to lose the weight not to be put down. My man, my mama and everybody can do that. I thought you are supposed to motivate me not tear me down."

I get on the treadmill and walk. I look at each of them pitiful women who have lost their way not only with the bulge but life itself. I see my face in theirs years ago a lost broken element.

"You carry yourself like you deserve it. You walk around here; shit all of you like you don't care about yourself. I was you, ladies. I was a mutt. I didn't care about me. I looked like a hot ass mess and I stink. Hair not did, lay in the bed crying so much my eyes swell shut. When I started to love myself I ate right and lost the weight. I did my hair. I dress up. I made sure I looked my best for me. People will treat you as you treat yourself. I treat you like mutts because you treat yourselves like mutts. You want me to treat you like a queen then show me queen like qualities. Ray Lexus get in there and wash your ass, change your clothes I have some of Michelle's old clothes that may fit you."

She walks to the bathroom and I hear the shower water running. The rest of the women step on the scale and weigh themselves. They write their weight on the board.

I conclude the meeting.

Ray Lexus is dressed in a pair of Michelle's old jeans and blue sweater. She smells of Caress. I bring out a kit of Avon products and hand it to her. She weighs in and in at two eighty-five. Shayla weighs in at two seventy-five, Danita weighs in at two hundred and fifty-five and Angel who is the smallest of the group she weighs two hundred and five pounds.

I know that each of the women is a perfect recruit. They fit every criteria of a possible recruit. I can change their lives, program them to kill the men they love. Can you imagine a bunch of women paralyzing the Queen City? I just squirted in my panties that some sexy shit.

There are many women who want to do what I do but just too damn scared to paralyze, destroy and any man or woman who breaks their fat hearts. Fat Girl Vigilante in full effect. I throw on my girl, Kelis

INSANITY AT ITS FINEST!

"I'm Bossy". I dance around the room. I'm laughing; I'm drunk off my own power.

I feel like taking a man and just cutting his dick off while I perform oral sex on him. Just when his veins are pulsing and he's ready to cum. I run my razor across his scrotum watch his eyes bulge, as he is shocked that he has come in contact with a boss bitch. Instead tonight I'll cool out and chill Buffalo needs a break from me. Then I'll go and find my next victim. I have one question that's been pondering me all night.

Who killed Markel King and use my signature?

BETRAYAL OF A SISTER!

Is Miyama still taking my shine like she did with Daddy? Miyama has always been the apple of Daddy's eye. The very reason he lived and breathed. I was secondary in his life only being allowed to visit on holidays and summer months. I was the cause of the arguments that he and his beloved wife had. Miyama had the beautiful home, fancy clothes and shoes while I lived in roach infested apartment. I ate beans and rice with chicken backs.

My mama struggled and sacrificed everything. I didn't see that I was blinded by the fact of loving my father so deeply. In my eyes he was King and Mama was a peasant. I was the "*mistake*" he made by pure infidelity and lust. I reminded him of his indiscretions against his loving wife every time I showed up with my green eyes like my mother. Miyama hated me but I loved her. She paraded around with her fancy clothes and toys. While I walk around in my Woolworth's fashion and hand me downs. She would never let me play with her toys and I can remember crying all day long.

I'd hang out with her and she talked about me to her friends. She'd beat on me and pull at my hair. I tried my best to make her love me. I tried my best to let her see I would do anything.

She knew what would happen as she led me there for hide and seek. She never once said she was sorry. It cremated my faith in the church and in God. Thomas had never been the same until he lodged a bullet in his brain to forget. He the only one who tried to save me and protect me. In that shed behind the church holds so many chubby girls and boys secret. My secret the only one that brings tears to my eyes.

INSANITY AT ITS FINEST!

SHE STRIKES AGAIN!

I've called it a night I'm off duty and go home. I let my dog Bullet out in the backyard. I live on a quiet street off Richmond and Elmwood. I watch him as he runs around in the snow. He loves the snow and the cold air. I toss the ball at him and he catches it. He brings it back to me. I've had Bullet since he was a puppy. I found in a drug house covered in dirty clothes and took him and made him mine. I throw the ball and it lands in the snow. He grabs it with his teeth and brings it to me. I throw the ball a few times more before going in the house with Bullet. I grab a Heineken, the fireplace is on and sit in my favorite lounge chair, kick off my boots and cross my legs. I turn to the game because if I look at the news it may mean me coming into work. I turn on the Bills game and they are actually kicking ass. I feel my cell phone vibrate on my thigh. I reach in my pocket and flip it up and the number is from the Adams Mark Hotel. I answer, "Bishop, speak to me."

"Hi, Bishop! I know it's out of the blue, but I don't know I just thought I give you a call. I'm sorry to have bothered you! I will not call you back."

"Wait, Michelle, don't do that. I'm actually happy you called. I am sitting here looking at these Buffalo Bills and Jets. They are actually kicking ass."

She chuckles,

"I am happy they are winning."

"What are you doing at a hotel if you don't mind me asking?"

"You've already asked so it really doesn't matter if I mind. For your info, Sir I just needed some rest and relaxation. I just can't find that at home right now with my Mom there and all."

I take the rest of my beer and gulp it down. Bullet is laying in front of T.V. and the scent of fart enters my nose.

"So you are going to stay in the room all night alone or are you seeking company?"

"Yes. I hope you don't think I was calling you to come over."

"No, but I do think you called because you are just little interested in who I am."

"Maybe"

INSANITY AT ITS FINEST!

"Maybe or you are too scared to say, "I'm the guy who has you blushing."

"A little conceited aren't you?"

"Far from it, dear! I have this nappy fro and this thick ass beard on my face and…

She cuts me off,

"You're a handsome man and have the most beautiful eyes I've ever seen and on that note Mr. Bishop, good night." She hangs up the phone and leaves me stunned. I rub my hand through my beard and scratch it.

The Bills beat the Jets by two points; I flick through the channels and realize nothing is on the boom tube but reality TV and infomercials. Shit, I pay all this money for cable and this all I get. I flick it off and recline back in my recliner. I close my eyes the phone rings again. I look at the caller id. It's my partner Hernandez.

"What the fuck is going on that you call me on my night off. Just tell me it's because your wife is sending me a plate of her delicious food.

"Bishop, we need you at New Deaconess Baptist church on E. Ferry. There's been a crime committed."

"Let me guess my suspicions are that the Fat Girl Vigilante is still loose and now we have corpse with a missing dick. Am I right?"

"Yeah, but make that two dead men with missing parts, fried like a piece of chicken. The Captain is pissed because once again you are right."

On this particular night I wish I wasn't. I haven't had a day off in two months and living on three hours of sleep per day. I was hoping to God to get some shuteye and a peace of mind from this whole case. I curse out loud and say.

"Fuck me, I'm on my way! I guess that is a no on dinner, Huh Hernandez?" He laughs.

"Si Papa and after you see this shit you're not going to want to eat?"

"Spare me the details until I get there." I set down my beer and put my badge around my neck, put my gun in my holster and throw on my coat. I lock up and jump in my truck and off to yet another scene of the crime.

INSANITY AT ITS FINEST!

FOUR HOURS EARLIER

MAKING PEACE WITH MY PAST

As I stand in my red thigh high boots and a body suit to match this church holds many memories the ones no child should have to remember and endure. Thinking to myself just a few hours before they were begging me not to murder their sorry asses. Tears streaming down their eyes praying for mercy and professing they are men of God. The sounds of Donnie McClurkin's "we fall down" plays in the background. On his hands and knees I ask my famous question, "Do you remember me, Deacon?"

Sweat pours from his forehead, lips and chin trembling as blood leaks from his arms. At first I was going to murder him in the church but even a sinner like me has respect for the house of the Lord. His eyes rapidly blinking, the pulse in his necks throbbing and veins pulsating.

The Deacon whispers, "Ma'am I want no trouble. I know your spirit is wounded but if you kneel down and say this simple prayer with me. We will pretend as if this never happen. "He extends his hand out to me the way he did that afternoon. I step back and memories of him holding my hand and hugging me flash before my eyes. His lips kissing me, his body on top of mines and those words of "pretend it never happened" echo in my ears. I look at him he has aged gracefully his hair now a salt and pepper color was the only sign of his age. He face was still smooth, his slanted eyes, his thin lips and thin goatee. I remember when women had fights over who would be the great Deacon's wife. They would pamper and shower

INSANITY AT ITS FINEST!

the Deacon with meals, washing his clothes and paying his bills. None of them qualified because his heart was sold to the Pastor. He lured me the same way he knew my weakness was food and cakes.

I put the shot gun to Deacon's head and he whimpers. The more I look at them the more I want to rip out his esophagus and feed it to them. I hear a pounding in my ears and head, my pulse is elevated, my skin is hot and I want him to bleed all over God's temple.

"Take off your clothes and shoes."

"I have money, diamonds, jewels and whatever you want just take it and go. All will be forgiven." He announces as his voice shakes.

"You can't bribe me anymore to stay silent. Do as I say and shut the fuck up. Deacon, put the damn cell phone down don't even attempt to call the law on me because I will slaughter your ass on the Lord's Table of offering put the phone down."

"You shot me already what more do you want?" He barks.

"Justification of your sins I want to sleep at night without seeing your faces. I deserve that just walk to your car and don't touch me."

He raises his hands and walks to the Cadillac Escalade. Shivering, leaving blood trails in the snow. I force him to drive he knows who I am. He remembers me I can see it in his eyes.

He mutters,

"Please forgive me. I am held by a demonic spirit and God loves you." I cut him off and spit in his face. I walk him out of the sanctuary, the wind blowing sideways, snow covers his naked body and he is trembling. He gets in the car. I duct tape him to the seat."

"Please forgive me, Satan has me sick and lusting for the wrongs things."

INSANITY AT ITS FINEST!

"Fuck you and his forgiveness. A demonic spirit is about to take your ass out."

After twenty minutes I let him open the door and disarm the alarm. Pastor is sitting in front of T.V. watching C.N.N. He was still the same ugly man, short, now bald, his ears pointed out, one of his eyes crossed, tiny holes in his face, his skin was blue black and his eyes bulge out of his head.

My body tenses, the hairs on the back of my neck raises and I spit at him. I lift the shot gun with a potato attach to it. I shoot him in the chest three times and he slumps to the side of the chair. I turn around and Deacon attempts to run I shoot him in the back three times. I pull out the hunter's knife and cut off his dick and put in in the Pastor's mouth. I stab the Pastor over and over again until I am drenched in his blood.

"Why yawl destroy my life, huh? You made my Daddy hate me. You stole my innocence and belief in God from me. Why did you do that to me?" I…I…didn't deserve that. Thomas, and the rest of us didn't deserve to be molested."

I walk into the kitchen and I find cooking oil I pour it all over their body, empty seasonings from garlic, paprika, red pepper flakes, oregano, to onion powder and chili powder all over them. I will let them marinate because I'm going to roast these pigs. I want to smell their skin burning and hear it snap, crackle and pop. I go to the bathroom take a shower, wash my hair and dry off. I walk around their mansion the poor parishioners have paid for Italian leather, granite top, floors covered in Cashmere rugs and top of line window coverings. I go in their closets lined with suits of various colors, shirts, ten Rolex watches, diamond pinky rings and twenty- five pairs each of black, blue, gray and white shoes.

I open the refrigerator pull out the birthday cake Wednesday Scott Holmes made of a bible, I go in the freezer and scoop out vanilla ice

INSANITY AT ITS FINEST!

cream. I turn on the television and flip the channel until I reach the classic show with Nell Carter called, "Gimme a Break". It is the episode when Nell goes home and her father is dying. Memories flash back of visiting my father on his deathbed and his last words, "I love you but you are a liar. Men of God would never harm you and touch my daughter."

I put back on my boots, I put on Deacon's brand new sweat suit and my boots. I look over at the picture of his son, Steven. All of these men from various generations in the same family destroyed the good in me.

I sing the Happy Birthday song. I dip my gloved finger in their blood and write my name all over their wall and doors. I set the Pastor on fire first and let his chest burn. The Deacon I watch him burn for a minute and then put them out with the extinguisher. I drag each of their bodies to the car, the smell of their body makes me gag. I cover my nose and throw them in the back.

I drive and turn the corner memories reappear of my birthday, the sound of my sister laughing, Thomas face and the Pastor and Deacon having sex with one another. I cried for Miyama to help me and if it wasn't for me they wouldn't have hurt Thomas. When Thomas and I limped out she said,

"Now the sin is washed away from you."

Every Sunday for an entire summer the Deacon and Pastor had their way with us claiming to cleanse our souls from sin. No one ever believed us. My father went to his grave believing his little girl was a slut. Miyama, the Pastor and Deacon took away my father. He no longer talked to me or could look at me. He packed up my bags, placing me in the station wagon a week after my birthday and he said, "I love you but the lying I will not tolerate."

His reply was,

INSANITY AT ITS FINEST!

"Be well and may God cleanse your soul. He loves you but I can't love you."

They made him hate me. I cried for six months straight and every time I called he would never speak to me. All I was to him was a financial responsibility and his troubled child. The truth remains buried in that shed and the shattered hearts.

It's okay because I paid them back. I've done what society should do to all of the child molesters' castrate them and make them eat their dicks. Stuffing them in prison with the option to be free and hurt another child. The option to carry on to plot. Plan and fantasize about a child. Fuck that!

I pull up to the church, the temperature reads zero degrees. The snow is frozen solid, the streets are sheets of ice and a driving ban has just been issued. I park in the spot and step out. The doors of the church are wide open. I drag each of their bodies in sit them on the pulpit.

I pop in the DVD given to me of Thomas suicide and saints that are sinners. The Pastor and Deacon had been raping and sodomizing him for years beyond our childhood that after a while he thought it was a natural act. I pop it in and press play.
The video shows the two men in a room with Thomas as they take turns raping him. Thomas face is flush red and covered in tears begging the men to stop. The Pastor and Deacon are kissing and holding each other. The video then shows Thomas pointing the gun to his head saying
"I try to tell you Mama, but you wouldn't listen maybe now you will believe me now."
Thomas pulls the trigger and shoots himself. I rewind it back. I sing amazing grace Thomas favorite song. I pull out his picture and kiss it
I whisper, "They'll believe you now my friend and if nothing else justice has been served for you."

INSANITY AT ITS FINEST!

I set the third pew on fire and the alarm goes off. I walk out through the back knowing no one will see me on a frigid night of -11 degrees. The sirens of the fire trucks and police cars are pulling in. Fat Girl Vigilante signature painted with the Pastor and Deacon blood. I drive off without a care in the world. Two less sick motherfuckers erased from the face of the earth

INSANITY AT ITS FINEST!

THE SAINTS ARE SINNERS

I pull up to the Crime Scene Unit truck and step over a mound of snow. I almost slip and bust my ass on the sheet of ice. The four media trucks are outside and the S.W.A.T surrounding the area. I hear each reporter giving their tale of the events that went on tonight. The first officers who arrived on the scene are rookies the tall lanky white one is vomiting all over the sidewalk. While the other one Samisen is trying his best to impress us with detailed accounts of the events.

Hernandez and I walk up to the situation. Samisen gives us the details of the scene.

"The Pastor and Deacon of the church were found shot, stabbed multiple times, burned and castrated sitting in the pulpit. That is not all wait until you see the video on the screen it some mind blowing shit, Bishop."

I brace myself for what I'm about to see. I lift up the yellow tape and walk in I look at the video my mouth drops open. The Pastor and Deacon are taking turns performing oral sex on a man. They turn him around and take turns fucking the young man in the ass. I feel sick to my stomach, swallow the lump of truth that's being dished out. The same man now on the video a lot older with gray hair and sunken eyes is crying and said, "I try to tell you but you Mama but wouldn't listen. Maybe now you will." The sound of the gun and the blood splatters all over the wall and the screen.

I look at Hernandez who is the one who yells,

"Shut that shit off and put it in evidence, dust for prints and whatever else you can find." He shakes his head and spits in the tissue he has with him. The video is etched a sketch in my mind for a lifetime just like the little girl dying in my arms. The sight and smell of death are all too familiar now.

I can taste gasoline in my mouth, the smell of flesh burning and blood has my stomach in knots not because I'm not use to the smell but because these sick bastards were molesting children.

Two more pillars of the community discovered for doing the unthinkable. The first thing I notice is how the pattern has changed. Did someone else do this and using her signature? It was not her usual pattern, one more obstacle to overcome with this case. The pattern is broken she didn't shoot the other victims. She burned the third pew."

Did they run from her when she tried to set them on fire? I looked at their wrist no rope burns or signs of being tied. The blood is still fresh; it's still running from the victim's body. She had done this within the past few hours. I look on top of the organ and there sits a letter, I walk up to the organ pick up the letter scented with a sweet perfume. I open it and the words jump at me written in red pen,

Dear Officers of the Law,

By now you are here trying to figure out who I am. I'm doing your job. Stopping rapist, stopping adulterers, stopping the bullies and all the abusers. I'm cleaning up the streets up for you. It's okay don't be embarrassed just thank me for doing your job. I'm here representing for every fat girl like me who's been used, abused and mistreated. I'm taking them sorry ass men who's ever did a woman dirty and cutting off their dicks. Oh, wait! Don't get it twisted I'll kill a bitch too if she did me wrong consider her dead and gone. Oh shit! It rhymes too anyway back to what I was saying.

You'll learn that we are not your toys. We are not going for anyone's shit. I'm one of many. You may catch one, but you won't catch us all.

FAT GIRL VIGILANTE

I hand it to Hernandez and he reads it. He laughs, "She's confident we won't catch her ass."

"Very, gives me a reason to want to catch her even more." I stay at the scene a little longer. I tell Hernandez, "listen I'll be back."

I put on my latex gloves walk into the Pastor's office and I look around for clues in his office files. Look for pictures of members and children. Several hundred pictures are found of chubby children naked ranging in various ages. I feel a salty feeling in my throat and rage burning in the pit of my stomach. As I look through the

INSANITY AT ITS FINEST!

pictures, I see one of a young boy and girl. The little girl has on a yellow dress on and ponytails. The young boy in a suit and a bow tie. I study the picture and realize this boy was the man in the picture who was on the tape.

"Hernandez come over and look at these pictures. This sick bastard was taking naked pictures of these little girls and boys. Shit, these sorry Mofos deserved to die."

"Yeah, I wish I was the one who pulled the trigger. Amigo, anyone ever messes with my girls I murder his soul. I'll lose this badge."

He spits on the ground and bags the pictures... That little girl face, it like I knew her. This was an old black and white photograph. I show it to Hernandez

Isn't that the young man we saw on the video and the little girl who is that?" Hernandez stares at it closely.

"Yeah, that is him, now that I think back he was the dude who committed suicide four years ago at the Adam's Mark Hotel. We later found out from the medical examiner's report he had large amounts of crack cocaine in his system. We question the parents, but they say he had issues and kind of shrugged it off as another addict dead. This video never surfaced until today she or whoever did this murder had this video."

"Looking through the file Thomas family have been members since 1962. The wife was on the choir. She is active in tithing and in the church committees. She didn't know they were molesting her son. Damn! I want to wake them up and show her this video and ask her how the fuck you didn't know they were boning your child in the ass."

Hernandez looked at me,

"Let's do it, you can tell they were keeping her busy with her church duties. She was clueless I bet." I dial Michelle number it rings three times before she picks it up. Her voice sounding sleepy,

"Hello."

The questions I want to ask her get stuck and I clear my throat, dead silence and no way to ask. I hang up. My mind wants to rule her out as a cold-blooded murder. My father taught me when I first came on the force there is a difference between a killer and a murderer. A killer is reckless and does it without a plan. A murderer strategizes for days, months and even years to off their victim. The Fat Girl Vigilante is a murderer with a purpose. This is more than revenge she feels like what she is doing is justice for all fat girls? Is that Michelle? I've got to get to know her my guts telling me she going to solve this riddle. That she knows something just like her aunt. Is Miyama holding the secret? My mind is leaving no stones unturned but still no exact answers.

We reach the address of 100 Humboldt Parkway and step into the frigid air. The cold cuts my cheeks and the wind blowing snatches my breath away. I bang on the door. I see a light flick on and someone peeks out the window.

"Who is it?"

"The Police Ma'am." We place our badges to the window and she cracks the door.

 "How can I help you late in the night?"

"I know it's late, but we have some important information about Thomas McMillan. Are you his mother?

"Yes, but he's been dead four long years."

"I'm aware, Ma'am, but I have the reason he killed himself and thought you would like to know." She gathers up her housecoat and said,

"He committed a lot of sin. Homosexuality, poisoning his body with those drugs and then…. Listen Officer, my son has been gone long before he died. I don't need to know anything further. Good night."

I wedge my foot in the door and proceed to ask,

"You mean you don't want to know what the two people you trusted the most did to your son? Your beloved Pastor and Deacon were molesting your son. Is the truth too hard to handle?" I pull out the picture of her son and the little girl and show it to her

"Is that your son in that picture? Do you know the name of the little girl? Her face frown she points her finger in my face.

"How dare you come here and lie about my Pastor and Deacon. True men of God they've done nothing but uplift the community and take care of our people."

"By molesting children. Listen, you want to sit and protect these sons of bitches you go ahead. Here's my card I have the real truth on tape.

INSANITY AT ITS FINEST!

Come to my office and look at what they did to your son." I throw my business card in between the door."

I walk away and she closes the door. I get in the truck and Hernandez follows. I hold my head.

"This is some phenomenal mess right here, cousin. I mean she doesn't want to see what these fake ass saints did to her son."

"I know, Amigo we're still going to talk to Miyama maybe these dudes may have messed with her. Let see what she has to say."

I call ahead to the holding center to bring Miyama down for conversation. Hernandez and I pull up into the parking garage. I sit in my car and finish off my cigarette. I step out to pull up my collar to cut off some of the frigid wind on my neck. I flash my identification and badge. Hernandez goes in the room first and decides he is just going to listen while I interrogate her. I turn left and enter into the investigation room; I stand against the door. Hernandez introduces himself and motion for me to take control of the interview.

Miyama is in an orange jumpsuit, more of her hair missing. She doesn't smell of urine this time around. Her lips are dry and cracked. I lend against the door and I scratch my beard.

She asks, "What question do you have for me today because I don't have the answer."

"Yes, you do and today I don't feel like hearing no riddles because let me first inform you the FAT GIRL VIGILANTE has killed your Pastor and Deacon. She shot them in the head, back, stab them multiple times, cut off their dicks and burned them. Oh, yeah and the Pastor and Deacon were dicking each other in the ass. So at 2 a.m. on my day off I'm pissed off and need fucking answers. "

"No, not them."

"Yes them!"

"You're lying, they're not dead the spirits would have told me. No, you playing me and my Pastor and Deacon isn't dead. I don't want to live anymore. She's out of control. She wrong, Lord. Stop the daughter of Satan. Bishop, she did this? Satan's daughter killed them. They served the house of the Lord. They baptize me, gave me food

INSANITY AT ITS FINEST!

and took care of me. I've been going to this church since I was a baby. I won't believe it."

I bang my hand on the table and kick the chair aside. "I have no reason to lie to you. Who the fuck is Satan's daughter? You keep saying that shit and right now I need a fucking name and Satan's daughter isn't cutting it. You know who's doing this and the one thing I hate is someone playing with my intelligence. Remember you called me so I can stop the Serpent of Arms from killing. You said I needed to stop her. How many dead bodies before she finds a way to get to you?"

She looks at me her eye now cold.

"Detective, don't you get it? I want to be with my Lord! I want to die. You want me to do your job and solve your murders. I won't do that because none of you wanted to help the many times I called. You let my baby girl be abused by her Daddy. You are so close to the answer, you just don't see it. Satan's daughter does her dirt right under your nose and you can't even smell it. She is colored with green and envy. Bishop, you're supposed to be a minister not a detective. Isn't that what your grandma wanted you to be? Kenya that is the name of the little girl you accidentally killed. My eyes widen and Hernandez looks at me. I turn away and bang on the door.

"I'm done with her."

The ride is silent and Miyama is playing with my mind. She gets in my soul every time and the sick shit is I allow her.

I finally reach back to the precinct and Hernandez and I go over the clues.

"Okay, so all of these men were killed on their birthday. She burned them and castrated them. She only shot the Pastor and Deacon. On my ride over I realize none of them are connected through work, family or friends. Also, she writes her signature in the victim's blood. Yet, check this out her leaves no trace of fingerprints, no bodily fluids or hair. She planned every detail of the murder so…." I rub my hands through my hair this case is exhausting. She hasn't slipped yet. I look over at Hernandez and he is smelling tissue and the envelope.

"Yo, Bishop smell this perfume." I sniff it and it's not cheap. It nothing I've ever smelled before.

INSANITY AT ITS FINEST!

"This scent has been at every crime scene. I'm particular about smells whoever doing it wears this particular perfume. It's not something you buy out of the store. I'll take it to the lab and see what they come up with. Right now, we call it a night get some sleep and rest. I feel as if we are getting nowhere. Five hundred to five thousand could have that scent.

SARGE/ MICHELLE

I wake up in a wig and heavy make-up. I'm naked trying to figure out what I did last night. The phone is ringing and the caller id flashes Mama's name. I turn it off because I'm almost afraid of what she may have done. Who she may have killed, I turn on the news. The new reporter is standing by a church and the words flash across the screen "Fat Girl Vigilante strikes again". I look and there is this man wallet. I run to the bathroom and there is no blood. I take a sigh of relief. Sarge remained a good girl.

I hear my phone and there is a text and it reads, CALL MAMA ASAP! I delete her message. I grab my IPOD and towel. I put on my baby blue workout yoga pants and matching tank top. I turn on Notorious BIG and hit the treadmill. My mind is on my workout and who was here. I look at the tall and bald security guard and he walks up to me.

"Can I get back my damn wallet?" His face cold and callus told me I didn't let him get far.

"Sure."

"Sarge, how you played me last night was fucked up. I mean you call me up here and then you belittle my dick and put me out. I didn't want you know how."

I breathe a sigh of relief that I only curse him out and not killed him. Sarge appeared again and now that it was water under the bridge I get on the treadmill.

I remember that in my fat days I couldn't be on it for five minutes now I'm doing forty minutes on an uphill. I look at the mirror and my body is transforming right before my eyes. The music has me in a zone and I start to run. I do crunches. I hit the weights. Sweaty and feeling good from putting in a good workout.

I go back to the room. I strip and admire my body. I look down at my toes. After losing the weight, my feet is an inch smaller. My stomach is flat. I still can't get a man to fall in love with me.

I feel sadness form up on me. I jump in the shower. The color of the day is sky blue. I put my red hair in a bun on top of my head. My favorite lipstick and the perfume Mama made for me. I top my lips off with raspberry lip-gloss. I look at the wig; the outfit I would not be caught dead in and those hooker boots.

I get on the elevator and check out. Sitting on the green couch is Mama, her legs crossed and she looks like a model. I watch as she conversing with the handsome security guard. My Mom who's fifty-five years old looks only thirty-five. My mother skin is a beautiful deep cocoa brown and her face clear from blemishes. Her red hair in a pageboy styles, her makeup flawless, her body strong, long and tone. I'm not where Mama is at yet. I walk up to her thinking if that guy knew what I knew he stay far away from her. He and Mama exchange numbers. He kisses her hand and winks.

"Good Morning, Mama!" She dressed in chocolate brown jeans and baby blue tunic. Her wool coat, which is a baby blue, brings out her boots.

"Good morning to you why haven't you called me?" I take in a deep breath and answer,

"I was asleep. I didn't hear the phone." She smirks and licks her lips. "You are a horrible liar. Come on we need to talk, go get your car. I left mine." I get my car and hand the same guy who Mama was talking to the ticket. I want to tell him don't do it that beautiful woman in their will fuck you, cut your dick off and fry him like a piece of a bacon. Instead, I drive around in a circle. I step out and switch sides so she can drive. She always has to be in control. I sit down and I feel her hit me across the face three times.

"Don't you ever ignore my calls? Do you understand me! I'm your mother and when I call you answer." Blood is dripping from my nose. The Sarge side of me wants to smack the shit out of her back. I hate her with a passion.

INSANITY AT ITS FINEST!

Tamyara Brown

She is my mother the woman I love and despise her at the same time. Love usually winning over the hate. I let her treat me the way she wants to. The woman who gave me life so on the other hand I have to respect her. I look directly out the car window.

I hear her voice echo, Sarge saying, "Smack her ass back that's why she keep beating on you like a little kid."

Mama is smiling and the excitement in her voice let me know she was reporting to me of the crime she committed, wish I couldn't hear so I would not have to soak up the bullshit.

"As you know, I kill the Pastor and Deacon. They screw me up inside, fuck up my whole thinking, took away my relationship with GOD. I waited years to off them. At first Michelle, I was planning to stab them to death then I decided to seasoned them, oil and flour them. After I shot them to death, and then girl you should have seen how I cut off their dicks with one swift move of my knife. It was a beautiful crime if I must say so myself. Wipe the blood off your face I taught you to never have a dirty face." I follow her direction and clean off my face. This ride seems like forever.

"Why you'd kill them?" I had to know.

"For Thomas, for me and every other child he hurt."

"Mama everyone in the community love the Pastor, the church, and the Deacon. They did nothing to you." She pulls in our driveway. I only have seen my mother shed a tear once and that was over my Daddy. So to see her express that emotion was so weird. I wanted to console and hug her. Instead, I let her cry,

"Michelle, Michelle, Michelle. You have no clue as to what those men who you called pillars of the community have done. They took my Daddy away from me. A Church is where I was supposed to feel safe and because of them I no longer believe in prayer. My relationship with God was taken away from me, don't I deserve to be close to God? Just like Miyama that selfish phony bitch. She pretends to know God and love him, but she would have never ever let them take away my innocence that was her gift to me. She told me to hide in the shed and wait for her. I wanted so bad to be accepted and liked by my own sister. I went in the shed even after Thomas warned

INSANITY AT ITS FINEST!

me not to." She pulls two Kleenex from the box and dabs her eyes. She looks at me and says,

"They took turns sticking their dicks in my mouth, my ass and pussy. She never told Daddy the truth. He sends me back to Brooklyn. He never called and he never wrote. All he ever did was send a check. So I killed them their two nuts in a bucket and fuck it. They took from me and I took their lives. They'll never rape another chubby kid again. That's all they ever prey on. I did the police job by sending them to hell." She wipes her eyes and clears her throat. I'm crying with her and when I reach out to hug her she pushes me away.

"I'm sorry, Mama. I didn't know how to fix the hurt in you." She grabs my face and squeezes it real tight.

"Just know every person I've ever killed had it coming to them. Believe that if nothing else. . Please, Chile hear my promise I'll kill you too without hesitation. Don't let that brief bit of emotion fool you. Now fuck around and get loose with your lips. Now that's all cleared up. Are you hungry, dear?"

"No, I have to go to a book discussion over at the coffee shop."

"Enjoy and don't eat anything fattening."

"Yes, Ma'am."

I watch her walk into the house. I refused to go inside with her besides tonight is her revolution meeting. I begin to back out of the driveway because she has told me the most devastating news about her childhood and she wouldn't let me hug her. She fears any type of affection from me. She hasn't since the day she killed my father. I grew up craving for love from anyone but more importantly desiring it from her. At home, she called me a mutt and a fat rodent. I live with the foolish belief that one day she will love me. She has killed in front of my eyes and never once have I shared her secret. Never once have I tried to kill her for taking away my daddy. I stopped Sarge every time she attempted to hurt her.

I decide to go on Elmwood Avenue. I realize I haven't eaten yet and go into Tim Hortons. I order a bowl of oatmeal and French vanilla cappuccino and an apple. I sit in the corner and watch the snowfall. I think back to what Mama said. Did Auntie Miyama do that? It's unbelievable, now if the situation were reversed I wouldn't have any doubt in my mind.

INSANITY AT ITS FINEST!

Tamyara Brown

I pull out the Challenger newspaper and begin to read it. Bishop walks in and orders a coffee and a banana walnut muffin. He doesn't even notice me as he walks out. I have a face people tend to forget about. A man as handsome wouldn't want an ugly and overweight woman like me. I would be lying to myself to think any different. Another morning alone, I look at the couple sitting holding hands and kissing, I want a man to love me the day he loves her.

It's like all I ever get is the men who mistreat me. I drink some more of my cappuccino and eat a spoonful of oatmeal to erase the ache in my heart. I hear a deep baritone voice and I look up and his handsome face is staring at me.

"Good Morning, Beautiful?" I turn my head and see Bishop big smile.

"Good morning to you."

My heartbeat speeds up and I look away from his handsome face. He sits across from me and I feel like my temperature on this winter morning is ninety degrees.

"Hi, Michelle. I'm sorry if I scared you. I had to come back in and say hi." He touches my chin so he can look me in the eyes. I feel as if he has put me in a trance. To break the power he has over me I ask, "Are you following me? I feel like you are. You show up everywhere I am."

He parts his lips and he is doing it again smiling. He rubs his hand through his thick beard and pulls on his ear.

"Honestly, No. We just seem to meet up. It pure coincidental. Maybe it is meant for us to get to know each other" He touches my hand.

"So how are you, Bishop?"

"Overworked and underpaid but all is good. You look like you have a lot on your mind. You smell wonderful. What is that scent?"

"It's a perfume my mother bought from the Cayman Islands. She got it made when she went on vacation"

"I love it. So, Ms. Michelle, I was wondering if I could request the honor of taking you to dinner tonight or whenever you're free?"

He's still touching my fingers and he is never takes his eyes off me. He finally removes his hand and folds them.

"Is that a yes Or are you going to turn me down cold?"

I look at him. I want the words to come out, but nothing is able to reach my tongue. I'm filled with excitement and overjoyed with someone asking me on a date.

"Um, Yes, I would like that. What's good for you?" He pulls out his I phone and looks at his calendar. He touches the screen and smile, "If you're free how about tonight let say 7:00 pm?"

"Sounds good." He smiles and he has the nicest teeth.

"Well beautiful, I have to go so tonight I'll see you."

He kisses my hand and I feel as if a bolt of electricity inside of me.

"I'll see you tonight."

I watch him pull out a cigarette light it. Even the way the cigarette hangs is sexy. He goes into his truck backs out and disappear. I think to myself maybe Miyama right the man of my dreams is coming. Just maybe it is him.

Bishop

DAY OF CONFESSIONS & DISCOVERY!

I put on my Bluetooth and dial Hernandez number. He answers, "What you got good, Boss?"

"Shit, the perfume we smelled. Miyama's niece had the exact the same scent. She said she her mother brought it from the Cayman Islands. Can you pull up the chemist who may have design this fragrance? It's not a coincidence."

"Hell no! We're on to something, Bishop! So what are your plans?"

"I just need to figure her out and see if she is the serial killer. I have a date with her tonight. We kind of being running into each other."

"I don't know what if she figures you out? "

"I have to do what I have to do to catch a killer, Hernandez. You act like I am going to fuck around and fall in love, have a baby and make her my wife."

"Shit happens, Bishop."

"A date and conversation that's it. We have to put a dent in the case!"

"Is she fat?"

INSANITY AT ITS FINEST!

"No, she has a voluptuous body. I was thinking last night what if fat girl vigilante isn't overweight at all? What if she lost the weight and is now seeking revenge on people who have teased her, bullied her and so on and so forth. I'm on to something and it smells damn good. We close to solving to catching her."

"Thomas mother came down and she wants to talk to you. I know it's been like twenty-four hours since you've slept. She may help us in giving us the name of the little girl in the picture."

I yawn and shake my head. Sleep is weighing on me heavy but not as much as who is killing all these men in the Queen city.

"I'm on my way. Did forensics find any prints on the tape?"

"Yes, just the prints of Thomas."

"So Thomas came back from the dead and blasted them." Trying to make light of the situation.

I pull into the parking lot of the precinct and park. I walk in and pour a cup of coffee. The old woman I saw last night is now wrapped in a wool overcoat. Her head held high, thin eyes, and bright red lipstick. She looks at me and turns her head away.

I greet her, "Mrs. McMillian, you can follow me in the room right there. Ralph, can you bring the cart with the TV and the copy of the tape marked *2019 THOMAS MC* evidence in the room for me, please?" She sits down and I offer her coffee she declines. I wait for Hernandez to come in the room. I observed her she is well dress and her hands folded in her lap.

She speaks, "The little girl had the greenest eyes and dark skin. For the life of me I can't remember that child name. Her sister Miyama is another crazy somebody walking around barefoot. A city slut came and spread vicious lies on the good Pastor and Deacon. Men of God would never do the unthinkable."

"The young lady spreading lies about what?" She waves it off and takes a big huff.

"It doesn't matter they are all dead. Show this video so I can denounce the lies of the good men in the community."

If I had some hours of sleep I would have come back with a smart-ass remark, but as the saying goes let the video do the talking.

INSANITY AT ITS FINEST!

Hernandez walks in with Ralph who brings in the TV and VCR set up with the tape.

Hernandez ask, "Are you ready for this, Ma'am?" I answer the question for her,

"Oh yes, she is ready as she will ever be. She needs to denounce our fictitious tales on the Pastor and Deacon."

I push play on the remote and allow the tape to begin. As the scene plays the Deacon walks in and he begins to undress. I hear the Pastor tell Thomas to kneel before him and he pulls out his dick and command Thomas to perform oral sex on him.

You see tears in his eyes as he refuses. You then see the Deacon strike Thomas in the face and stuff his dick in Thomas' mouth. Looking at this I get angry all over again. When I look over at Mrs. McMillian her mouth drops open, tears fall down her face. I hear her whisper,

"Turn it off, please" I ignore her soft voice pretending she didn't say a word. This part of the video she needs to see and hear. Thomas voice cracking and in between sobs said,

"Mama, I tried to tell you for years what they were doing to me. You didn't believe me. Maybe now you will."

He has the gun pointed to his head and the sound of the gun going off. The blood splattering all over the walls and screen. Her screams and crying to the Lord causes me to turn off the video.

"Ms. McMillian you can now denounce the lies to my partner."

I throw the remote on the table and walk out.

I head home and pray I can get two hours of sleep. I haven't been at home in twenty-four hours. I look at Bullet who running in circles. I let him out and let do his business. I fall on the bed. My body is exhausted, my mind restless and tired all at the same time.

The video haunted me and like always educated me it was fucked up people in the world. The innocent smile on someone's your face and behind closed doors while breaking several commandments in the bible. They are doing someone's child dirty while preaching the word of God. It almost shocks me people would take the word of their Pastor or whomever over their flesh and blood.

I thank God every day for my parents. Not many folks are blessed with what I have in them. So many dudes I put in jail have had the

INSANITY AT ITS FINEST!

same tragic shit happen and no one willing to face the truth. I switch my thoughts over to Michelle.

I think of her smell, her smile and the way Michelle's hand felt in mine. Her appearance soft, sweet and innocent. Good girls kill people too. If she is the murderer of she had to have a reason, right? A method to the madness she is creating it is the belief I am trying to wrap my head around.

Is it her mother? Is she overweight and angry at the world? My gut clenches tight. I feel like a fire that has started in my chest, I pop an antacid in my mouth swallow without chewing. I chase it with water and burp. My cell has Hernandez ring.

I look at my phone and it's Hernandez. There goes sleep I think. "What you got good for me Hernandez?" I grab a cigarette light and inhale what's killing my lungs. It relaxes me, but it doesn't calm the insanity in my heart and mind.

"I swear I feel like today is the day of confessions. Ms. McMillan was all tore up she had to be sent to the hospital after the video. Your favorite psycho wants to talk."

I jump up and grab my keys off the nightstand. I pat Bullet on the head.

I lock up and the nosy neighbor greets me. I nod my head and jump in my truck and pull off. I see a long line of people in the visiting area. I show my id and ask, "Hey Anne, what room is Miyama in?" She licks her lips and begins her usual flirting "She's in room two and I am available for you anytime."

"Now how should I take that, Ms. Anne? She smiles and comes close to my ear and whispers.

"Let's just say I aim to please and I do it well. You will think you are in pussy heaven after the tip of your dick gets wet, Detective Bishop." I chuckle.

"Stop playing your husband would be pissed off at me for taking his wife and turning her out on this right here. Have you calling me Detective Pussy slayer." I grasp my dick. It's true if she wasn't married I would have given it to her in the worst way. For an older woman, she is damn fine.

"Why you bring him into it?"

"He's your husband so he already in it. Now had he been just your boyfriend I would have taken you up on your offer."

I wink at her and walk through the metal doors. I prep myself for the bullshit Miyama's going to feed me today. I prepare myself mentally not to curse her out or jack her up. I'm tired, horny and just fucked up all across the board. The guard opens the door. Miyama is reciting bible verses. Snot all over her nose. She is rocking back and forth. I look at her and stand against the door. I hand her a tissue from my pocket. She refuses it.

"You called for me to come down here. What is it that you want, Miyama?" She clears her throat. I wish she'd wipe her fucking nose and she didn't smell like piss. She speaks softly,

"It's my fault, Bishop. I did this to them, to Satan's Daughter. I want to share the story of jealousy and how Satan feeds off it." She rocks back and forth in the chair.

"I'm not in the mood for bullshit riddles and predictions."

"Just listen, please. I have to tell the truth because God only likes the truth."

"You're truth better be a lead to a suspect and not some old fuckery." I cross my arms and pull my hat off. I glare at her. She is staring at the table, pulls the booger from her nose and puts it in her mouth. I turn up my nose and suck my teeth. Nasty ass I thought to myself.

"Every summer she'd come up to visit Daddy. I was filled with the sin of jealousy. She was fat but pretty. I didn't like all of my friends wanted to play with her. They thought she was special because she came from New York City. I was Daddy princess and no one was going to take my place. I was mean to her. I would get her in trouble."

"I'm not understanding how a sibling rivalry will help me catch a serial killer?"

"So I told the Deacons she wasn't saying her prayers at night, told him that she didn't believe in God. So on her birthday Daddy bought her this beautiful yellow dress and shiny Mary Jane's shoes. My Mama presses her hair and she had all these long pretty curls. I was so mad everyone was ignoring me and treating her like a princess."

I think back to the picture of the little girl in a yellow dress and ponytails. I rub my hand over my face and blow out air.

INSANITY AT ITS FINEST!

The Deacon told me to send her to the shed so he could pray over her. I told her I would play a game of hide and seek with our friend Thomas. I made her hide in the shed because no one would find her. I heard her call my name and I refused to go in there. I wanted her to be free of sin. I wanted her to go back to Brooklyn so I could have my Daddy back and my friends back." Her head hung low and the snot dripping on the table.

"Exactly what are trying to say to me, Miyama?" I pull at my ear because I know she wasn't about to tell me what I thought she was. She sniffles and cries some more.

"They didn't mean to hurt them. They were taking Satan out of them. They'd ask me to bring them to the shed in the back of the church. It's where they pray over bad children especially fat girls and boys. They take them in there and locked them in until they said, "Hallelujah".

I grab her by the shirt and shake her. I want to stomp her ass out for polluting my mind and allowing these sick animals to hurt children.

"How sick of you to believe they were saving their souls. Did it ever occur to you that they were hurting them? You brought those children into that shed to be..." I can't let the words out of my mouth. I shake her again and allow her to hit her head on the back of the chair.

She sobs, "That wasn't what I sent them in there for I was helping them get the sin out of their blood." I let her go and back away from her.

"It is the same shit you killed your husband for, Miyama. Each of their innocence stolen." She sobbing uncontrollably pulls at the root of hair, scratching her skin and mumbling,

"God, I am sorry. Please forgive me."

"Who, who was the children?" I bang my hand on the table.

"I don't know who."

"You do remember and you better tell me."

"Thomas, Linda, Bobby, Tateyama, Goldie and...'" I blow hard and exhale.

"And who else?"

"Satan's daughter. She was one of them. I was just trying to save her honest to GOD. I wanted to get the Satan out of her. I mess her up I made her kill people."

"You are right. You let whoever the daughter of Satan is and you destroy her soul. You put her in the state of mind to kill. You help take away her innocence. I got to get out of here before I beat the hell out of you." I bang on the door and the guard lets me out.

I yell at Anne, "I want her transfer out to the psyche unit. I want her under twenty-four-hour watch. She's talking suicide.

"It's a waiting list."

"This isn't up for discussion. She is the link to me solving this crime." I look at my watch it's already after two-thirty. Yo, I need to get out of here because what the fuck is going on in Buffalo? I called Hernandez emotions on overload. My body infuriated with anger to the point I've smoked two cigarettes back to back.

"She fucking sent those kids in there to be molested by those perverts. She calls herself cleansing their souls. She knew it, man. She had to I mean she knew their names and everything." I puff on my cigarette make rings with the smoke. Hernandez becomes the voice of reason,

"She was just a kid herself this happen in the late sixties. Maybe these sick bastards had her believing she was saving souls."

 I sigh and rub my temples. I think I need a strong shot of Hennessy to even phantom some of the shit I've been combating.

"It's logical but I still believe she knew about it. She is a psychotic Bitch, man."

"Boss, you need a break from this case for a minute. You are overwhelmed. Go home shower and go to sleep, Man. Really call it a day." I look in my rearview mirror my eyes are bloodshot red.

"You're right this is taxing on me." I look at the clock it's now going on five.

"Good man, Bishop!"

INSANITY AT ITS FINEST!

Bishop

DATE WITH THE SUSPECT

When I finally reach home I jump in the shower and just let the water wash over me. The steam opens my nostrils and release the smell of Miyama piss stench. I close my eyes as the water runs over my head. I'm burnt out and need the hands of a female to massage away the hell I've been through to solve this case. I know that if I allow my head to hit the pillow it, I won't wake up in time.

I think I should call my father and just vent. My father could help me find some resolve to this craziness. The decision not to call him was based on the fact it was my mother time with my father. She had to listen to endless night of cop tales and situations.

I turn off the water grab a towel and wrap it around me I lotion up and throw on some Cool Water Cologne. I put on a pair of jeans, luxury thermal with velour trim. The Oak well Mock Toe Boots by Timberland. Take a bottle of five hour shot to the head so I won't crash and burn. I clean up my beard and give myself a nice gold tee. I put in my diamond stud. I cut down my fro and give myself an edge up. I feel like a different man.

I put my gun in the holster just in case of emergency. I profile for Bullet. I look human. Tonight I'm going to multitask and be an officer and a gentleman. I check the clock and put some Visine in my eyes to clear the red out. I call Michelle. It rings three times and she answers,

"Are you canceling out our date?"

"No, I called to see if you were ready. Why would I cancel?"

"Oh, I thought you might have change your mind?" She gives me her address, which I already knew. I step out and drive approximately ten minutes to her home. She standing outside in a chocolate wool coat with boots to match. She is stunning her red hair cover with a wool hat. I step out the car and open the door for her. She slides inside like a true lady. She has on the perfume I smelled, no makeup but lipstick. She speaks,

"Hello Bishop." Her voice soft yet her tone seductive. She sits back and buckles seatbelt. She looks at me. Her green eyes are shaped like a Siamese cat.

"Tonight, you choose the place you want to eat. Wherever you like to go".

"A place called May Jen's I hear is excellent. It's a Chinese restaurant out in Kenmore." I plug it into my GPS and get the directions. I start the car and turn on my mix CD of the late eighties and early nineties love songs.

I start to sing as if I've got Johnny's skills. She interrupts me,

"Listen to you singing. You sound good no Johnny Gill but you got a little something."

"Don't hate on my voice, Girl."

We laugh as we pull into May Jen's Restaurant on Kenmore Avenue. I step out and open the door for her and extend my hand to help her out. I take her hand and lead the way. I open the door for her and she walks in. The restaurant décor is beautiful. The beautiful fans on the wall and Oriental flower décor.

I assist her with taking off her coat. Her body is thick and curvaceous. Her sweater dress caresses each curve. I feel my nature rise. I hang it up and when we reach the table I pull out her chair.

"You are quite the gentleman and I appreciate that."

The waitress dressed in black and white brings a beautiful teapot and two small cups. She hands us the menu to order from.

"My father taught me you never treat a woman with disrespect. It's the way he treated my mother."

"How long have they been married?"

"They've been married for thirty two years and still in love with one another."

"Wow that is a long time. " She pours some tea in a cup and sips it slow.

"What about your parents?" Her eyes shift. She sighs.

"My father died when I was eleven and my mother well she's alive. So do you have siblings? I clear my throat and sip on the glass of water.

"One brother. He's forty he just recently got married."

INSANITY AT ITS FINEST!

"I have no siblings."

The waitress comes over and ask if where ready to order. I order the ginger garlic chicken stir-fry and she orders the tangerine chicken. I select a vegetarian dumpling for appetizer. She seems nervous and her cell phone has been vibrating for the past twenty minutes.

"So is the food good here, Michelle?"

"Excellent. I love the Ginger chicken stir-fry it's my favorite."

I yawn and shake my head. I continue,

"I'm sorry I've haven't had much sleep."

"I can tell your eyes are red. Are you gigolo?" She chuckles and I laugh.

"No, I am not. I am a mental health counselor." She shifts in her seat and folds her hand.

"Is it hard trying to figure out someone? I mean it has to be hard to figure what or why they did what they did or do." I sip more of my water and take a minute to prepare my lie.

"Yes it is. I mean dealing with it and having to be strictly confidential. You carry a lot of people's secrets and unable to say one word about it."

"Tell me about it." She mumbles

"I'm sorry did you say something?" The waitress brings our entrees I think back to what she said. I don't push. She bites into the chicken. She said,

"This is delicious. Have you tried it?"

"No will you let me try some? She picks up the fork and put a piece of chicken, tangerine and snow pea and carrot. She feeds it to me. I put some of my ginger chicken on a fork. I feed it to her.

"You're right the tangerine chicken is good. What about the ginger chicken?"

"I'm not a fan of spicy food but this really good." We eat in silence. Her phone rings again she looks at it and excuse herself. I see Hernandez walk in with his wife. He and his wife walk over.

"Hi, Maggie. You look beautiful as usual. Hernandez what's good with you?" We shake hands.

"You clean up real good, Amigo. Everything good?"

INSANITY AT ITS FINEST!

"Yeah, we're good." They walk back to the table and Michelle walks in and sits down. She wipes her eyes and sits down. She looks down so I won't see it's apparent she's been crying."

"Are you alright?" She shakes her head and answers,

"Yes, just a little disagreement with my mother. She thinks no … I'm sorry I'm on a date. Maybe she is right." She lets her tears roll down. I take my hand and wipe her eyes. She turns her head and smile.

"The dessert here is good too." I turn her head back towards me.

"You want to talk about it?"

"No, Bishop. I'm fine. I'm sorry she always does that. She just overprotective that's all."

We get ready to leave and my phone receives a text from Hernandez asking if all is well. I text back yes and I will call him later. I help her with her coat open the door for her and she sits. Her phone vibrates and she turns it off.

I look through my CD's and put on my old school jams. I hit track number three of Mint Condition.

"I'm about to cheer you up by singing or make you laugh." She looks at me and I wipe the tears that have fallen. She smiles. I start singing and sings along with me. I stop the car and though it's cold as hell. I'm going beyond the call of duty, because it's obvious she's hurting.

"Come dance with me in the middle of downtown." She raises her eyebrow.

"You are serious aren't you?"

"Very. Now come on!"

She steps out and I take her hands and wrap it around my neck as we gaze into one another. Our body sways to the music, though the snow is falling we keep each other warm exchanging body heat. In our own world we share a moment that will forever be remember I see people looking and in the parking lot as we dance. She is no longer crying and her head rests on my shoulders.

"You don't have to hurt right now. Let me take over and I'll make you see I'm what you're looking for?"

She shakes her head. I hold her closer and I can tell she needed that. I needed her to see she deserved to be held and pampered, I don't really know her yet we have a connection I cannot explain. . I hear people saying, "I wish my man did that for me?" She is no longer crying but instead with a big pretty smile. I find myself not wanting

INSANITY AT ITS FINEST!

to let go. She felt right in my arms. My gut didn't tighten. I break our embrace and for a moment we stare at one another. I put her hands in mine and lead her back in her seat. I get in next to her. The whole ride I kept looking at her and her beauty is breathtaking. We finally pull up in front of her house.

"Thank you, Bishop."

"No need it was my pleasure." She smiles. I see the light come on upstairs she sighs.

"I really enjoyed tonight. Even though you said don't say thank you. I appreciate you showing me that there is at least one gentleman in Buffalo. It's very rare." She looks up at the window. She sits and leans her head back.

She asks,

"Have you ever felt like just going away and not coming back?" I turn the music down.

"Honestly, Yes I have! It's why I came to Buffalo. A woman I loved once had an abortion. I was so wrap up in work and didn't even realize it. I never knew it would actually affect me. It hurt because I've always wanted to be a father. I close my eyes and she puts her fingers in mine.

"It wasn't your fault."

"I don't know. Everyone at one point or another wants to get away from their past so they can forget." I close my eyes and see the past flash back again. I turn and look at her.

"Yet, Bishop you can't get away because of the memories in your mind. It's like it's chasing you and finally catches up when you close your eyes to sleep.'"

"Exactly. You can never forget." I yawn and shake my head. The five energy drink is wearing off.

Bishop, Good night and get some rest." She kisses me on the cheek and we hug. I feel this connection and I have to avoid it.

"Good night, Michelle. I'll call you tomorrow. I look up at the window I see a shadow of a slender woman staring down at me. Her arms folded and her hair hanging over her eyes. I back out and my gut clenches. I look up again and she's gone. I may have hit the jackpot.

Michelle

BREAKING ME DOWN

He has taken me to dinner and danced with me in the middle of Downtown Buffalo. I walk up the stairs and open the door and I pray Mama is sleeping. The moment I've waited for all my life for a man to make me feel special. I'm greeted by Mama's slamming me against the door. "Who the fuck was that?" She punches me in the stomach and I bend over.

"Mama, he is just a friend." She bends down by me and smacks me in the face.

"You need to do your workout to burn off those extra hundred pounds instead of going on a date. So you feel you want to be a whore, huh? Run out with a man you hardly know. How would you like if I kill him? Cut off his dick and set him on fire the way I did your Daddy." She laughs.

"Mama, I'm sorry. I won't defy you again. Just leave him alone, please. Whatever you want?"

"Whatever I want, huh? I'll get back to you but for now go clean yourself up. I want you on the treadmill for an hour, then a hundred sit ups and pushups" I follow her command. I look at my face in the mirror swollen and red.

I hear Sarge say, "Fuck that bitch up! How long you going to let her keep doing this to you? Kill her the way you killed Markel. Stop being a punk bitch."

I whisper, "I am not a killer like you and Mama."

She replies puts her hand on her hips.

"I am you, stupid. You're a murderer face it. With her gone we will be happy. The only way I die if you kill me and vice versa. Kill Mama, cut her up and bury her in the dumpster. Don't be afraid."

I turn from the mirror. I think of Bishop, his hands touching mine and his hug. He and I dancing. I sing to myself, "*You don't have hurt no more. Baby, it's over.*"

I put on my red workout clothes. I look and I see the woman I don't want to be. Her voice begging me to off Mama. I get on the

INSANITY AT ITS FINEST!

treadmill and warm up by walking. I don't look at Mama as she's doing reverse crunches.

"So Michelle, did you fuck him? You need to run instead of walking. Increase your endurance." She is doing one-hand push-ups.

"No, we just went out to dinner."

"How much did you pay?" I roll my eyes. I start to run just so she won't start hitting me again.

"He paid, Mama. You act like no man wants me. Am I that ugly?"

"You're still fat and no good man with common sense wants a woman looking half ass decent. You think because you lost those hundred and some pounds that it's okay to be fat. Hell no! You goal weight is supposed to be 120. "

"I'm trying real hard, Mama."

"Bullshit. I found Oreos under your bed. Do you want to be obese again? Fat is ugly like you. Beauty is thin like me and the other women you see."

I want to reply every time I turn on the T.V. the truth is spoken in volumes. Their definition of beauty isn't me. Beyoncé is what every woman craves to be secure, powerful, sexy and the right body weight. She is what every man dreams of at night. If I had her beauty, brains and power I would be accepted and loved. I see her and believe she is perfect in every way no flaw at all.

"I want you to have her abs. Have you been bleaching your skin and bathing in bleach like I told you too?"

"No, it irritates my skin. You don't have to be thin and light skin to make it. There are so many dark skin and curvaceous women who are beautiful."

"You think Beyoncé would be as successful fat? We already have against us that we have dark skin. At least if you have a nice healthy body it will get you in the door even if you're ugly."

"Do you think I'm ugly because of the weight or my face?" She kicks me in the knee.

"There is a bunch of pretty fat women with hypertension, diabetes, and fat around their heart. You see them with a decent man? Hell no! You see they can't walk or breathe? My mother she had the long hair and green eyes but no man wanted her because she was over four hundred pounds. You are ugly as long as you're fat."

It is not true, Mama. I know women who love their body and confident."

"Yeah, right. If you're thin some prince charming can sweep you off your feet. You never see a rich black man with a big chick on his arm. Don't you understand I just want better for you?"

I weigh two and twenty pounds. I lost a whole person and changed my diet. I work out five times a week but to her I'm still need to lose more because I am not Beyoncé. She believes she is perfection. She idolizes her. Her skin is clear, it has a natural glow, and she never carries a body odor because she takes a Body Mint and Chlorafresh.

"What about Monique? What about Oprah? Mama, she is the most powerful woman in the world. She started out fat. They are big women who have men who love them regardless of their size."

"Stupid they have money. Money changes the rules when you're rich and famous. For your information, they both have lost the weight. They also can buy and sell a nigger. You my dear, don't have the confidence, the strength or any talent to make it fat. You are a weak failure who will die alone and never have a baby. Nobody wants you because you don't like you. I don't like you and that the motherfucking truth."

"Is that what you think of me?" I hold my tears back. I put on my coat on and my red boots. She smirks at me and comes in my face. "Yes, I do."

I slam the door and I run down the stairs. I get in my car and I cry like a two-year old. She takes the joy out of me. I drive around nowhere to go. There is her truth flat out and again I had no strength to defend myself. I had no courage to tell her how beautiful I am at any size. I ask myself who will love me? If my mother doesn't love me how can I expect someone else to?

 My cell phone is ringing. I pray it isn't Mama. Bishop name flashes and I wipe away my tears.

"Hi, Bishop! I thought you were tired."

"I had a few hours of sleep. I'm sorry to call so late but wanted to make sure you are okay?"

INSANITY AT ITS FINEST!

I tried to fight back the tears and the sobs. I try to contain all the pain I was feeling inside. What I was feeling would run him away. "I'm okay."

"No, you're not, Michelle. What's going on? Are you home?"

"No, I'm driving around. I just needed to get out the house. I'll be alright." I pull over.

"Where are you? I will meet you."

"I'm at the McDonald's at Grant and West Ferry."

"I'm on my way promise me you won't leave." I feel so powerless. I ball up the tissue in my hand and rip it apart.

"Okay!"

I order a Big Mac, large fry and two apple pies. The woman hands me my food and I stuff a handful in my mouth and take a bite of the sandwich. The knock on the window startles me. I look at the man with a gray hoodie its Bishop. I let out a huge air of relief. I unlock the door. I look in the mirror my face is swollen. My hair's a mess. I run my fingers through my hair.

 I lower my head and hide my fries. I start to cry again. He lifts my chin with his finger."

"Talk to me, Michelle."

I don't want him to know my mother is a psycho maniac who get off on murdering men or beating me up when she feels like it.

"Can you let me cry on your shoulder?" He unbuckled my seatbelt moves closer to me.

"Why don't you come home with me? You really don't know me and I'm not going to hurt you. I promise you. Or we can sit in the car your choice. In this condition I can't allow you to drive and get hurt. Whatever you want to do besides drive." He puts his arms around me and holds me tight.

"I'll go to your house. What about my car?"

"I'll have friend of mine drive it back to my house." I hand me keys and I have no clue why I feel safe with him.

Bishop makes a call and gets out the car. He walks around to open the door. I step out. I realize I haven't taken a shower, my hair is a mess.

"I look a mess. I was working out and…." He cuts me off

"You look fine."

He opens his car door and I get in. He checks my door to make sure it's locked. When he gets in the car. "You feel like some music?" I shake my head yes.

We drive listening to Jesse Powell. I break the silence.

"You love music don't you?"

"I do it soothes me. More of the old stuff and the nineties, the stuff today is pure garbage except a few artists." Tony Terry comes on.

"This brother should have won multiple awards."

"This is one of my favorites by him. He had another song head over heels that I love too."

"Yeah, Yeah I have his whole CD at home." He pulls up to Wilson farms and park.

"I need a pack of cigarettes, you want anything?"

"No, I'm fine thank you for asking." He walks in and shakes the hand of the male clerk. They converse for a few minutes. I watch as he get two cups of coffee and his cigarettes. He gets and hands me the drinks to hold.

."I know you said you didn't want anything but I got you a cappuccino. I hope French vanilla is good for you."

How you know I like cappuccino?"

"In Tim Horton's it was what you were drinking yesterday."

He pulls up to his home. I hear the dog barking.

"I have a dog? Are you scare of dogs he won't bite unless I tell him too? He only understands German."

"You speak German?"

"Yes."

He opens his door and turns on the light. He is beautiful. He rubs his head and snaps. He sits down.

"Put your hand out and let him smell you."

I pull my hand out and he sniffs it. He tells the dog something in German. He snaps his finger twice and the dog walks over to me.

"Go ahead, Michelle. Rub his head. I touch him and rub him.

"What his name? He is full blood German shepherd I can tell by his coat."

"Bullet".

He sends him to the basement. He and I walk to the living room. I take my shoes off because he has this beautiful beige carpet covering

INSANITY AT ITS FINEST!

his floor. It is soft like cotton. His long fingers touch my face tracing the red bruise decorating my face. It stings when he touches it and I winch.

"What happen to your face?"

"Do I have to talk about it?" He sits next to me. I take a deep breath. "Yes! At this point in the game you have to. I need to know what's up." I take the tissue and twist it.

"My mother and I had a big fight. It is okay she just lost control. I mean she just gets angry and she hits me. She just thinks any guy I come in contact with will try and take advantage of me .She always saying nobody wants me because of my weight."

I get up and reach for my shoes. He stops me and stands in front of me. I sit back down and I cover my face with my hands. My throat is dry. My head is pounding I can hear it in my ears. He stands against the wall hands in his pocket staring at me. He looks like he's searching for the right words to say. He sighs,

"I'm sorry, Michelle that you're Mom feels that way. How do you see yourself?"

"I see what she tells me. Who she thinks I am. I mean what she said has some truth behind it men don't marry fat girls. When I was bigger no one called me pretty, asked me out on dates or pay me any mind. My skin color isn't…." He cuts me off

"Let me stop you right there. I'm going to keep it all the way with you. This whole time you're talking, you've told me how your Mama sees you and society? I have yet to hear your own opinion? So again let me ask you, how do you Michelle see herself?"

"I'm all right. I'm not perfect. What do you think of me so far? I bet you think I'm weak." He sits on his coffee table in front of me and takes my hand in his. He looks deep in my eyes and moves closer to me.

"Michelle, listen to me, please if I tell you what I see will you believe me? Will you throw her distorted thoughts out your mind?" He clears his throat and licks his lips. "I can…" He places his finger on her lips.

"Let me finish what I see is a beautiful black woman. If Michelle saw it too. She wouldn't allow her Mama or no one else to define who she is as a person."

"It's all I know. It was all that was taught to me that you were ugly if you're fat." He takes his finger and wipes my eyes.

"Michelle, I'm going to teach you something tonight. My grandmother may she rest in peace taught me a valuable lesson about how you think about yourself. You are the owner of your thoughts. I don't care what people put in your head it's up to you and only you to own your thoughts?'

"Some thoughts I want to disown like my father dying"

"If you don't mind me asking how did your father die, Michelle?"

I look at him and I want to shout my Mama did it. I can't because as psychotic as she is. I never broke a promise to her. I pray that he doesn't see right through me. That the truth is written all over me but I let the lie spill like the liquor spill on Daddy's grave. I feel his eyes on me and there I begin my liquor spill of untruth,

"He was killed in a car accident. That's all I know."

. He walks over to me with a washcloth filled with ice. He places it on my face,

"This will help the swelling go down. I have guestroom and you're more than welcome to stay."

"You're just being nice to me. I seem so pitiful don't I?" He rubs his gold tee and raises his eyebrow. He sucks his teeth and stands up,

"Okay, real rap don't sit here and tell me what I think of you in a negative sense. You're sitting here making false accusation about how I feel. You're not going to do that in my house. I don't think you're pitiful. I think you're human who has a right to express her emotions. So are you staying?"

"Yes. I'm sorry."

"Don't be. You and I need to get some rest keep the ice on your face while I make up the bed."

I lean back on his couch. I close my eyes because they hurt so badly. I feel wet hot breath on my face. I open my eyes and it's Bullet. He lies on my lap and I rub him. He looks at me and me at him. I scratch his ear and I see Bishop step out and snaps his finger and say something to him in German. Bullet jumps down and goes into the basement.

INSANITY AT ITS FINEST!

"Michelle, I put extra blankets in there it a little drafty, you can turn the heat up. I'm tired and you need some rest. Good night".
"Good night, Bishop."
I watch him go into his room. The door closes. I go into the room wrap up the blankets and hope once I close my eyes this night will be over.

OFFICER DOWN!

His shriveled dick did nothing for the sexual desire burning in my loins. The odor of sex, weed and body musk lingers in the air. I hate his loud ass snoring and whistling sound from his nose is annoying me. He has the nerve to call himself Big Willie what an understatement, his 6"6 frame was muscular and built for a career as a basketball center versus an officer of the law. I look in his wallet and there is a picture of his wife, three children and his badge. Another sorry ass smug motherfucker breaking a woman's heart, I take out his license, the money in his wallet and his American Express card.

He's sleeping peacefully and has the nerve to be cute. I awake him by massaging his dick, stroking him until his volcano begins to erupt. I release his stick, take the handcuffs and lock his hands to the bedposts. Spread his legs and tie his feet to each post.
"Big Willie, wake up and sex me the way I deserve." His eyes bulge he notices his hands locked to the bed and feet bound."
"What the hell are you doing? Let me free, I told you last night I'm not into bondage." I smack him in the face and lick his cheeks.
"Listen to Mama! First, you are not in the position to tell me what to do. Secondly, the plan for today is I'm going to fuck you, cut your dick head off and set you on fire. Oh and stuff my dildo down your throat."
"Your that bitch killing all those men. Why me? I don't even know you. Listen, Listen you don't want to do this. I'm a police officer. Don't bury yourself in the grave, Lady."

He starts shaking the bed trying to get free. He's making too much noise. So I turn up the music. I start singing the song my head bouncing up and down on his chest. The fear in his eyes is a turn on. I stop turn down the music and say,

"Shah!! Shah! Stop that you're messing up my vibe Big Willie. Mama doesn't like that at all and for the record that's the very reason why I am killing you because you're an officer of the law." I climb on top of him and lick him all over his face, then I plant small kisses all over him. I pick up the bottle of lighter fluid pour it all over his chest watch as it coats his dick. I begin to massage it on to him.

"Originally, I never plan on killing you. Killing you would classify me as a lunatic to take one of Buffalo's finest and kill him three blocks from Attica Correctional Facility. I thought about it for a minute and realize why the hell not? Why shouldn't I cut off your dick? Why shouldn't I fry you up like bacon to see if your fat meat is greasy?" I laugh out loud as I watch as he defecates on himself. I think to myself and he calls himself an officer of the law. He's weeping, kicking banging the head post against the wall.

"Baby, you need a colon cleanser and to change your diet. Your shit smells horrible. I would offer one of my remedies but I am going to kill you."

"This is my first time I swear to God. I mean us, you and me connected. Oh God! Please don't kill me. I won't tell anyone who you are. I'll get up out of here and disappear." I tune his lie out with the song rubber band man by that T.I guy. I start dancing and singing.

"Rubber man wild as the Taliban. This is good shit right here." I move to my overnight bag pull out my brand new sharp ass Hunter's knife I purchased off the Indian reservation.

"I hate when men pretend like this is their first time cheating on their wives. Like it's my first time peeling a man's dick like a banana. Happy Birthday Big Willie! Happy Birthday Big Willie! Happy Birthday to you."

I go to cut his dick and that son of bitch kicks me. I fall to the floor hitting my head on the dresser. I regain my balance and I swing and cut his big toe off. I start swinging the Hunter's knife all over his body, stabbing him creating new orifices in his body.

INSANITY AT ITS FINEST!

Tamyara Brown

The massacre scene is straight out of a horror movie. I look at his foot almost detach from his ankle. His stomach slit open, blood running likes a faucet. Damn, I missed the head of his Dick. I walk over to him and cut it off. Roll it around like it's a dice and shake it up twice. I throw it against the nightstand. "Craps out, Officer! Ay, who I be? Rubber band man. Wild as the Taliban 9 in my right 45 in my other hand. (Who I'm is?) Call me trouble man. Always in trouble man."

I walk over to him and pinch his nose watch as the blood drips down. I kiss his lips. I run my gloved hand through it and write on the door Fat Girl Vigilante. I shower and dress. I look at him staring at me and his death is intoxicating me. I put back on my coat and black latex gloves. I pour more gasoline on the floor. And set him and the house on fire.

I take off my clothes the power of lust and the high of murdering an officer makes my pussy wet. I take my fingers and touch my breasts and pinch my nipples. I moan as my other hands touch the lips of my pussy. I masturbate until I come with a force that brings tears to my eyes. I sigh and shake a little. No man has ever made me come that hard alive. I walk out the door and I get in my car feeling electric.

I clean up and prepare for my afternoon boot camp class. It's funny this time an officer, which has got to put me on the map as the most psychotic serial killer of all time. He is the officer of the law. One of Buffalo's finest killed near Attica Correctional Facility. The police are two steps behind me. I'll admit I'm out of control I have every reason to be.

I think back to the old man and woman staring at me while I drove off. The look on her face, the big toothless smile. I wore my pink wig and black latex gloves. The look startled me and no one ever startles me.

INSANITY AT ITS FINEST!

MOURNING THE DEATH OF AN OFFICER

"Bullet, sitz platz!" He sits down beside me I stand and stretch. I smell food cooking which is an unusual fragrant in my house. Always on the beat I never cook breakfast at home. The scent of fresh brew coffee awakens me I inhale and Michelle is standing at the stove. Her braids are flowing and she looks sexy standing in my tee shirt.

"Good morning and what do you have smelling so good in here?" She turns around and answers,

"French toast, fresh strawberries, and fresh brew coffee. I thought because you was so nice to me I'd fixed you breakfast?" she puts her hand on her hip.

". Thank you this is a first for my house." I pour a cup of coffee for her and me. She fixes our plates and sit next to me." I pray over my food and she follows my lead. We eat in silence. She looks at her cell phone.

"Everything okay."

"Yes. I really don't want to go home but I have too." I look up from my plate and wipe my mouth clear my throat.

"You and I can hang out for the day. I'm off and have nothing plan, except doing some laundry and sitting in front of TV watching football." She releases a breath.

"I still have to call my Mama to let her know I'm alright." She excuses herself and walks to the other room. My cell phone vibrates and it the Captain,

"Bishop!"

"I need you ass down here now that sick bitch took down an officer."

"Who?"

"Get the fuck down here in Attica now. An officer is dead Big Willie!"

INSANITY AT ITS FINEST!

"Fuck!" I throw the coffee mug against the fridge. I get up and punch the wall. I take a breath and light a cigarette. Michelle walks in and begins to clean up the coffee.

"What's wrong?" She has a puzzled look on her face.

"No. Plans have changed I just got called into work. So you have to go." I grab a cigarette and light it.

"Okay. Did I do something?"

"I don't know. No, I'm sorry am just frustrated. My friend bought your car. You have to go" She turns and goes into the room she slept in. A few minutes she's dressed and I hear the door close. I call her phone she answers,

"Bishop what did I do?"

"I was wrong and I shouldn't have took my frustration out on you. I promise I'll call you and explain later. I need you to promise you'll text me and let me know you are okay.'

"I promise."

"Talk to you later." I call Hernandez.

"What happen?"

"No one knows all I know is the shit happen three blocks down from the prison and it was a cop. Also, I checked Michelle's car." I cough and spit out the phlegm in my throat.

"What you find?'

"Crime scene found traces of blood on the mat and seat. I put her DNA on file. Yet, her driver record is clean and this car is the only one register in her name.

"Okay are you at the scene yet?"

"I'm about ten minutes away."

My drive is a silent one. Yet my thoughts are loud as a motherfucker. Did she just play me? Is Michelle a killer? Or is her mother the doing all of this? The signs, the details everything isn't always what it seems. Is that her strategy? Is she charming the shit out of you with her million dollar smile, dimples and cat eyes that sear through your heart? Is she on to me? Is that her angle? Make you fall for her, she sex you, then sting you and seep her poison in your vein. Cloud your thoughts and before you know it you're kissing Jesus feet. She put you to sleep, cut off your dick and burn your flesh. Was I set up? Was she playing on my sympathy?

The scene is highlighted with red and white. Painted in yellow tape. I smell the wood burning mixed with road kill. The smell I was becoming accustomed to was death and fire. I look at the scene and see the black crow fly over my head. I flash my badge and the Captain is on a rampage. I put out my cigarette. I walk up to him and he jumps in my face. He screams,

"What fucking leads do you have, Bishop? Go in their look at his blood all over the place. Look at this innocent officer dead, his foot cut off and cock head shredded. I want all manpower on this. You, Hernandez and every fucking one of you better get me this bitch so I can inject the poison in her veins and spit in her face. This man had a family, Bishop. Jesus H. Christ. "His finger in my face, his breath smelled foul of old cigars and garlic bread. Sweat pour off of him in the midst of the cold. He talk before I can answer he pushes me aside and walks away. I put on my gloves and prepare myself for what I'm about to see. I walk through the door. I walk through the rubble and there is Big Willie still handcuff. The stench of Big Willie burnt body smells like hogs shit on a farm. His hands handcuff to the bed, his foot detached his big toe on the bed and the head of his dick leaning against the nightstand.

The Crime scene investigators tag and bag all of Big Willie detached body parts. They comb through the rubble looking for the tiniest bit of possible evidence. The officer calls Hernandez and me outside. He points to the white woman in her nightgown holding her baby.

"Good morning, Ma'am"

"Good morning!" She is holding her baby rocking him.

"I understand you heard something last night?"

"Yes, loud music and a woman screaming. I know because it woke up my baby."

Did you hear what the woman was saying?"

She covers her baby's ears and her face blush red "She was saying, "He was going to fuck her good."

"Anything else Ma'am?"

"She had loud music playing. They must have been doing that until about five this morning." I hand her my business card.

"Did you see anyone who came in or out the house?'

INSANITY AT ITS FINEST!

Tamyara Brown

"I just saw a white Toyota Corolla pull out of the driveway. I couldn't see who it was. After about a minute I saw smoke. No I mean I smelled smoke." I write down the name of the car.

"Which is it you smelled or saw it?" She wipes the snowflake off her face and covers up her baby with the blanket.

"I saw it." The snow is coming down heavy.

"I don't want to keep you out here with your baby. If you can remember anything else here's my card call me.' She walks away.

The old woman walks up to me and taps me on the shoulder.

"Yes Ma'am!" She puts her teeth in her mouth. She pulls her housecoat close.

"That man who lives there brings all kinds of whores in there. He was crooked cop, he had drugs in there too."

"Are you sure he's an officer of the law with a family?'

"Yes, I'm sure and I'm aware he is an officer of the law but he also had whores, drugs and liquor in that place. No one can call the cops on a cop."

"How are you aware what went on in his house?" She puts her hand on her hip and clicks her teeth.

She pulls me by my jacket and whispered, "Look, I see things all I have at seventy-five years old is my sight. I saw a black woman with pink hair get in the car the lady told you about. She was about 5'9 and had on black gloves real shiny."

"Did you see her face?'

"No. Just the hair and she had on a brown trench coat." I write that down and hand her my card.

"Bishop, come here." I walk over and he points to the bloody torn coat." I call over the crime scene investigator to bag it.

"She's slipping, Hernandez!"

"Yes she is. So now where looking for a white Toyota Corolla, a woman with a pink wig and a torn brown trench coat so close but no fucking cigar."

 I look at my phone and it's a text from Michelle.

I'm all right. Are you? I text back.

 Yes. Taking care of something. Call you later.

Hernandez and I walk to the car.

"We know your girl isn't a suspect on this one. Do you think she set you up? It looks to me like they're working together? I think back to last night her calling me. Her face bruised.

"Is she aware of that I'm on the beat? Fuck it I'll play her game and lock her ass up." I chuckle.

"I need to get deeper in her mind and…"

"Her pussy." Hernandez finishes my sentence. I crack a smile

"Never that. I've never had relations with a suspect compromise everything I stand for."

The ride back to the bricks. I park and go upstairs. Look at all the evidence presented to me. I look at everything and in truth I have nothing but circumstantial evidence. I comb through every picture, no prints, and small clues leading to Michelle's Mother. I hit the table three times and kick the chair. I look through the reports. I've talk to Miyama and no luck there. She talking all this crazy off the wall shit which makes no sense. I don't know what to think about Michelle accept they are all connected. The phone rings interrupting my thoughts,

"Homicide."

Is this the Detective Bishop Jones working on my husband Markel King's case?"

"Yes who am I speaking to?"

"Tucker King. Can we meet and talk?"

"About?" I ask her. She sighs and answers,

"I know something that I should have told you and could help you catch the bitch who murdered my husband." Her voice cracks.

Maybe she has what I'm looking for so I can stop her dead in her tracks. I say dryly,

"Can you meet at headquarter in fifteen minutes?"

"Yes, I can. Officer Friendly"

"My name is Detective Jones and I have not a damn clue who is Officer friendly is."

I go down and let the desk officer know she's coming to text me. I go outside and take a smoke break. I dial Michelle number and it rings three times.

"Hello."

"Hi Bishop!" I let the smoke come through my nose.

INSANITY AT ITS FINEST!

"I'm sorry for the way I acted. I just was upset and frustrated that on my day off I had to work. I wanted to spend time with you and as usual the boss is grinding my gears to come to work. I'm a little overworked and among many other things I don't snap off like that normally. So can you forgive me for my irrational behavior?"

"Yes. Whatever I did I'm sorry. Bishop, I really appreciate you taking care of me the other night. I was a mess. It's just so much…. I don't know. I always mess up with guys" I see this woman step out of a white BMW with a silver fur coat and sandy brown hair. She steps out and walk towards to me like a cougar on the prowl.

"Michelle, you did nothing, Hon? I was in the wrong. Listen, I have to get back to work I'll call you later." She stood in front of me, extended her hand, her wedding ring was now gone. Her fingernails manicured, the scent of strong perfume, she licks her lips and smirks.

"You must be Detective Bishop Jones or wait I prefer to call you Officer Friendly. I could never forget a face. You are fine, damn fine. When we met before I was in distress but damn Officer Friendly you are gorgeous."

"Thank you, go on in. I'll be right with you."

She smells of Chanel no.5, her hair touches my face as the wind blows and the snow blows sideways. I finish off my cigarette and walk behind her. I take her to my desk and offer her coffee.

She nods her head no. She sits in the chair and crosses her legs. Her legs are long and muscular. In the dead of winter has on a dress that clinging to her curves and high heel boots. I raise my eyebrow, we lock eyes and move closer to her. The sexual tension is so thick that it chokes me. I clear my throat and wipe my forehead.

"Okay, so you said you have some information for me. What you got for me?" She leans into the desk take her long French manicured fingers and make circles in my palm. She looks at the crotch of my pants and my nature is at full attention. She speaks softly,

"My husband was having an affair with a lot of women. I knew it for years, I had my own thing going on too. Yet, it wasn't about the affairs it was the type of women he slept with"

"Really, what type of women?" She leans back in the chair and uncrosses her legs.

"He's always had affairs with fat women, it was his fetish. He used to throw them in my face by showing me their pictures saying they were the only type that satisfy him sexually. These women are beneath me, their looks are hideous and I can see if they were pretty in the face. I was his wife he chose me and I couldn't satisfy my own husband." She wipes the tear before it falls and shakes her head.

She hands me the pictures. I look through hoping none of them were of Michelle. I look at each one of them dressed in lingerie, some naked and some in sexual poses. She sucks her teeth and picks up the picture of the nude woman. She looks at it and throws it on the ground, steps on it. Some of them look sexy and the others look grotesque.

"That's what he wanted over me. I was just his showpiece. Here I was in the gym five times a week, eating a sensible diet and I had to beg my husband to make love to me.

"How do you know?"

I look at each picture carefully and none of these girls resemble Michelle or Patricia.

"One day I caught my husband dick down her throat that's how I know. I gave him an ultimatum to put her out or else I expose his prostitution ring of fat chicks in Niagara fall. Yes, everyone's favorite philanthropist was pimping Fat women."

My eyes pop open wide and a prostitution ring of plus size women. She was the light to the truth.

"Markel as rich and successful was an undercover pimp?"

"Yes. No one ever caught him because his goons ran the whole operation.

The bitch came around threatening to kill him. She busted out our windows in our home" I spread the pictures out on the table again

"Which one was it?" She picks up the picture of the lady dressed in a bra and thong. Her hair is cut short looking like fire flames.

"Her. She lived there for about a year until I evicted her ass just before he died. Her name is. Deana McMillan. She now lives on Perishing.282 that's the number." She leans closer to me; she traces her lips with her tongue. I look at an additional picture of her this time she was dressed in thong and pasties. . I think back to what the

INSANITY AT ITS FINEST!

old woman had said about the pink wig and black clothes. She wasn't as attractive as the rest of the women.

"So is that all?" She rubs my face and moans.

"No, actually it's not all. How many inches is your cock? Her hand begins to massage my dick. Her eyes fixated on it as if it's her favorite lollipop. I exhale and let out a moan, look around and clear my throat. I remove her hand and turn from her.

"You couldn't handle it?" I say she hands me her business card, kisses the back of it."

"Officer Friendly, this small body can take the whole thing. I hope those pictures help solve the case or put that bitch Dena in jail for life.

I'll be seeing you soon. Real soon." She stands up and I reply,

"My name once again isn't, Officer Friendly. I'm far from friendly, Mrs. King."

I look at the picture of Dena. Run her name through the system. She has a record as long as my arm. She recently got arrested for starting a fight with a clerk in ALDIS. They gave her probation. Deana was one of his many women I look at her picture to see if her face looked familiar to me. Tucker sashays away and looks back at me. The smirk on her face and seductive eyes said, *"Please fuck me now."*

I have business to tend to. This case takes precedence over sleeping with my dead victim's wife.

"The plot is thickening." I hear Hernandez voice. He breaks my trance.

"Boss slipped up on something. You want to hear it now or wait until tomorrow?"

"Nah Man, go ahead because I got a lot of good for you too!"

"I gave up on sleep a long time ago."

"Well I did a check on your girl. She lived at one of Markel's home on Delavan near Census. The lady who lived upstairs said she was a sweet woman who always spoke. Also she confirmed that he was abusing her and the mother beat him up and threatens to cut off his dick. She said that through the vents she could hear Markel beating on her and belittling her. The lady said one day on November 14, 2007 he stripped Michelle naked and threw her out on the streets.

The next day he moved in with another woman Dena McMillian. The following day her mother came and whipped Markel's ass threatening to cut his dick off. She said the last time she saw Michelle she had lost a lot of weight. I slapped him up.

"This must be the spot he was moving all of his lovers in. His wife came in and brought these pictures of all the women he slept with. She said that she thought it was some woman name Deanna McMillan. Also," I show him the pictures of all the women and point out Deanna. As per Mrs. King her hubby ran a prostitution ring of plus size women out in Niagara Falls."

"Wow, I remember the article written up a few years back about that. All these dudes of power have dirt buried deep in their closet."

"What are you thinking?"

"Markel use his apartment as his love nest. He had over ten women alone who lived there in a ten year span. All plus size including Michelle. I think that as we add different pieces to the puzzle we are getting a clearer picture and that the few pieces missing are with Michelle. My gut is riding on the fact the mother may have done him in. Also, Michelle is aware of the fact her mother's offing these dudes. That's the secret those two are holding." Hernandez asked.

"It makes no sense that they protect her. I got to get into her. I got to dig deeper into this." I put on my coat. I walk downstairs and Ms. Tucker is waiting for me. As much as I want to release this sexual frustration. I've never like a woman chasing after me more or less giving it up eight days after her husband was murder.

She calls me over.

"What's up?'

"I have set out a plan for us tonight, I demand you come to my home and sex me now."

I pull my collar up to my neck. Light a cigarette and smoke

"You're demanding me to come see you, Huh? Sorry, Hon not tonight."

"Why"

"Your husband isn't even cold in the ground and you're worried about fucking me. Secondly, I suggest you check how you ask for anything from me. I'm not some soft ass nigger you can demand to do anything. On some real shit maybe the reason your dead husband was fucking around on you was your attitude. Come correct with me

INSANITY AT ITS FINEST!

or don't come at all. Have a good night and thanks for the information."

I get in my car and slam my door these Buffalo women are a trip. I'm going home pull out my Vaseline and watch Porn Hub. I guess my date is my hand. .

Michelle

REFLECTIONS

I lie in the bed and listen to Maxwell. The street light on the snow look like tiny diamonds. No one to call and nobody to talk to except Sarge she has been my friend since the day my Daddy died. She comforts me and protects me. I have always been the odd girl the one with the crazy mother. The quiet fat girl, who no one wanted to be around. When someone attempted to be my fiend Mama would locked me up in the house. If I went outside I was never allowed to leave the front porch. Whenever I'd make a friend, which was deemed acceptable she would never let her in the house. I was never allowed to go to birthday parties, events she'd say, "She could never find anything suitable to cover my gut. In the summer I stay in my room locked up with books, she say, "Since you are hiding cookies and shit in your room all you will eat is an apple, a scoop full of oatmeal. Lunch was three celery sticks, four carrot sticks and a cup of beet juice. Dinner will be a garden salad. It was Sarge who I played house with and talk to. She was my secret friend, when the girls would tease me it was her who made me stand up and fight. Sarge would get mad at me for days and not talk to me if I wouldn't do bad things or get in a fight. I'd bang on my head and she'd ignore me. Like one time when the kids were calling me Porky pig and I started crying she began making oink sounds in my head all night. I just started to close up my world to everyone including Sarge. No one liked me and no matter what people would pick at me. Running home to Mama would only result with the speech of losing the weight and horrific beatings with sticks.

One day I begged Sarge and told her I would be mean if she just be my friend. It was Sarge who convinced me to feed my sixth grade class with brownies laced with ex-lax after they'd kept calling me, "Porky Pig." It was her who convinced me to steal the boy's gym clothes and urinate on them for calling me an ape. Me, always being quiet and staying to myself no one ever thought I would do anything

INSANITY AT ITS FINEST!

evil to them. No one ever suspects the good girl. The truth is I never wanted to do it.

Sarge knows that at the right time when I'm at my lowest she has control. That is why Markel's dead. He took my unborn child away. It seems every time I'm almost close to love someone takes it away. Losing is all I seem accustomed to. No one should ever get use to that. No one should get use to believing someone will take it away. It all started with losing my father,

Whenever I think of my father I remember him reading to me Cinderella and Snow White always calling me his beautiful princess. I remember him telling me I was beautiful no matter what size I was and God didn't make an ugly child. He would take me to Coney Island in the summer and the Aquarium. We go on rides, eat Nathan hot dogs and cotton candy ending our day with ice cream.

My memories filled with returning home Daddy holding my hand and me begging him to let me him live with him. My Mama standing at the door with tears in her eyes and a love for the man who left her for someone else? I would be sent to my room and it was only at that time I would hear Mama beg Daddy to come back home because she and I needed him. She would repeatedly say,

"I'm trying to lose the weight. See I bought a new dress. I know what happened was wrong. I should of have told you the truth. Please, just love me."

Daddy would say, "It's over Pat, you and I are done. I have another woman and I love her. Look, I just want to be here for my daughter. She doesn't deserve to hear the truth." I always wondered what the truth was and until this day I don't have a clue. He'd kissed me goodnight and always promise to see me next week.

It is when Mama began to stop visitation; it was when she would beat me for crying for him. All access was denied for him to even speak to me on the phone. No more seeing Daddy on a regular basis. No more trips to Coney Island, he made every effort to be in my life. He'd sneak by my school and stand by the gates blowing kisses and waving at me. It's why I love him because he never stopped trying to see me. My last vision was of his body burning. The smell of his flesh and his screams of help me. I shake my head of the memory and wipe away my tears.

The night is quiet except for the music and my thoughts are loud. He's being nice to me, he'd never see me as his woman. I'm waiting for my dreams to catch up to my reality. I want normalcy in my life. I want someone to see when they're around me that I'm fun to be around. I deserve to be loved. I want to shout out, hold me, love me and care for me.

All of my life I've given all of me. I never intentionally mistreated anyone.

The moon is full and I don't feel like crying. I feel like talking. I feel like laughing. I look in the mirror at my face. Tears are there and I didn't even know I was crying. I have no clue what to do with myself. I want to go out but not alone. I pick up the phone and dial Bishop's number.

"Hang up and stop sweating this dude." I hear Sarge say,

"Make him want you. That dude likes to chase. Be easy."

"Sarge, I like him already."

"I know but I promise if he ever hurts you or make you cry I will kill him."

I think this is pitiful I'm having a conversation with myself. It's all I got right now. I try to prevent myself from calling him. I turn away and lay back down. I think of all the ghetto drama that has entered in my life. I'm tired of feeling captive and swimming downstream and everyone swimming upstream. Lonely and Loveless is how I feel.

I look around in this room filled with memories of Mama locking me in not allowing me to eat or crying myself to sleep surrounded by thoughts of missing my Daddy. Mama punishing me for being overweight, Markel ridiculing me for being overweight and more importantly me hating myself for all those years for being abnormal. The torture you go through for not loving yourself enough, disliking what you look like but who you are. The journey is ugly especially when you have everyone you love confirming your suspicions of yourself. One voice of a loving individual isn't enough especially when the negative thoughts drown them out.

I crave for my Mama. I craved Markel and so many people to just love me. Love, not money or cars. Just love.

INSANITY AT ITS FINEST!

Now what is the issue with me? I lost the weight but Mama still has reason to be the way she is towards me. She still has this hatred towards me; she not only tells me but also shows it. She carries her pain, her anger and shares it with others. When she wakes up in the middle of the nightdress differently, she comes back satisfy to have killed another man. I want to tell but then as sad as it seems I can't phantom her leaving me too. Knowing that I have no one around would devastate me.

I also see the good in my Mama when she opens the living room to help women lose the weight. I see her when one minute she curses and pushes them to the edge but then buy them new wardrobes and give them makeovers. I see when she talks to them, nurture them and lead them to succeed in their weight loss plan. Why can't she nurture and love me? Why can't she shower me with a small amount of love?

Is that how she loves? Was that how she was taught to love? Those men who raped her ruin her spirit and left her dead. She became cold at the age of twelve. I think if Sarge had let Markel still live would he have made me cold and callous? Would he have ripped the very existence of my soul and who God had intended me to be? Those men did that to Mama. Yet, in my heart I have this strong hope one-day she'll let go of that, tell me she loves me and hug me so tight. We'll have a loving relationship.

I read somewhere that loves starts from within. What if the perception of love is twisted and ugly? What if you believe that you can buy love, or beat someone, or mistreat him or her? Is it that child's fault because remember she or he never asked to be born? What if they lack affection and a kind heart for the human kind? If they are broken vessels from the very start, no one loving you from the day you are conceived to the day you where birth out of the womb. Birth by a woman who has lost the will to love. I feed off that thought often. It's the question I fear asking my mother.

I want Bishop or any man to fall in love with me. After all that have ever happen in my life the abuse, the mistreatment and whatever else. I still yearn to be loved unconditionally. I still want to know before I die what it feels like to be the apple of a man's eye. The sunlight is shining and the snow is still covering the ground. I hear Mama's familiar knock she yells, "Class is in session in ten. I expect you to be there."

I hate those FAT GIRL REVOLUTIONS MEETINGS. It's like a big pity party and exercise session. I take a shower and let the water run down my body. I hear her footsteps, my heart pound. She pulls the shade open, she stares at me, and "Some man is here to see you." I step out wrap the towel around me.

"Who?" She gets so close to me pushing me against the sink.

"Some man is here to see you. Don't let him in my home or I will gut your ass with a fish hook..."

At that moment the air escapes. I throw on my Grey sports bra and basketball shorts. I slip on my Grey slippers. I let my hair hang. I walk and as I get closer I hear music outside. I peek through the window and I see him. I look at Mama she rolls her eyes. She sits the mats on the floor. I throw on my coat and when I open door he is looking right at me. He winks at me as I walk to his car. He steps out and opens the door for me. I get in and he closes it.

"Hello."

"Hi."

I bite my bottom lip unprepared for the moment. I pull my coat close to me. He touches my hand.

"I met your mother and let's just say she..."

"A she-devil in wolverine clothing. Whatever she did or said to you I'm sorry in advance."

He adjusts his baseball cap and look down at me. He answers, "When I ask for you she spit at me. I wiped it off and smeared it in her face. That's when she went upstairs to get you. Enough about her what are you getting into anything today? I've turned off my cell phone so it can be you and I."

I look at her Mama in the window arms folded and her evil green eyes piercing. I sigh and I want to say yes but my mind said to say no. So I won't get wrapped up in this man only to lead myself to heartbreak. I go against my thinking.

INSANITY AT ITS FINEST!

"I have to work out and after that we can hang out." He licks his lips and nods his head.

"That sounds good. In about two hours, since I need to check on something anyway. You promise pretty lady?"

He rubs his hand on my cheek. His finger fall to my shoulder down my arm and sparks are igniting something I haven't felt in a long time."

"I promise. So I'll see you in two hours."

He walks out and opens the door for me. He tips his hat at my Mama. He touches the small of my back and before he turns to go to his car his kisses me on the lips. I look at the hate in Mama Eyes and the smile on my face is brighter than the sun shining.

She said,

"So he is the guy who has you missing meetings and losing yourself? I'll admit he is fine, damn fine but the hell does he want with you?" I take off my coat and hang it up. I put on my sneakers and bring out the case of bottled water. I answer,

"He's a friend, Mama!"

"Friend my ass, you are so stupid he only wants to use you. Why would a fine ass man like that want you? You are three steps from being overweight again. "I inhale and exhale. I'm not going to fight with her today. I go in the kitchen and prepare the vegetable platter. I cut up the celery. She walks in taunting me.

"You're mad because I'm speaking the truth. This man doesn't want you he only wants to get in your panties, he wants something more out of you. Look what happen with Richard and Markel? How long are you going to be a fool?" I take out the broccoli, carrots and yogurt dip. I set the vegetables on the tray. I walk back in the living room and open up the folding chairs. She follows me.

"I ought to smack the shit out of you just for being a silly ho. you're a silly ass derelict stuck on love. I should kill…" I smirk and Sarge voice instead of mine comes out. I point my finger towards her and shake it.

"Watch your words Mama they may just come back on you. What are you going to kill me like you did my…..." I roll my eyes and Shayla stands at the door.

"Um, Hi, I knock but no one answered the door. I'm sorry for walking in on your meeting" I look at Mama and she's in the mirror painting her face black and white. Shayla sit-downs since the last time I've seen her she has lost about twenty pounds. She has her hair braided. She always quiets.

"My Mama does the same thing to me."

"Do what?" She opens a bottle of water and sips it.

"She belittles me. If a man looks at me she reminds me every day that no man wants a fat girl. Or that I'm ugly. Like I don't know that but it's okay maybe they're just speaking the truth." The sadness forms around her eyes and she hangs her head low. I sit next to her and lift her chin.

"You are not ugly and you're losing the weight. It's not right what they are doing to us. I've live with that thought every day. Mama ensures me every day that I am ugly.

"I know but it's all I know too. Look at me Michelle I'm not a pretty woman and the weight doesn't make it better.

That why I'm here so I can feel better but also so people can stop being ashamed of me."

I touch her shoulder and can remember feeling those exact same feelings.

"Shayla, you are losing the weight and you look good. It took me a long time; I was close to three hundred pounds. Just don't quit okay.

"I thought you was never overweight."

"I'm still a big girl. I still feel like that woman who wore a size twenty-six. Even though you fix the outer in a year. It takes years to fix the inside. How it's going with getting your children back?"

"It not going well. I feel like I'm going to lose, you know. I'm doing everything they've asked the parenting classes, rehab, and got a better job, sign up for school and losing the weight. My lawyer said my home is an unhealthy environment. I need to clean up more."

"I'm sorry, Shayla. I'll come over and help you. Any time after work I'm free."

"You look like your Mama but you sure are different. I'm too embarrassed."

"Don't be this is to help you get your children back. Everyone life is a mess whether it's on the outside or inside. If you want we can work out together?" she sips on her water.'

INSANITY AT ITS FINEST!

"Thank you Michelle. I'd like that. Here's your Mama and the rest of the ladies." The meeting was long and tedious. The workout even harder, some of the ladies vomited she was punishing me for having Bishop come by the house. I don't miss a step with the thought that in a couple of hours I'll be with him.

She'd come up and sit with me. I try to help her she was just so eager to be loved."

.

THE LOVE NEST

I knock on the door of 218 East Delavan the lady looks out the window. I flash my badge. She opens the door. "Can I help you?" she asks. "My name is Detective Jones and you remember my partner Detective Hernandez we are here to ask a few questions about your deceased landlord Markel King." She waves her hand for us to come in. She closes the door and we walk up the stairs. Have a seat Officers. Can I get you some coffee, tea or pop?" Hernandez responds

"No, thank you. Now you'll remember I came the other day to speak with you about the women who lived in the downstairs apartment. Can you elaborate?'

"Sure, sure. That man was just an animal. He gets these big girls in his apartment. He let them live there for a year or so. After he finish having perverted sex and abusing them, he'd wait until garbage day to put them out. Some of them women were nasty and rowdy. It was only one nice girl her name was Michelle. She was respectful and clean. I hated what he used to do to her. She had the prettiest green eyes, too. He beat on her and verbally abuses her. To add insult to injury he slung her out like cat shit.

"No. She too weak in her heart, she is one of God's angels come up here cook for me, cleaned my house and go to the store and her crazy Mama would beat on her too. I tell you one thing she never hit her Mama back. She honored and respected her mother. "When the abuse was happening why didn't you contact the authorities?" She places her hands on her thigh and leans forward.

"I've live here for thirteen years rent free. I was paid to mind my business. I couldn't help her because she didn't want to be helped. So, I stayed out of it. Plus, her mama put a serious whooping on him. The day after he put that child out in the snow butt naked."

The woman teeth fall out of her mouth. She pushes them back in. Hernandez looks at me. I clear my throat and shake my head.

"What did she do to him?" she starts laughing and her teeth once again plops in her lap and again.

"She drove up on the sidewalk busting all of the windows of his BMW. She jumps out those green eyes wide and crazy. She punches him the jaw and flips him on the ground. She started stomping on him to the point you could hear. He tried to get up but she pulled out this butcher knife telling him if he moved or called the police she cut his dick off and feed it to him. I think she killed him." Hernandez asked,

"Do you think Michelle would have killed him?"

The woman teeth fall out of her mouth. She pushes them back in. Hernandez looks at me. I clear my throat and shake my head.

"No, Michelle is a weak woman and heart is pure."

"What did she do to him?" she starts laughing and her teeth once again plops in her lap and again.

"She drove up on the sidewalk busting all of the windows of his BMW. She jumps out those green eyes wide and crazy. She punches him the jaw and flips him on the ground. She started stomping on him to the point you could hear. He tried to get up but she pulled out this butcher knife telling him if he moved or called the police she cut his dick off and feed it to him. I think she killed him."

Whatever else I needed. Now her Mama she's evil. I knew her Mama from back in the day and ain't nobody ever fucked with her. I wouldn't believe it. It's not in her nature." We stand up.

"Thank you for your time. You've been a great help. We walk out and down the stairs.

INSANITY AT ITS FINEST!

"What are you thinking, Bishop?" I pull out my cigarette and light it. Inhale and blow out the smoke.

"Michelle's mother is the serial killer and Michelle knows it but, is too scared to tell. I'll get her to tell me. And you?"

"I'm thinking right now the same thing but, at the same time how that lady teeth kept popping out her mouth. It took everything in me when they fell on her lap not to fall the hell out." We start laughing.

"I was thinking the same thing man. Listen I have to meet Michelle. I promised I chill with her today. See if I can work on her talking to me." Hernandez raises his eyebrows.

"It is deeper than her being a suspect. You like her, Bishop?" He read my mind. It did upset me and I do like her. I know it's going against every code in my book but I do find myself wanted to get closer to her. Maybe it's because I'm lacking female companionship. Instead I say to Hernandez.

"I want to solve this case. I think she is cool but it's all police business."

"Okay Bishop, you tell an ugly lie my man. Let me ask you if she wasn't a suspect would you sleep with her?" I smash the butt of my cigarette in the ground. Look in the air and open my car door. Before closing the door.

"Yes."

I need some mood music. I pop in my Tevin Campbell, Joe and R.Kelly CD and ride out on a nineties vibe. I ask myself why she would allow herself to be treated like that. No matter what size you are you deserve to be treated with respect and admiration. It baffles me that a woman that fine doesn't know her worth.

Some women would rather let a man beat on them for the sake of saying they got a man. It makes no fucking sense to me. . If I had a sister and man put his hands on her I'd break every rib in his body. I clear my thoughts a pull up in front of Michelle's house. She outside talking to some woman. I beep my horn and her mother is standing outside too. Michelle and her mother look alike the only difference is her mother is much smaller in height and weight.

Michelle has her hair in two ponytails; she is dressed in dark blue, I notice that she matches with everything she wears including her footwear. Her mother in Grey even her sneakers.

She comes to the car door. I step out and open the door for her. "Look at you looking like a little girl." She blushes. "I forgot to take this out. Let me go back in and fix my hair." I stop her.

"You look cute like that? Leave it, I hope you up for some fun. I decided to take you to you Laser Tron." The smile on her face speaks yes.

"Okay. That does sound fun." We pull off and her mother in the window. She looks at me and me her. I tip my hat at her. I back out and pull off.

"You have a large collection of music. I love this Kenny Lattimore song. You ever feel this way for someone. I mean like getting married." I cough in my sleeve. I turn it down.

"Only once. I've been more committed to my career than anything. Have you ever loved liked that?" She shifts in her seat.

"Yes .the only difference was they didn't feel the same."

"Why do you believe that?" She sits quiet and Tank comes on. The expressway is especially busy for a Sunday.

"I wasn't their type of woman." It was the sound of cars passing by and the music. I break our silence.

"Talk to me, Michelle. What do you want from love?"

"For it to love me back and for a man to love me at the same time that I love him."

"Ever been married?'

"No. Always single. This may be hard to believe but I've only had two men in my life." I think back to what the woman was saying about her innocence. I laugh,

"Your Mother ran them off?' She laughs with me.

"You already know. I wasn't the type of girl guys wanted. I was overweight back then and ugly. Does that turn you off?"

I make a turn into the parking lot of Laser Tron and find a parking space. I unbuckle my seatbelt. I turn her face to mine. I get close to her and I say,

"Michelle, look at me and listen well. I can't convince you that you are a beautiful black woman. That's not my job nor is it my responsibility. I see that already and the problem is you don't. If you

INSANITY AT ITS FINEST!

were three hundred and eighty pounds that wouldn't bother me. I want to see where this goes, but I suggest you get over your hang-ups about your self-image. I came here tonight to have fun with you not worry what size you were in the past and even now. To answer your question no it doesn't bother me?" I kiss her on her cheek. Step out and walk around and open the door.

"I promise Bishop that I'll try. It's hard you don't understand what I've gone through. I know that can be annoying. I never been on a date besides you." Her eyes glossy and at that moment I feel for her. I wrap my arms around her.

"It's alright you don't need to cry. Come on let's have some fun." I take her hand and we walk in and I buy tokens. They dress us in the vest. Hand us the guns. They give us a tutorial. The purpose was to have fun but see if she knew how to shoot.

In playing and running she missed every shot. It gave me proof that she didn't kill the Pastor or Deacon. She can't shoot. The person who shot the Pastor and Deacon's temple was clean. She brings me water.

"I had so much fun, Bishop! You were the last man standing. Where did you learn to shoot like that?"

"My Father. He was a cop retire from the force. He took me out to the gun range every weekend and also he was in the gun club."

"My Mama was a part of a gun club with her old boyfriend. She is one of the best in the women's league." The bell goes off in my head. I make a mental note of the club

"Wow, so I was thinking of ordering something and a movie." She shrugs her shoulder and sits next to me. She folds her hand. She looks me in the eyes,

"Can I be honest with you?" I nod my head and put my arm around her. She continues,

"I would prefer to eat in. You eat out a lot and that's not healthy for you and neither are those cigarettes. You are grown but I'm just saying."

"You're just saying, huh? You're right. So what do you plan on making when you get to my house? I have no culinary skills at all."

INSANITY AT ITS FINEST!

"What about a buffalo grilled chicken over pasta, with vegetables? It's good I promise. I have to go to the store. I'll buy dinner because you don't have no food in your fridge."

"You don't have to Michelle?"

"I want to. I've had such a wonderful time. Let me cook because it's clear you can't." she jokes.

I 'm trying to see this evening for what I want it to be. Trying to investigate a crime. Getting closer to the truth on who's killing all these men and why. With her right here she feels good in my arms. This feeling has to pass. I want her to be innocent. I want her mother to be the criminal and all the clues lead to this woman. So why is there some doubt of her being innocent? She taps me on my shoulder breaks my thoughts.

"I lost you for a minute. Are you okay?"

"I'm fine lost in my thoughts that's all. Ready to go and have one of my bad habits."

I hold the door open for her. I pull out a cigarette and light it. We walk to the car and let her in. I smoke and think some more. I drop it on the floor crush it, get and the car and pull off. We stop at Wegmans and I let her go in and shop. I call up Hernandez,

""Que. Paso buddy?"

"BUENA PARA MÍ?"

"Aye, aye been hanging around me too much?

"Listen, I can't talk long but her mother was in a gun club. Michelle said she was one of the best in the female league. I need you to find out where, is she licensed and if she has any guns register under her name. Michelle didn't kill the Pastor and Deacon either."

"Why you say that?"

"She can't shoot. We were at Laser Tron and she is taken out within the first few minutes. I'll do more research on my end. Call me when you get any information. Gracias."

She's talking to a man who hugs her. I roll the window down and it's a heavyset dark skin guy. I know that guy so I immediately roll my windows back up he'll blow my cover. I arrested his brother a year and a half ago on a murder charge. I see her walking towards me. I close my eyes and pretend to be sleep. She puts the groceries in the back seat. I jump up.

INSANITY AT ITS FINEST!

"Oh. I didn't know you were in the car. I would have help you with the bags" she sits next to me.

"No it was fine. It wasn't that many bags. I was a little long. That guy was my ex boyfriend's brother he and everybody were talking about the cop being killed by Attica Correctional Facility. The news and everybody said she cut up him and it was a black woman they last seen leaving the house. It's all over the Buffalo News. Did you hear about it?"

"I did. They never said whether it was a she was black or not. You know something I don't know. She stutters,

"I mean my ex brother said he was black. I don't know." I look in her pretty green eyes and saw right through her lies. She knew something and I intend to get it out of her.

Michelle looks out the window. She is extremely quiet on the ride back. I pull up to the house and park. I open the door and Bullet is barking. I say, "Den Mund halten."

I grab the bags and bring them in. She takes off her sneakers. She goes to the sink washes her hands. She starts dinner. I feed Bullet and take him out. By the time I come back she has the salad ready and soft bread.

"You've been quiet since the drive from Wegmans. You alright?" she bites into the breadstick, her green eyes filled with worry. She drinks her water.

"Like you I became lost in my own thoughts. I'm okay."

She looks at her plate not looking at me. She sighs heavily. Her micro expressions tell me different. If I push too fast or hard I might scare her away. She looks up at me and she said, "Is the food good?"

"Yes it is! Excellent."

"Bishop, I suddenly don't feel so well. I was wondering if you could take me home. I'm kind of tired."

I slide my seat back. "Sure. Is there anything I can do for you? She shakes her head no.

I drive her home when I pull in her mother is in the window. I walk out and open the door for her.

"I hope you feel better. I'll call you tomorrow." I hug her and kiss her on the cheek.

"Good night Michelle."

"Good night, Bishop. Thank you for showing me a good time."

"You're welcome." Michelle looks up at the window and sighs. I wait for her to go inside. Yep! She knows something. The question is what. I turn the corner. I get home and put on gloves take the plate, the fork and glass. I bag it. I take it to the lab. Put her DNA on file. I think that tomorrow I 'll. pay a visit to Miyama. Get a sample of her DNA too. Bullet looks at me. I pat him on the head. The T.V will eventually watch me. Bullet will be curl up beside me. This shit is sad.

TOUGH LOVE LETTER

All of us are standing at attention with our hands saluting a fallen officer William O'Sullivan better known as Big Willie. His wife filled with grief trying to maintain herself for her children. The Irish pipe band playing amazing grace his casket brought inside followed by his family and dignitaries. Today we are only one color and it's blue. Listening to his six year old plead with God breaks every officer's heart. He yells,

"Please God bring my daddy back."

Officers from all over New York State took up six blocks long. The beat of the drums saddens my heart; Fat Girl Vigilante took the life of a fellow brother, an officer. The people are lined up with signs of love and admiration. I wonder if she is in the crowd among us looking on as the man people all knew and love.

I think she may come after Hernandez or me. My father use to say that every dead officer is personal because it's always a thought in your mind you may be next to die and it's your wife their handing the American flag to.

The snow is falling heavy and as the flags are half-mass. The sound of tears mixed with the bagpipes has me in a different state of mind. The funeral procession ends at Weldon Cemetery and we are relieved to go.

I walked into ECMC and on the one side of the wall are inmates dressed in green, hands and feet shackled. We get in on the same elevator the Correction Officer standing next to me. I get off and flash my get into anywhere I please badge. The nurse buzzes me in and I give Miyama's name.

Her room has two officers in front of it. Her orders is to be handcuffed to the bed Last night they found Miyama eating her own feces and throwing it the guards. She is clean dress in a whole gown, her hands in restraints as she lies in the hospital bed. She seems calm today. I pull up the chair and sit next to her.

INSANITY AT ITS FINEST!

"Hi, Miyama." She turns her hand. She tries to move her hands but can't. She also had another seizure last night. She finally speaks, "Still think I'm a lunatic?" In my mind I think hell yeah. I look at the plain white walls, the smell of stale air and the paper bag in the garbage can.

"I don't know what to think to be honest. What I'm trying to figure out who is Fat Girl Vigilante." She sucks her teeth and rolls her eyes. "You are such a liar, Bishop. Have you ever dated a fat woman?" I look into the air.

"I've a dated a plus size woman. Why is that important?"

"It's important because it's why all this is happening, the killings. Bishop you men don't want us to love or care for us black women. You men are all alike just from different sperm donors. You use us for what you want then abandon us like fat pieces of shit. You forgot that we need love too. Satan's daughter wants only one thing and that is love. I didn't give it to her instead I mistreated her. I was her big sister and I was supposed to protect her. Jealousy is an ugly feeling that makes even the most saved person evil. I messed her up all because I didn't want her to be loved by my daddy."

"Miyama is the person doing the killings your sister?" She takes a deep breath.

"No, she is long gone from here. She gone, just like my daughter, just like my Daddy." She has a single tear in her eye.

"You know we black women take so much shit off you men? To be loved! That is it? You know how to fuck us. You know how to make babies with us. You call us whores, sluts and Bitches we who look like you. You know how to beat us and choose every woman under different races and leave us lonely and broken. You forgot to love us black women. We are the butts of your jokes. We are no longer considered beautiful to the black man. You lie to us and expect something for nothing." She stops and yawns. I stand up and take out a tissue from the box wipe her face. I exhale and take the angry love letter she is speaking to me. She continues,

"You want to know why we are pissed off. Black men disgrace us more than any race in the world. You break our spirit and murder the love in us. Who told you beautiful was just straight hair, light skin and light eyes? You'll give any other woman of a different ethnicity respect but us. It hurts like hell and it isn't fair."

INSANITY AT ITS FINEST!

"You're right it isn't fair but what gives her the right to take innocent lives?" I stand next to her.

"They're not innocent Bishop and I never said what she's doing is right. Yet, understand these men preyed on us, too. I love my husband with every bit of my heart. You hear me? I loved him when he was doing time. When he had no job I went out and worked two. When he got arrested it was me who took my tax refund to bail him out. I took care of him when even his sorry ass family told me he was no good. I was there. He thanks me by performing oral sex on our child.

He left me and his child with nothing." She moans loud, grabbing the sheet.

"What he did wasn't right I agree with you. She isn't right for taking someone's life. I really need your help on this. Is she your sister? And if she is what is her name?" She turns away from me and she said, "You have the answers already."

"I'm assuming. I have no proof." She touches my finger.

"Not every assumption is wrong I know you care for my niece Michelle. Please don't hurt her."

"Does she know that I know you?"

"No, but God reveal to me your heart Bishop. She is scared and she needs protection. She is just hurting. You need her but not solve who's killing those men. You need her to love. To care for you."

I inhale because at that moment she has no reason to go into my head. I clear my throat.

"Is there another sister?"

"Bishop, my sister is dead been dead since she was twelve years old "My eyebrow rises.

"What are you saying?" she looks in the sky and hums a tune.

"I'm saying that there are a bunch of fat women broken by society. The crime you need to investigate is given people permission to kill a woman's heart. To murder a woman's spirit and violate her thinking just because of her weight and the color of her skin. We should be accepted because we stood by you. We healed you when the white man and woman hated you. Us black women have been here and will always be there. We loved you chained and beaten by the Massa. We are there when they from different races rob you for your riches and when you have nothing. We are here forever and no one loves harder than a black woman."

"You are right we have assassin our black women to fit our needs. Some of us have committed the unthinkable of breaking a woman's spirit. It is not a crime but murder is."

"The little girl you accidentally Kenya killed is in heaven playing with your daughter. Malika aborted her because you didn't care. It is why Satan's daughter is killing everyone she loved didn't show how much they care. I know you cared but like all men you don't know how to show it. Your daughter who died will come back but she's coming back to you as a boy. Michelle has a purpose in your life, Bishop. My Jesus is with you all the time." She begins laughing and then singing, "God has all the answers. He has all the answers." I hit the door and they open it. I look at the officers and shake my head.

She knew about Malika, the baby and the little girl. I pull out a cigarette. My cell phone was ringing. I needed to ignore it. I stood at the front entrance. She knew too much about me. My life, which I kept under wraps she exposes me and my truths. I look and there is Tucker King. She walks up to me.

"Detective Bishop! You look delicious dress in full uniform. You must be coming from the detective's funeral, sorry about your lost?" Her hungry eyes are on me. She smells of Chanel no. 5.

"What's that for?" I lick my lips. Her voice low and deep, she comes close to my ears and whispers,

"It a sign that I want you to fuck me. No excuses, I want your full size hard, thick and long cock inside me. So can you do that for me, Detective?" I think to myself what black woman in this day and age uses the word cock. She enjoys saying the word and I enjoy hearing it.

My dick is as hard a rock. I need this I think. I'm going against everything I believe in to relieve this tension. I look at her run my hand down her chest.

"Okay, am I getting in your car? Let's go."

INSANITY AT ITS FINEST!

Tamyara Brown

I walk to my truck and check for condoms. I don't have any. I think about what Miyama said, "Protect Michelle's heart. I will, we're not together.

I walk to her car she gets in. My dick and I follow. I don't treat her like a lady like I do Michelle by opening the door for her. I sit in and buckle my seat belt. She drives off and as the car goes down Grider and Delevan. She stops at Rite Aid. I sit back questioning whether I should go through with this. I'm not thinking straight and with the wrong head.

I'm tired of masturbating; I just need to be in some warm pussy. Release the stress and tension on her. Let go of what I heard from Miyama because her thoughts, her words are sinking into me. She has done that since I met her play with my mind.

Deep in my thoughts I watch Tucker come out. She opens the side of my door. She bends down and kisses me. She unzips my jeans and rub the head until I lotion her fingers. I close my eyes and moan. The thought of changing my mind flies away.

"I'm going to fuck you good, Bishop."

"You better." I reply. She drives down Delavan until we hit Main Street. We drive three blocks from Canisius College."

"Is this where you and your husband lived?"

"No, actually this is my apartment complex. I rarely saw Markel. He always had his dick stuck in some fat bitch pussy. Always leaving me unsatisfied and alone. I had flings, shit he isn't even lukewarm and here I am about to fuck you. So I'm not innocent. Markel and I relationship was strictly what it was money, power and half ass decent sex. Those girls he fucked were his pleasure. They received the dick but I got all the money. He'll pay me and I'll fuck someone else later. We lived separate lives."

She fumbles with the keys until she finds the right one. I glanced at her beside me and she is beautiful. She finds the right one and opens the door. Her carpet white and fluffy, we kick off our shoes at the same time. The portrait of her in a red leather strapless dress was sexy. She had pictures of herself on every wall. I notice she had none of her husband or family.

"You sure do love yourself?"

INSANITY AT ITS FINEST!

"I love me better than anybody else. I'm beautiful, smart and the woman every man on earth wants. Want a drink?"

She dressed in her expensive maroon pants suit. Her breasts sitting high like mountains. Instead of answering her I throw my jacket to the floor. I push her against her door. I kiss her neck, rub my lips there. I travel with my fingers and open up her blazer pushing it off her shoulders to the floor. I pop every button on her shirt, no bra on. She's had a boom job; I touched and felt enough silicone-injected tits to know hers was too perfect, too rubbery. I hear heart racing like an engine. She slides to the floor and takes off her pants and panties at the same time. I take off my clothes with an intense urgency to get inside of her. I reach in my pocket and pull out both condoms. She licks her lips.

"You are so damn sexy and hairy. Your dick is long. Too bad I don't suck dicks, you'd be the first."

"Shut up and let's fuck."

I kneel and crawl to her. She spreads her legs wide ready and open to receive me. My cell phone and her cell phone ringing loud and at the same time. Fuck that phone I need to cum. I pulled her face towards me to kiss her; I put my hands in her hair. She has weave I can feel the braids and thread getting stuck to my fingers. I slid my hands slowly until I reach her breasts. Her nipples looking like pink cotton candy. I massage and then pinch her nipples. She moans, "Damn you gone make me cum just by doing that."

I followed with my tongue nursing her like I was a newborn baby. She pulls at her hair and arches her back.

"Damn you, BISHOP!"

I stop dead in my tracks and rip open the condom with my teeth. I put it on and growl,

Turn on your stomach and spread your legs." I take my fingers and I massage her pussy lips. I start at the right side. She moans and bites the carpet.

"You like that Tucker?" She is at a loss for words as I go and massage the left side.

"I ask you do you like it? Let me hear the answer.'

"Yes, Can you please taste me?"

Hell no I thought! I don't know you that well.

INSANITY AT ITS FINEST!

Tamyara Brown

I rub the head of my dick from the top of her ass to the very entrance of her pussy. She shrieks, pulls at my hair. I do it again rubs it on her ass, then I smack it. It's flat and hard. I straddled her and stop teasing her. I enter with a force, her skin is hot and slick. If it's supposed to be a secret she's told half the entire complex I am fucking her good. She lifts her body and gets on all fours while I am still inside of her. She bucks her ass and I match her rhythm. She hisses and growls. She pulls up pieces of 50.00 a yard carpet. I bite her ass alternating with smacks.

I pull her weave and she screams, "Pull it my hair and fuck me harder."

I go at pace that gives my knees rug burns, sweat pouring off me onto her.

"You are fucking this pussy good Man! Omigod, I'm cumming, Omigod, I'm cumming hard. EEEEK."

I feel her squeeze me and I feel myself pour into the condom. The sweat pouring off of me. I watch her fall to the floor. I lay on my back breathing hard and catching my breath.

By the time I was done my phone had rung sixteen times. She silent and I both. I look at her and put on my clothes. She stands up still naked. She wobbles as she tries to stand. All I kept thinking was how good it felt to fuck. Who was calling and why.

"Damn, I'm weak. You got a good piece of dick there. Let me freshen up so I can take you back to your truck." I smiled at her. I was disappointed she allowed me to do all the work. No interaction, no real movement, she hardly touch me.

I hate selfish sex. She is bragging as if she really did some justice.

"I know my pussy was good probably the best you ever had in your life." I look at her and just plaster on another fake smile. She hits the bathroom and I look at my missed call three from my brother, three from Hernandez and one from ECMC.

I hit the voicemail key and its family checking up on me. It's the last one that knocks me off my feet. Miyama passed away this afternoon. I hear the words over and over again. I just saw her two hours ago. We talked she told me my unborn child was playing with the little girl

I killed. I look at Tucker who walks out hair and make-up fully done. I rub my hands through my beard.

"For a man who just had the best sex of his life you look like you just lost a friend?"
"Actually, I just need to go handle something. Are you ready I need to go?" She looks me up and down.
"Well alright!" I follow her out.
By the time we reach ECMC the press is all over the place. I step out and wave. No kiss! No goodbye! No nothing! I walk around back and enter the hospital. Hernandez text me that he saw Michelle here. Guilt shower over me as soon as I see her. I look at her eyes are red from crying she is alone .Her mother is not there to mourn her sister's death. I want to console her and hold her. Not while Tucker's scent is still on me. I turn around and walk out the door. I get in my truck and drive off. All that kept ringing in my head was what Miyama said. "My sister is dead." What did she mean by that?

INSANITY AT ITS FINEST!

DADDY'S LOVE IN NEED

Michelle walks in the door and she doesn't even speak to me. Who the hell is he? This man pretending to like my daughter and he is sneaky. I can smell the lies and deceit on him. He has yet to attempt to introduce himself to me. What is that he wants from my child? She turns on the shower and the smell of Carol's Daughter's Almond Cookie shower seeps through the bathroom door. I look at her pictures in my album book.

If I'm honest with myself I was blessed with a beautiful child. She reminds me of him. Damn him for doing that to me all over again. I hate him for spilling his sperm in my womb and planting a seed, as a constant reminder of him Michelle hates me for killing her father. I dislike her for being a constant reminder of the person who hurt me. I hate that her dimples are just like his. I hate she evens smiles like him.

Michelle thinks we are different, that I never yearned for my Daddy. The sun and moon set on my father. I couldn't wait until the birds came out chirping the days were longer and the warm weather hit. It was my sign that Daddy was coming in his station wagon to pick me up. I made sure I was perfect in my best dress and Sunday go to meeting shoes spit and Vaseline shiny.

He'd never come up the stairs; I didn't care because I was going to Buffalo, N.Y.to be with my Daddy. I loved that man more than I loved my mama I'll admit it. I now understand the hurt she felt when I chose him over her. They say you never understand a mother's pain until you are a mother yourself facing the same exact situation Karma is a ugly Bitch and damned if the same cards weren't dealt to me two times fold.

The truth settled in that he loved my sister more than me. She had him every day. I had him only in the summer months. She hated me for being in her space, for being his daughter and being the outsider. She would pour urine in my bed saying I wet myself. She had no issue with lying on me. The days my father would spank me with wire hangers for being a disobedient child. I swear I was a good girl who said her prayers, stay being nice and kind. Miyama hated me for no reason but loving our father. She was the one who curse, stole money from the collection plate and then blame it on me.

She couldn't share him for two lousy summer months. I remember the day she cut my hair off and he told me I was lying. He chose her over me and believed I would do this to myself. I was just the child from the woman he no longer loved or may have never loved. My mother synopsis is that they fell in lust at first sight. They made love, created me, his wife approach her and she cut her in the face and he began to hurt her and me.

When men run from being a father it's because he can't stand the constant reminder of how he chose the wrong woman to have a child with. I was the bastard child with green eyes who reminded him of his sins and infidelities. He could never deny me as his child. I resemble him in every way. I would hear him tell his wife he was sorry for making a mistake. I wasn't a blessing or a gift. I was classified as a mistake grew up with that word all of my childhood. Imagine that word being said to you being a vivid picture if he had a choice in the matter you wouldn't be here. My mother reminded me every day how she tried to have an abortion because if she couldn't have daddy she didn't want me. Nasty reminders of how from the time of conception I wasn't accepted or wanted by either parent.

The truth is I don't know how to love my daughter. I bury that feeling many years ago. I can't give her what she deserves emotionally. I died a long time ago along with Daddy and I killed the emotion to trust someone at the age of thirteen. I made a decision that no one would take away anything from me again. You hurt me, I kill you it is simple.

I've been ridiculed, tossed to the wolves and trampled on by those who pretend to love and like me. I sit here before the world the woman I chose to become by people's actions. They help make me the evil bitch that I am. I was designed by all the hate they pressed upon me. In theory it isn't my fault. You know how many God fearing people destroyed me? How hearing the word "Hallelujah" makes my soul cringe. I hate God not because of what he allowed to happened to me, but for every woman who was broken by so called Christians.

So-called Christians pretended to love me but would sit in the pews talking behind my back. I tried building a relationship with God but let's keep it funky and tall I've been betrayed a thousand times. They made me hate because they took my love and like an asshole they fuck me with lube. Funny, with lube you think that it won't hurt much but pleasure is all for the other person easy entrance. It still hurts. Whenever I trust people they have a way of throwing it in my face. I'm suspicious of anyone and if you come to close I'm cutting you off by the balls and your clit.

Michelle is angry too; I see it in her the desire to kill me. She just too weak to do it, she let her heart rule her mind. Let her anger overcome her and she may try me. It is why I remind her daily that I will kill her before she ever kills me.

I pull out my album book of my husband and I see the good times we shared when I was smaller. He loved me once and as the weight piled on he began to despise my body and me. Every time he told me I was ugly I ate. Every time he wished me dead I ate and ate. When he would remind me that he should have married a white woman or a light skin woman because my skin color sickened him. The more I loved him the more he hated me just like Daddy, just like my sister and everyone.

He took advantage of me, had me on an emotional roller coaster never knowing when he would leave me or hate me. I was unsettled and uneasy with the color of my skin and how fat I was. I would bathe in bleach, take diet pills and wear lighter shades of foundation. To keep my husband I paid him to stay. I did whatever he told me to do and with all I gave he wouldn't love me. I deserve to be loved and accepted it was all I ever fucking wanted.

I deserve for God to love me and he had to hate me for him to let his Saints rape me. I've tried to figure it out what I did to our Lord and Savior why didn't he stop them. Out of all the bad people in the world why did he let this happen? How can you break a soul when it is dead?

INSANITY AT ITS FINEST!

The most dangerous woman is the one who has nothing to lose. She already at a place where she believes God hates, her man's gone and no one to love her. That's me in the nutshell anything of value especially love was stolen from me. I kill for the joy but it helps me to forget the pain I went through. It's my sexual and unusual high of seeing someone take his or her last breath. Watching his or her heart stop. I know I'm psychotic but it brings me more joy than opening presents on Christmas Day.

Again, people have created me to be a psychotic beast and the truth is I love it. The courts never persecute the son of bitches and the bitches of bitches for messing up a person's life. Ever read the news? He or she came from a dysfunctional background but that doesn't give him the right to walk up in a school and kill everybody.

Why the fuck doesn't it? I came to people to help me and hear my cries and they shrug my rape off because men of God wouldn't molest a child. That Bitch Amanda called child protection on me because she said I was drowning and overwhelmed with parenting. Stupid cunt thought I forgave her because I would share made up stories. Like the fat pig she was she ate it up. I pretended to forgive her and I even bought her gifts to show her tokens of my appreciation for further fucking with my psyche. The fact that C.P.S worker cursed me out, call me a weak Bitch and said I look like a gorilla. Whether they both know it or not they gave me motive to murder. Gave me motive to stop trusting these mofos.

I was losing control, I let people take advantage of me and they added the dash to break me into being a murderer. She left her bag unattended I tainted her sandwich and salad with rat poison nothing brought sandwich. me sheer pleasure than watching her foaming out the mouth and dying in front of her colleagues in the cafeteria. I felt no remorse for her death she tried to get my child taken from me. She would lie to my face talking about,

"She loved me. She liked me. She cared for me and all along I was her case study for her thesis. I overheard her telling her colleagues she hated looking at me because my eyes and dark skin sickened her."

She wasn't the first person I killed actually my mother was the first to quench my thirst. She wanted to die. She lived in misery, she stop bathing, she never went outside and sank deeper into depression. My

INSANITY AT ITS FINEST!

mother hated her cinnamon brown complexion, hated being a black woman. She believed being darker than a paper bag was a sin for women.

I watch her cry every day for ten years over Daddy. She watch Casablanca all day long. She had diabetes, hypertension, weighed 400 hundred pounds and was on oxygen. She sit weeping and she would say,

"I hate my life. I hate living and I am nothing. I should have died." Nothing I said or did helped. I had to put her out of her misery and besides I got tired of smelling her. I prepared all of her favorite foods ham, pigtails, potato salad, macaroni and cheese, fried chickens, ham hocks, collard greens, spare ribs and a 7up cake. I went to the library researching ways to kill her without it showing up in her blood. It was her birthday December twenty seventh, she sat looking at Carol Burnett all day long. I kissed her forehead, hug her and said,

"Mama, you will not suffer another day maybe once you're dead you can have Daddy."

"Death is better than this hell on earth. I hate being a black woman please God if I come back on this earth make me white, blonde hair and blue eyes."

I draw up the solution mixed with her insulin. My hand shakes, my heart pounding and I count to ten. I push the needle in her forearm. Within three minutes she smiles, her chest rises, foam runs from the side of her mouth and she kicks one time. She is dead and I am murderer. I feel nothing but joy because she is free. I sing to her a song by the Stylistics and one tear falls.

"God, you've never answered any of my prayers but let her rest in peace and come back as a happy white woman."

I tried counseling and this one quack therapist spoon fed me motivational quotes and affirmations. She never listen to a word I said. I'd speak and she throw some more quotes at me. She had a habit of sharing her great life with her husband, family and vacations,

"Would you fucking listen and stop interrupting me."

She simply said, "Woman up and trust God. Jesus will fix it."

INSANITY AT ITS FINEST!

I needed fucking help not a motivational quote or self-affirmations from a book. I needed her to help convince my Daddy those men raped me. I needed her to believe me when I said I didn't urinate on myself or cut my hair. Or rip up Miyama's clothes.

What the fuck was medication going to do for me but put me in a vegetated state? I came for help and they turn it around on me. They said I was crazy and when I agree they said I wasn't. Fuck them I'm my own therapist. I got my back if everybody lived that way the world wouldn't be so many people evil like me.

I won't let that man take my child away from me. He wants her for himself. I scream out, "hell fucking no."

I will kill her before he takes her away from me people keep taking from me. We have our shit, I bust her ass but it's because of me she looks half-decent and I am the only one who can protect her from this cruel world.

"What is it and why the hell are you calling me at three in the morning?" She was mumbling and breathing hard. She catches her breath and said

"Dena is going to drop the car off at the usual spot."

I roll my eyes.

"Good."

"Why do we have to rent cars for you?"

"Bitch, because I am helping your fat ass out with some cash."

"I don't need no problems with the law."

"You're already in trouble with your nasty ass house, popping morphine pills and being ugly ass shit. That's what going to take your ass under not me. I'm your gift of getting your life together."

I hear her weak ass crying over the phone.

"I am going to kill myself."

"You've attempted to do that and failed. You are pathetic, Mutt. I'm going to give you a few tips on suicide. If you was going to do it you would have done it already."

"I am."

"You don't have to worry about killing yourself. You have to worry about me murdering your ass." I hang up on her and I hope she does so it will keep one less murder charge off me. Pity, she was just fixing her life.

INSANITY AT ITS FINEST!

I hear a knock on the door and it's Michelle. She sits next to me knowing how I feel about someone touching me. She looks me in the eye.

"Mama, Can we talk?" Her hair still wet and wavy smelling like almond cookie. I cross my leg and lean back on my bed.

"What do you want to talk about?" She lowers her head and then she looks at me.

"Mama, I want you to stop the killing." I file my nails and blow on the tips of them, cross my legs and smirk.

"I'm not killing anyone I'm avenging crimes committed against me and others. I'm an enforcer not a criminal."

"Aren't you scare of the consequences of getting caught?" I look at her and slide close to her.

"Do I look scared? Do I look worried? Since you giving out advice on what I'm doing as a grown woman who birth you out my pussy. If you ever call yourself telling on me because the guilt is eating at you I will kill you and that that man of yours. Don't tell me to stop I'm the victim. I know you don't believe me. I'm on a mission and I have a few more people who need to die." She starts tearing up and turns her head. She knows how I hate any sign of weakness.

"Mama everyone gets caught. You're not invincible."

"I want to get caught and stop crying with your weak ass."

She turns away from me her arms folded.

"Why won't you stop killing people, Mama?"

"For every fat girl whose lost their souls and nobody heard them. Every time I was bullied or teased because of my weight and dark complexion. To let them know that it's not okay to disrespect us and mistreat us." She walks out without a response.

THE SCENT OF DEATH

I walk into the hospital, the waiting room filled with sick people, prisoners in green jump suits, chained by the ankles and legs. The security guard at Erie County Medical Center is watching the Bills game. My legs feel weak, my heart heavy and everything seems to be moving in slow motion. I take the elevator to the ground floor, the grey walls seem to be closing in on me. Each step I take echoes in the air and the scent of strong bleach. Lined against the wall is gurneys waiting to carry another dead person.

The coroner has a white lab coat, covered in what looks like jelly stains, he is tall, bald and has freckles on his face. He looks me up and down.

"Whose body are you here to verify?"

"Miyama Grant."

He flips through the clipboard, runs his finger down the sheet and flips the page over.

"And what's your relation to her?"

"I'm her niece."

He hands over a clipboard and a pen.

"Fill the paperwork stating you are verifying the body."

He nods his head and walks over to the third gurney. He pushes it to the front of the glass, removes the white sheet and the tube is still in her mouth. She is absolutely beautiful as she sleeps. I look at Miyama and she is smiling. She is at peace she no longer carrying secrets, carrying the pain inflicted on her by Mama. I kiss her forehead and my tears rain on her face. The room is freezing cold, I shiver and my hands are numb. The guards look at me and the doctor pulls me in the private room.

"Your Aunt ask me to give this to you before she passed."

I take the envelope with my name printed on it. His eyes travel as I stuff it in my pocket. I walk out without a feeling in my body but the heavy weight that the one person who loves me unconditionally is gone. The one-person who just didn't see me as the weight I am but

INSANITY AT ITS FINEST!

the woman I was inside. Mama wouldn't even allow her to say goodbye. How hurtful the only other living relative and you can't pay your condolences and identify the body.

I sit in the lobby and the whole emergency room is full but to me I don't see anybody. I open the letter and but my tear filled eyes won't let me see the words. The guard who was at the morgue hands me a tissue.

"Thank you." He pats me on the shoulder. I blow my nose and try to compose myself. I pull out the letter and it reads:

Dear Michelle,

God asks me to write this letter to you. I know you have dealt with a lot of pain and hurt in your life. Please accept my apology as I never meant to hurt anyone and that Satan made me do it.

I know that but first let me tell you GOD loves you unconditionally and he gave his only begotten son to save our lives. I'm here to tell you that he has not given up on you. He has his angels watching you. I ask that you recognize you were never unloved by him.

I love you and think you should understand that God never gives us nothing we can't handle if it was that much to bear he would carry us. I have to tell you something because my sister wasn't always Satan's child; I played a part in that. The love you had for your Daddy well my love for your grandfather was just as deep. I had to share with your sister. I didn't want to. I had the sin of jealousy and that one sin will coax you to the unthinkable and act in haste. Your Mama was a pretty chubby little girl with those green eyes you have. I hated her and I did mean things to her. I torture her, cut her hair but most of all I did any and everything to make her go away. I would pee in a jar and pour it on her bed. I took her to the shed, the place where they free you from sin. Everyone who came out of that shed was closer to God. Limping out of the shed their clothes drenched in blood, tear stained faces yet I thought they had saw God. That's what the Pastor and Deacon had said to me. If I knew the truth then I wouldn't of done that to her. I would have never made her hide in there."

I heard her and I let them hurt her. I turned deaf ear and for that I will forever rest in hell. I didn't know Michelle. Your mother's heart was as pure and sweet as yours was. What so many others and I did to her I will forever be punished.

INSANITY AT ITS FINEST!

I chose to follow my Pastor and Deacon.

No one believed her not even me. I didn't want to I was just satisfied she was going back to Brooklyn and would never come back. I never realize that all she wanted was to spend time with Daddy and her big sister. She tried to be friends and I turned my back on her. It's the one thing in my life I regret allowing my sister to be hurt.

I'm so sorry I let that happen those raping her and so many children. I need you not to become your mother or me that happen to you because someone hurt you. Don't let that be the reason to take life without God's permission. I did it, your mother did it? Be a better woman because your heart doesn't have the evil that dwell in mines and your mother.

Love will come. A man will come in your life, let him in and let him love you. He will give you the most precious gift God can give a woman. I need you to get on your knees and pray tonight for your Mama. Let God lift the burden of all the hurt, the despair and pain. I've always love you. Those people that you encounter taught you a lesson. Taught you what love wasn't. A man is in your heart and he available to love you unconditionally, don't be afraid. He's already there he needs you and you need him.

You are burden with the decision to tell the police what your mama has done. Let God take care of that. Your mother wants to get caught. You have to be safe to carry out God's plan. Be careful!

I love you,

Miyama

I close the letter and cry. Why would she do that to her? How could she? I want to go in and scream at her. I stuff the letter in my pocket. The warmth of his coat and his signature smell of Egyptian Musk put his arms around me. I look up he's dressed in a Grey button up shirt and jeans. He kisses my forehead and he whispers in my ear.

"I'm here and it's going to be alright." I put my face in his chest and find security in his arms.

"Thank you, Bishop."

"Someone told me I needed you as much as you needed me." I sit up and look him in his eyes today they blend in with clothes.

"Who?"

"A good friend of mine. Come on let me get you home."

INSANITY AT ITS FINEST!

BISHOP

FALLING FOR THE SUSPECT

Michelle sits at the kitchen table and I bring her a cup of green tea. I sit across from her and give her a moment to collect her thoughts. I take the tissue and wipe her eyes. She is shaking, overwhelmed with sadness and anger. I want to take that feeling away from her.

"It's hard losing someone you love."

Her voice trembles and it aches my heart.

"She was the only person to love me unconditionally. Then she drops this bombshell on me about...."

I brace myself for whatever she may tell but not seem too anxious. I wait for her to tell me anything even if it's a small piece to the puzzle. I focus on her needs.

"Are you hungry?"

"No, but thank you anyway. Can I ask you a question?" I walk over to the counter and pour myself a cup of coffee and grab an apple Danish. I take a bite and say,

"Sure go ahead."

"What if someone you love and looked up to told you they did something to your mother. How would you handle that much truth?" I sip my coffee and answer,

"I don't know it depends on what it was they did or said. Why did your Aunt tell you something?"

She drops her head and whimpers. I wipe her eyes again and hold her in my arms. I want her to tell me whatever is on her mind. I kiss her hand gently, rub her back as she cries.

"My mother wants to cremate her. I want to give her a funeral, she would like that." She takes the cup to her mouth and slowly drinks the tea.

"Your mother must have final say on what happens?"

"Yes. I know why though and I can't blame her. I understand she wants to forget, she needs to forget." She again wanders off in another place where secrets have been stored. Where truth has come out and now it hurts, it's hurt like hell. She lays her head on my chest and cries rivers of pain, releases more than she wants to.

I've seen tears from the women who love me and me chose not to love them back. I saw tears from the woman I did love begging me to choose her and get a safer job. None of that faze me, she walks in my life for a few weeks and she is causing emotions to unravel. I've hidden the day I was sworn in as an officer of the law. I take a deep breath and wipe the tears from my eyes.

"If you don't want to discuss it that's okay. I'm not going anywhere." My embrace is tighter around her arms. Her tears wet my tee shirt

"Thank you. I trust you and I haven't trusted a man in a long time. I need to think of something else. I need to smile, feel good without crying. I am always crying and I don't know how to stop. Do anything to forget my past, to get rid of this pain inside of me." My hormones think lay her down and the couch and sex her until her pain becomes mountains of pleasure. Instead I take the gentleman route.

"I think I can put a smile on your face." Her eyebrows raise up and look at me with a weary look."

I take Michelle by the hand and lead her to my couch I turn on some Spoken word by my man Khari' Toure. I just received his CD off Amazon and fell in love with it.

He touches on a lot but this brother right here is the truth. I begin explaining his poetry and spoken word to her.

"Khari Toure he's been out for a minute. He is from my hood Oakland and on my free time I would hang out at this lounge but he's done his work all over the country. This is my favorite, it's called Thickness. Listen!" I sit and marinate on the words. After this finish. I turn it down and put the remote on the coffee table. The other poems may make me take this innocent evening to another level.

"Wow he is good. I never heard of him before. I would like a copy of this? "

"You sure can on one condition you have to show me a smile."

She smiles and damn I look at her in a different light and she has this natural glow. No make-up but that lip-gloss she's always wearing. Her beautiful cocoa brown skin, her cat eyes, long eyelashes, her full

INSANITY AT ITS FINEST!

Meagan Goode lips and deep dimples. Her beauty comes from all over her. I can't see how she could not see it.

"Hey, why did you stop that CD.? We can sit and listen to it." I touch her chin,

"Hmm, that brother speaks a lot of your story and other truths. You think you can handle all that truth."

"I could why do you think I couldn't?" I shrugged my shoulders and kick off my shoes. I pull her close to me and allow the CD to shuffle through.

"You ever date a plus size woman?' I think back to Malika.

"I have the woman I told you about. She was about your size, sexy, confident and I would have marry her."

"What attracted you to her because you know being from California brothers out there aren't checking for big women?"

"Every man's perception of a woman isn't that she be a size six with a light complexion and super model skinny. I love a woman with full hips, thick thighs, and full breasts. I like your size. I liked her size and the difference between my ex and Ms. Michelle is she doesn't like her body"

My voice trails off and squirt comes on and I try not to focus on my erection forming as Michelle leans back and her eyes ask that question. Have you ever made a woman squirt? My mind tells me to show her the answer. I want to tell her that I can make her orgasm have an orgasm. I want to tell her that if she looks at me one more time I'm going to kiss both sets of her lips. Instead I say,

"Are you okay, Michelle?"

She clears her throat and zip down her jacket and her nipples are piercing through her shirt. She looks down at my pants and wipes the sweat forming on her brow. She smiles and I don't know if it's because of my dick cutting through my pants or the fact I have that effect on her.

"Um… Yes just enjoying the music along with his words. This is beyond steamy, it's sensual and erotic!" I fixate my eyes to her lips the way she says each word. The elephant has barged in the room. She afraid to ask but I'm not

"Have you ever?" Her cheeks become cherry reds, she shifts and rubs her hand down her throat.
"Have I ever what?" She knows damn well what I'm talking about.
"Squirt." Her smile is bright and she looks down to the floor.
"Bishop, yes I know what it is. To answer your question no I've never. I think it's just a porno myth."
"Damn. It would be a wonderful experience for you. No, Love it isn't a myth at all." I laugh and blow out air.
"So have you ever made a woman? You know… um" I finish off her sentence and lick my lips again.
"SQUIRT! But of course?" She rubs her hand on her neck and clears her throat. I smile that sneaky smile that informs I have much experience in pleasing a woman I,

Cherish breaks the tension. She is no longer crying and for a few moments the sadness has been put to rest if even for a few hours. I go to the bathroom hoping after I relieve myself my erection goes down. I look and it stills full I lean my head back. Maybe because Michelle looks so damn sexy and I have this natural attraction to her. 'She's a suspect Bishop', I say to myself but my dick is saying she is a woman who you need to go ahead and give it to her.
I turn on the faucet splash cold water on my face and wash my hands. When I come out she is laying on the edge of the couch curled up like a five-year-old sleep? She looks angelic. I go into the linen closet and cover her up with my favorite blanket. I go in my room and turn on the TV which pops on YNN they're talking about the death of Miyama and the chain of events with FAT Girl Vigilante. Mayor Byron Brown pops up with the same dry ass speech he been saying since the beginning of the case. I turn off the TV and close the door.
I need to relieve this erection. I grab the baby oil and pour some on my hand. As I stroke slow Michelle creeps into my thoughts. I let out a moan. I hear the door open but I think it's Bullet. I quicken the pace and when the sensation feels good. I allow my pitch go higher my eyes pop open and I see her green eyes piercing at me. I should
INSANITY AT ITS FINEST!

be worry if she will kill me but the feeling is to cum and not worry. The light from the hallway shines and she can see my jism spill all over my hand. I fall back exhausted and curious about what she wanted. I hear my door close. It lets me know she was watching me and I hope she enjoyed the show.

My eyes are wide open as daylight creeps in. I need a few more hours of sleep but I have a shit load of work to do and a million thoughts running through my mind. I grab a smoke and light it. I take a drag and think back to last night catching her watching me. I should be afraid because maybe I was her next victim. I don't think it was in her thoughts. The look in her eyes told me she enjoyed it. If she had heart enough and wasn't worry what I'd think of her she would of came and finish me off and got hers too. I chuckle to myself. A sudden light tap hits the door.

"Come in." Her expression told me the truth she looks to the ground.

"Good Morning!" I let the cigarette hang from my lip. I beam at the thought she watched me jerk off.

"Good Morning, How was your sleep?"

"It was good. I was wondering if you could drive me to the hospital to get my car so I can go to work."

"Sure. Give me five minutes to throw on some clothes." I stand up and the head of it pokes out her eyes are fixated on it. To add insult to injury I'm hard as a brick.

"Michelle, last night did you need me for something?" She turns her head and her cheeks are bright red.

"Um, no I um… I" I lick my lips and answer,

"I could have help you with whatever you needed."

"Okay… um I will see you in five minutes."

"Yep." I blow out a smoke ring and wink at her.

We are now in the car and I can tell I have embarrassed her.

I ask, " Do you mind if I turn on some music to wake me up?'

"No, that's fine! Bishop before you do I just want to apologize for walking in your room while you was um…"

"It's not a problem. So what exactly did you see?" She looks away from me again.

"Only you sleeping at least I think.

"Was that all?"

"Umm. Yes it was dark and I walk away immediately."

"Okay. I wasn't asleep. I was indisposed and I am aware of what you saw. Like I told you before Michelle I keep it real at all times. We're adults and what I was doing I'm not at all ashamed of. You shouldn't be ashamed for me either."

"You're handsome so you should never have a problem getting a woman to satisfy you sexually."

"I don't have a problem with getting women, I guess I've been busy and though I've had sex I'm attracted to you but right now we are still getting to know each other. You don't need the stress of me trying to pursue you sexually with so much on your plate. I found myself wanting to go there but…"

"I understand. I thank you for that Bishop respecting me and all."

I pull into the hospital parking lot and I get out and open the door for her. She steps out and I hug her. I hold her for a minute. She kisses me on the cheek. I watch her walk to her car. She gets in and pulls off. I realize I'm breaking my own rules falling for the perp.

INSANITY AT ITS FINEST!

Tamyara Brown
Patricia

LOVE AND INSANITY WILL NEVER MIX

She made me love her deceived me into believing she was a man. Her muscular frame, large hands, big Afro, converses. He told me her name was G-man. I should have known something was wrong when he only wanted to perform oral sex on me and use a dildo. I found out the night I found blood running down her leg. She had missed her hormone shots.

"So basically I'm a man but born in a girl body. Listen, babe you have the best of both worlds. Don't worry I'm looking into getting dick implants."

Goldie and I are like liquid cocaine potent and deadly when mixed together. She is stronger than me, she is a professional assassin I can't kill. So I went after her daughter. Pretty Mia, as I pulled each of her teeth out, cuts off her tits, carved my initials in her face and left her for dead. I felt a gratifying sensation of joy. The minute it took for the smell of smoke and the fire to fully ignite. I'm gone, the deed of taking her life is because I couldn't kill Miyama. Goldie, will be horrified. She was a distraction and a reminder of the fact I was sleeping with a woman. Dare I say it? In this day and age when love is irrelevant. It has been for a long time. When you're a cold-blooded murderer that one feeling will throw you off track making judgement based on a feeling.

Within fifty minutes I'm on West Eagle Street and call over to the homeless man. I give him twenty-five dollars to hand the garbage bag to the lost and found at Police headquarters. He walks in and I pull off. He'll never be able to describe me today my wig is purple. My face covered up with a beard. I drive the long way home thinking about my life.

I sit in my living room naked, all the lights off and I cancel my meeting. I pray that traitor ass daughter of mine stays away. I don't

INSANITY AT ITS FINEST!

want to hear a sound. I don't want the hum of the refrigerator so I unplug it. I have the nerve to feel hollow and ashamed of what I have done. I hear the sound of the key turn the lock, I sit up and the door opens. I see Michelle stand over me and her green eyes staring at me; she flicks on the light. She asks,

"Mama, why are you naked?" My first reaction was to backhand her and cut her hair off. Instead I spread my legs open and answer,

"This is my house I do as I please. I watched that bitch burn?" She sits next to me and tries to wrap her arms around me. I must be hormonal because tears of the past have flooded and broken the levee. Now my tears are uncontrollable. Michelle hands me a piece of paper folded. I snatch it from her and read each word quickly. I look at it again and again.

I scream,

"You wait until you're on your deathbed to admit the truth. Fuck you, Miyama. Fuck you five times in the ass the way they did me. Never once did that bitch mention what happen to me. Not once Michelle and that shit hurt me. Ate me alive inside. She invited me back in her life after Daddy died and left us this house. I help her even after she repeatedly had the runs and shitted all over me. I help her lose the weight and I waited for years so she would just say,

"Sister I'm sorry. A simple sorry would have healed me. My husband, the Pastor, Deacon, my Mama, Camilla and Goldie. Sorry is such a sweet word."

"Get away from me, Michelle?" I move to the other end of the couch, I ball up and hold my knees to my chest. I cry and lately this has been a habit.

"Mama, I am so sorry that has happen to you. I understand why you are the way you are. You close me out and now I understand. You need help, Mama." I look at her and say,

"How in the fuck can you understand having two men rip your ass and pussy open? Huh? Them repeatedly fucking you in every open whole. Watching them take the only person who tried to protect you and running a train on him. Your sister, your flesh and blood standing out of the door laughing, playing rope. She lied on my friend saying we had sex. Took away my Daddy. You have no clue not even an inkling what I feel. You understand." I get up and flip

INSANITY AT ITS FINEST!

the coffee table over, throw the vase against the wall. I walk close to her and show her my ass, I continue,

"My own Mama, my Daddy and the damn police didn't believe that the good old Pastor Neck bone and Deacon Fat back would do this to me. It's okay! It's okay!"

I sniffled and walk upstairs. I slam the door and the house shakes. She couldn't understand what I was going through. Michelle talking about how I need help. I'm my own therapy. I turn on the TV and the news reporter said,

"A homeless man turned in a woman's breast in a plastic bag. They suspect that this is connected to the woman who they found at the Golden Arms Motel near University of Buffalo. More at eleven." I looked at her picture flashing. I throw the remote at the TV. The explosion doesn't bother me. Fuck it! I need some 8ball and MJG. I turned the music sky high.

"I throw on my red peek a boo dress. I find my red thigh high heel boots. And underclothes are absent. I put on my perfume, flat iron my hair and put on my diamond encrusted hoops.

I grab my purse fuck it. I've got on my make-up. I'm on a rampage with a smile. I walk down the stairs. My Michael Kors accessorize with my hunter's knife and my dildo.

"Mama, where you going?" I lick my lips put my gun in my purse.

"To find a birthday boy or girl at the club, and slice his dick in half. You know how I do." She grabs me by the arm and the look I give her. She steps back.

"Mama don't do this tonight, Please?"

"Oh okay. Since you trying to save a life. Here's a new flash for your ass your birth father is the Deacon of the church now marinate on that. Your daddy is your brother." She slams the door. The music blasting loud. I hear her tires screech as she turns the corner.

INSANITY AT ITS FINEST!

SAVING A LIFE

After Mama left I mediated on the possibility of the man who raped my mother to be my father. She's lying. I won't believe her. I get up and go through the photo album book look at each picture of Daddy and myself. I look like him. I have his deep dimples and smile.

I look at the one picture Mama has a heart around it and it's a picture of my grandfather and grandmother their wedding photo, next to it my parent's wedding picture. She is much bigger and she is smiling. She is happy. There is another picture of my Mama pregnant with my father kissing her belly and again she is smiling. My father with me in his arms and mommy smiling, the story the pictures tell is her being happy with Daddy. I look through and like a movie my life plays back to me frame after frame.

Until I get to the picture of me and a little girl who seems to be younger than I. She and I are dress alike holding Mama Hands and the lady Camilla Mama's former friend smiling. I lift the picture up and written behind it is our names my Mama, Camilla, Anais Nya (Michelle's sister, Michael's daughter) and mine. The tears drop down on Mama's face. I have a sister. Is this true?

. She is going to kill again, I got to stop her. I have to help her and save someone's life. I run upstairs and find the prepaid phone I bought. I program it and take a walk about ten blocks up. I call the police,

"Hello, I need to speak to the detective on the Fat Girl Vigilante case." They put me on hold and a recorded message of Mayor Brown and the Commissioner plays then a voice comes on with a thick Spanish accent. I hesitate and almost want to hang up but I put aside fear.

"Hernandez. Homicide how can I help you?" I feel my throat getting tight. I feel sweat running down my neck.

INSANITY AT ITS FINEST!

"Officer tonight a woman in a red dress and red thigh high leather boots is going to a club to find a man whose birthday is today and killed them."

"How do you know Ma'am?"

"She told me. I'm trying to save a life, she is very upset and when she's upset she hurts people. Please send some officers out to the clubs." I'm trembling now betrayal has nothing on the chill outside. In my thirty years plus I have never muttered a word to anyone of the murders she committed.

"Do you know what club Ma'am? Can I have your name?

"No. She has gun?"

"What does she look like?" I can't fully give her up. She'll know I told. She'll kill me if they don't catch her. I'm just trying to help somebody.

"She has on a peek a boo dress and these boots are sequined heels. With the letter P on it." I hang up and throw the phone in the trash. I run back to the house and close the door

Is the Deacon my father had she lied to me all those years? Lie to the man who supported me. He knew I wasn't his daughter but loved me. I'll make sure she'll get caught. She is evil and deceitful even when you try to show her kindness and love she literally shows me her ass for me to kiss. I can't save Mama. I don't want to anymore. Without her in my life I can finally move on. I will no longer live in fear that she may kill me or I her. It's no way for a woman to live. I have to move on with my life one way or another. I've been a little girl lost and running in the same direction with nowhere to go. Mama is going to kill me one day, if the Deacon is my father. I hear someone banging on the door. I feel my heart pounding rapidly. I stand and tiptoe to the door, I peek out the window and its Shayla standing at the door. I sigh and take a deep breath. I open the door.

"Hey what are you doing here?" She raises her eyebrow looks around the house.

"Isn't today the meeting?"

"No, Mama cancel it. You can come in if you want to?"

She steps in and closes the door. She flicks on the light. She sits down on the couch.

INSANITY AT ITS FINEST!

"Someone didn't adhere to their diet so she flip out." We chuckle.
"She needs no reason to flip out."
"You're right about that I was going to get a good workout in." I pick up the coffee table and grab the broom and sweep up the broken glass. My mind is running on high octane worrying if the police will show up at my door telling me Mama's dead. I grab two bottles of water and hand one to Shayla.
"So how's the court thing going with your husband?'
"It's not going at all. I go to this stupid therapist who analyzes every word I say. He did give me a compliment on losing weight. He always so negative to be a therapist. She takes a deep sigh.
"How are your children?"
"They still hate me and my ex has no problem reminding them of how bad of a parent I am."
"He shouldn't be bad mouthing you to the children."
"I know."

"So who is the fine ass man who picked you up a couple of weeks ago? If you don't mind me being in your business."
"He's just a friend but I like him. Girl, he is fine and so sweet. He holds the door open for me, took me to dinner and danced with me in the middle of downtown." .I wrap my arms around me and kick my legs.
"You are just a blushing talking about him. He must not be from Buffalo. If he is please tell me he has a brother?"' We laugh.
"No, he's not from Buffalo. He from California."
"No wonder our men here are ruined and the good ones are married."
"You ain't never lied."
"So how does your Mama feel about him?"
"She hates any man that I talk to. He's a good guy though." Shayla hugs her.
"I'm happy for you Michelle. You deserve that. You are a good person."
"Thank You. So are you. Can we do lunch Friday, Shayla?"
"Of course. Take care and see you Friday." Shayla leaves and I finally have a friend. Someone to talk to and converse with.

INSANITY AT ITS FINEST!

Tamyara Brown
"Thanks for water and you take care."

INSANITY AT ITS FINEST!

Bishop

I watch the woman as she leaves Michelle's house. The same woman
that she had been talking to the last time I came over. I lean back
because I know she is the one who made the call to Hernandez, he
played back the call and I knew her voice. I take a sip of my coffee
waiting to see if she'll walk out the house. I want to see if she was
steering us in directions to catch her mother or was Michelle indeed
the killer? Was she trying to save someone's life because she was
tired?

The lights goes off, she walks out of the door, locks it she walks to
her car. She gets in the green Honda accord. She pulls off, I follow
her for about seven blocks and she parks at Gigi's restaurant and
walks in. She is dress in the clothes she had on when I drop her off.
My cell rings and its Tucker King, begging for more dick.

I don't answer she was an experience and now the thrill is gone. The
moment she chased me I knew it was like a car accident. I'd hit it and
now it's time to run.

I let her leave first. I go in and the waitress at the counter has big tits
falling out her shirts, she licks her lips wiping away the excess
chicken grease.

"Welcome to Gigi's what can I get for you?"

I look at the menu and decide on chicken dinner laced with Mac and
cheese, candied yams and green beans." She takes my money and
winks at me.

"I know you hear this a lot but is that your real eye color?" I smile
and answer the question I get everywhere I go.

"This is my real color."

"You have pretty eyes. Another woman just came in with green eyes"

"Does the woman with green eyes come in here all the time?"

"When she was bigger she was one of our best customers then one-
day came in and beat her up in front of everybody, calling her all
kinds of fat hogs and Bitches. It was so embarrassing. Why do ask?"

"She is someone I am interested in."

She raises her eyebrows and twists her lips.

"A man as fine as you like big girls? You must be a creep."

INSANITY AT ITS FINEST!

She was all breast, a face like a pit bull, her big ass sloppy tits touching the bottom of her stomach.

I shake my head; I pull out my wallet and hand her ten dollars. She hands me my food. I tip my baseball cap.

"What's up?"

"Listen, an officer on the beat downtown saw a woman in a red peek a boo dress and shoes entering Club Diabolic on Washington and Mohawk... Red hair and sequin heels."

"I'm on my way make sure he doesn't approach the perp. Keep an eye on her."

I back up and speed off. The roads are icy and the snow is falling hard. Why in the fuck would she be there with no coat in this weather and a summer dress on? I hit the 33 and get downtown in ten minutes.

"I'm here Hernandez. Did you go inside?"

"Yes, she is dancing with two young men. Her body is incredible."

"You stay up close and I'm coming inside but I have to keep my distance so I won't blow my cover."

The club is dark but I can see Patricia dancing with two young men. One with dreads, another one with a piercing in his lips. Jamie Foxx, "Blame it".

She has moves like a young woman, she sticks out her tongue, gyrates her body close to him. She whispers something and he rubs his hands together. They walk towards the back and I follow behind them. She and the gentlemen go outside. She hands him a small white pill and he swallows it.

"Tonight, you are about to get the most memorable head of your life." She said.

I text Hernandez to go outside. She kisses him, unzips his pants, his eyes rolls in the back of his head. A beer bottle breaks, loud outbursts, screams and I draw my gun. I clear a path grab the big dude pounding on the guy with two piercing. I flash my badge.

"Get the fuck back or everybody is going to jail?"

I run to the back and she is gone. Like the phantom she has disappear.

INSANITY AT ITS FINEST!

Hernandez approaches me and the dude is slump over. He is still alive but drugged out.

"She is on the 33 and gone."

"Fuck!" I scream.

"We'll get her."

INSANITY AT ITS FINEST!

PLAN B

I call Michelle and she picks up right away.

"Hi, Sexy. Are you busy tonight, thought maybe you and I could spend time?"

"I need to get out of here. I just don't want to deal with her tonight. I thought I saw you at Gigi's tonight."

My jaw tightens and within a second I answer,

"I was there but didn't see you. A man's got to eat. Why were you there I thought you didn't eat food like that anymore."

"I do once a month or when I am stressed out. I just don't eat out every day like you Mr. Jones."

"I'm outside waiting for you."

Her mother sits in the car. Michelle walks out with a gym bag. She doesn't look her mother's way. She walks to the car and the routine I've created I step out and open the door for her.

Her mother steps out the car and walks in the door not looking back. She closes the door and in front of the window she undresses. She keeps on her shoes. For her to be in her fifties she had a body some women pay millions of dollars for. As evil as she is I have to admit she is beautiful.

She shuts off the lights.

I back up and drive to my home. Bullet hadn't seen me in hours. I look at the floor and he's used the bathroom. I popped him on the nose and say, "nein pouif! Vora He runs in the basement. She is standing in front of me. She has on the scent.

Today she looks stunning, the way her hair is hanging in her face. Her pink sweats that seemed extra tight, her round ass and her breasts seem bigger in the V-neck pink tee shirt. I watch her bend over and I become aroused. She cleaning up the mess Bullet made I want to touch her ass. I watch her dump it in the garbage. She walks over to the sink and squirts the liquid soap on her hand and then runs it under the water. I take my cold dinner and put it the microwave. I wrap my arms around her. She separates from me.

INSANITY AT ITS FINEST!

She walks to my living room and kicks off her sneakers. Her toe nails painted a pretty pink. The side she is showing is exotic. She is beautiful and why wouldn't any man want her? She doesn't have a hint of sadness in her face, though I know it lives in her soul. I look in the fridge and all I have is water. I grab two bottles and hand her one.

"Bishop, I didn't ask permission to stay with you tonight. So I was wondering? I cover her lips with my finger.

"You don't have to ask. It's alright." Carl Thomas "summer rain plays."

I take her hand and lift her off the couch. I pull her close to me. I pull her chest close to mine. She looks me in the eyes and I s. I swing her around and do some salsa moves a beautiful Mexican once taught me. I watch her swing her hips from one side to another. She and I meet and the closeness sets a spark we've both have avoided, I'm not supposed to kiss the perp of a murder investigation. Yet, I want to our lips seconds away from the moment we both can taste.

I hear the microwave beep. It's the interruption I need. I go back in the kitchen adjust my hard on. I grab two plates and dish the food on the plate.

She sits on the couch. I hand her a plate and I have mine. I sit the bottle of water on the coffee table. She looks at me with her green eyes wanted to say something but instead taking a bite of chicken. She licks her lips and her tongue is long. The look in her eyes is calling me to be intimate with her give her something she has been missing. I want to fulfill her request. If circumstances were different and she wasn't a suspect in a murder. I would make her my woman. My cell phone rings and its 585-area code and excuse myself.

"Hello."

"Detective Bishop?"

"Yes!"

"I'm from Rochester Homicide unit. My name is Detective Martin Wilson and I understand you've been investigating the serial killings of the Fat Girl Vigilante."

"I am how can I help you?"

"Well on November 14th at around 3:00am we got a call and found a woman who was killed here and burn in a house fire. She was badly

INSANITY AT ITS FINEST!

beaten and once we arrived we found on a door burned with the words Fat Girl... we have reason to believe she has a connection to the murder."

"My perp has only killed men. Why do feel she would have anything to do with it?" I sit on the counter wait for the answer my mind is running a marathon this is crazy to me.

"Well detective I believe it because the husband admitted to having an affair with a woman with pink hair and green eyes. The same identical looks and of the one who killed the officer in Attica. The husband gave me her name Dena McMillian was who he was having an affair with."

"Dena McMillan. Okay did they happen to see the car she was driving in?"

"Toyota Corolla. It was a 2005 model." I hang up and now this case is baffling the shit out of me. I hang up and Michelle is listening to Brian McKnight.

"Sorry, I had to take ta call. I see you're letting Brian relax you." She moves her hair from her eye.

"So Bishop, I don't want you to think about work, or stress out like I do."

"Touché. Can I ask you a question?"

"Go ahead."

"What's been bothering you? I know you just lost your aunt, the mess with your Mom?" she curls up like a little girl. Looks at the pictures of myself with my father and mother the day I graduated high school picture. She looks at my family portrait taken when I was eighteen-year old. She sighs and neatly places the pictures back on the mantel piece.

"You had a good childhood, I can tell by your pictures. A lot of friends, those, who cared about you, I was always lonely. Mama was too mean and the other people just made these cruel jokes about me. I wanted the good life." She stares off into space.

"I did, but I had hard times. My father was shot by a gang banger. My parents almost separated twice because my father chose his career over his marriage. We all have hard times."

"I know but I had to hold onto so much stuff. I feel like I'm going to explode if I don't talk to someone. I don't know who to trust. The family I have dying off. Mama doesn't want me" I move closer to her and wrap my arms around her.

"You can trust me." She leans her head on my shoulder.

"Thanks, Bishop. My mama has a lot of pain in her and she pushes me away. I'm not supposed to do this. You're on the clock remember?"

"You are right. I am so what do you want to do?"

"Talk." She whispers.

She walks towards the window looks at the snowflakes. In Buffalo when the snow touches the ground it looks like rare pieces of crystal and when light illuminates it I swear no diamond shines as bright as that first snow.

"I remember when I was a little girl and at the time I was living on Quincy Street in Brooklyn. I woke up and there was a little park outside with a slide and these little girls were dressed in white dresses. They kept telling me to play with them. I tried hard but I couldn't reach them. They were so pretty and having so much fun. I was dreaming but I never ever forgot that dream. I have been a very lonely person. Always the weird fat girl with no friends. Sometimes I wish we had the choice of the parents you wanted. I would have a meeting with God and choose the people in your life. You made a life plan before you went out in the world of happiness, peace and most of love. Everyone walking on this earth should be loved. I ask myself everyday would I have chosen her for my Mama. I think I would have as sick as it seems. I just would ask him to not let circumstances shattered her heart, that he would teach her how to love me for me, Hmm."

I have no words to say after that, maybe even a therapist couldn't respond. I stand behind her and wrap my arms around her. Admire the snow hitting the ground. She continues,

"Bishop, I want to be loved. People do things bad and at the end of the day they want acknowledgement that somebody loves them. I want someone to like me for me." I put her fingers in my hand. I squeeze it gently. I feel a rush of feelings sparking the fire I practice putting out.

INSANITY AT ITS FINEST!

"I like you, Michelle. I like you a lot. You just have to believe that. Do you?" She still is looking at the snow. Her eyes look away from me, her voice low and soft.

"I want to Bishop. I do but it takes time for me."

She lets go of my hand and steps from me. I move closer put my hand on shoulder and allow it trace her spine until I reach the curve of her ass. She shudders and closes her eyes. I turn her around her and when she opens her green eyes they have melted me. The moment where I am supposed to say goodnight and go to my room like a good boy. I've always gone against the grain. I kiss her lips and she responds by returning my kiss.

The moment stood still as our lips fell in love. I get wrap up in the moment. Her soft lips and the soft music create a moment that could be dangerous for me. I allow my tongue to enter her mouth and our tongues do a tango. I wasn't lying when I said I liked her. I wanted to save her from the pain if only for one night. Take away the hurt that weighs her down. I kiss her deeper and now my hands are around her and I hold on for dear life. We are afraid to allow one another to catch our breath. It could end the madness we both are about to embark on.

She moans when I slip my hand between her legs. I've gone too far and I don't want to come back. I'm crazy because she could be seducing me to take away my life. She's full of emotion, raw and open for what I'm doing; her nipples are hard as diamonds bursting through her tee shirt. I want my phone to ring; I want Bullet to bark, just the music of Maxwell, Michelle and I by the window kissing softly.

I let my lips travel to her neck slowly and I kiss her collarbone. At this moment I'm not a detective, and she is not a suspect under investigation. She is this beautiful woman who I want to make me feel good. I am this man wanting to introduce this feeling to her. I stop and I take her hand lead her to my bedroom for the first time. I speak softly,

"Do you want me to stop? I will go no further." She kisses me again and takes my breath.

"I need your answer, Baby!"

INSANITY AT ITS FINEST!

I whisper in her ear as I suck on it, I'm traveling down to her collarbone small lip pecks and nibbles. I say again,

"Do you want me to stop? I will go no…"
She whispers,
"Please don't stop."
I take off her shirt and admire her voluptuous body. I remove her sports bra. I touch her breasts they're soft and real. I suck on her nipples, push them together sucking both at the same time and graze my teeth on them. She is touching my chest and sucking on my neck. I want to take my time with her so I lay her on the bed. I remove her pants and she has on pink lace panties and I slide them over her thick thighs. Her pussy bald with just one strip of red hair, her clit swollen and pussy sopping wet. I kiss her again and I stand her in front of the mirror.
"I don't ever want to hear you call yourself ugly. You hear me. You are so damn beautiful and sexy. I am ready to cum just looking at you. Your breasts, your stomach and pussy is pretty."
She turns her head away. I turn her head back to the mirror. She looks and my eyes are on her. I kiss her forehead, her nose, her lips, her cheeks, and her neck. I stay there and suck on it; I kiss each side of her collarbone.
My dick has grown another two inches in anticipation of satisfying her every need. I want to make her understand how beautiful she is. She bites her lip and I pull out her ponytail. The Red Sea of hair falls all over face.
"Don't tell me I'm beautiful don't do…." I stop her by kissing her again.
"You're not going to take that away from yourself, not tonight." She sits on the bed and she unbuckles my belt. She lets my pants fall to my ankles and my erection has her name written all over it. She takes her hand and she massages it. I grunt and let out a sigh. I pull my sweater over my head. I want her to feel relax before I even enter her. I grab a pillow put it under her ass. She has the most beautiful ass I've seen in a minute. Normally, she is use to giving pleasure but tonight it isn't about me.
It's about her feeling beautiful and cared for. I intend to take care every inch of her body, mind and soul. I let my hands explore her
INSANITY AT ITS FINEST!

body and with each touch she moans my name, "Bishop, this feels good. Don't stop please."

I massage her thighs her legs and each of her toes. Her hand is on my chest. She craving to touch me the way I am she.

"I want you to enjoy this. Enjoy me touching you. You have probably always been the one pleasuring a man. Making him feel good and they neglected to make you feel the same if not better. Tonight, it's all about you, I promise you that?"

I spread her legs and from there I explore her pussy. My head and hands are all she needs. I remember I have some baby oil from nights of pleasuring myself. I pour a small amount on my hands. The excitement in her eyes tells me no one has taken her to this level. I begin massaging the mound and outer lips slow making sure I hit areas and spots of her pretty pussy making. Her lip form in an O and her hands holding on to the covers for dear life. I take my time she so wet, my fingertips slide into her opening. Yep, I massage that area there too. I see and feel her juices flowing and the smell she releases is intoxicating me to bring my lips to kiss it gently and I do. She pulls her hair and moans louder. She then grasps the top of my head moaning my name, "Bishop".

"Does that feel good? Am I making you feel good, baby?"

I whisper and then squeeze the outer lips using the thumb and index finger from one length to another work the other side until she is clawing at my head. I massage the inner and outer lips of her pussy. Her ooh and aahs told me she needed my tongue to massage her sugar walls. I stick just the tip of my tongue at her opening and I lick until her head is touching the floor. She pulling away her mind doesn't understand what it's like to have a man make her feel this damn good. I tongue fuck her until she is convulsing and screaming, "This feels so damn good. Oh my God."

"I'm not done with you yet Michelle this is just the introduction."

I gently use my thumb to stroke her clit clockwise and counterclockwise between each lick.

She said, "Bishop, I'm going to cum. I'm going to cum!"

I squeeze her clit it takes her into her second orgasm and a large amount of fluid wets my hand and bed. I let her come down from the high I just gave her. I wish I was done but I'm not. The moment has been joyous and she is still catching shooting stars after she has cum. She's panting, her heartbeat beating fast.

I insert my finger inside of her at first moving in circles and then telling her third orgasm to come here. She is sweating and I pull out of her and kiss her again. I slide my hands all over her body listen to her moan. My hands slick with her juices and sweat. I cover her and I push my erection that is now on overload inside of her. Her pussy is so hot and tight. She squeezes me with her pussy muscles makes me say," Michelle, your pussy feels like silk."

"Bishop, please take your time, go slow so this can last all night." It's not about me so I follow her instructions. Her moans make me stroke deeper, she cries out of my name make pull out all the way and rub the head on her clit. She arches her back and the good feeling is evident as her legs wrap around my back squeezing the pleasure s out of my pores.

We rock slowly and our bodies and our moans are in synch. As her pleasure mounts she holds on tight to me, her hands squeeze my ass and she bites her bottom lip. I put her legs on my shoulder and stroke faster, my sweat dripping all over her face. I wipe her face. "You are so damn sexy. Every kiss, every touch, the sound of your voice has brought all five senses alive. Come on and give me that last cum. I want it all." I kiss her again, stroke again this time I can't control my pace. My orgasm is coming from all over the place. I close my eyes tight, I cry out, "Michelle."

My whole body on fire as I stroke two more times as my seed overflows and she comes. She is convulsing and muttering obscenities. I lay on her both of us trying to breathe again, the room smells of sex.

I kiss her again this time slow, never moving my manhood from inside her, realizing I forgot the glove to cover up my stick. I play in her red hair. I don't worry about tomorrow or if she may be the one that is the murderer. I kiss her and caress her red hair while she falls asleep.

INSANITY AT ITS FINEST!

Michelle

I wake up and I'm still in Bishop's bed. I turn around and his arms are still around me. I snuggle against him to secure the moment and hope it won't ever end. Inside of me I wait for him to tell me nasty things, say I disgust him and this was just sex and nothing else. I wait and wait but instead he is pulls me closer, kisses my ear, my lips and face.

"Damn, you're beautiful in the Morning, Baby!" I run my hand through my wild hair and smile.

"Good Morning, Bishop!"

He kisses me and he holds me tight with small kisses on my neck. I feel like crying but I don't. His cell phone rings and he looks over at it. He hisses and reaches for the phone. He looks over at me and is in the bathroom.

It's 6:30 am in the morning. I find my bra, my pants and underwear. I go in the other bathroom and take a shower. I have to be to work at eight. He walks out the bathroom with a towel wrapped around and toothbrush in his mouth.

"What time do you need to go to work?"

I answer, "Eight" He looks at the clock and then me. I turn away from him to get dress back in the same clothes.

"Michelle, last night was amazing." He puts on his clothes.

"Will you forget about me know that we had sex. I mean I'm used to it and even okay with that." I put on my coat and he walks toward me, he takes my hand and kisses the palms of them.

"That is not okay for me. I want you while you're at lunch to tell me your worth. What is your value? What you deserve as a woman from a man but more importantly to yourself. No, baby this isn't it. I'm falling for you and this isn't about us being intimate. It's about how you make me feel. I haven't felt like that in a long time. You're kind, you're an amazing woman to me and I admire you Michelle."

"Bishop, I've fallen for you. I'm just afraid of it's just the therapist side of you kicking in?""

He slips on his leather coat and hat.

"No it's the man who cares for you kicking in. You ready to go." He kisses me again and if I'm dreaming please let me stay asleep.

While he does his usual routine. I think about his question, no one has ever asked me what I'm worth to myself. No one has ever had that type of conversation. When he pulls up to my job. He lends over and kisses me again.

"Think about my questions and I'll call you later waiting on the answer. Have a good day."

He steps out and opens the door. I look across the street at the green and White House where I use to live. He drives off and I hope he isn't lying about calling me. Today is going to be a good day.

INSANITY AT ITS FINEST!

BISHOP

I walk into the office trying to shield the fact from Hernandez. I broke my own rule. He is sitting at the desk with a cup of Joe and burrito.

"Buenos Diaz, Amigo!"

"Buenos Diaz, Hernandez!" I sit down and notice he has a cup of Joe from Timmy Ho's and a burrito for me to eat.

"Gracias. Listen I got a call from a Detective in Rochester and they had someone killed on November 14th about 3:00am. Markel King was killed around 8pm in the evening. He said he found a door with the letters FAT written on it. I think she had more than enough time to go and do each of the killings."

"Or your girl Michelle could have killed Markel while Mom was offing the chick in Rochester. She has motive, Bishop."

"I think maybe the mother could have done it. She is abusive to her but like the lady said at the house she did threaten him?" I sip some of my Joe and bite into my burrito." He looks at me and raises his eyebrow he sniffs around me."

"You and Michelle fucked? You were all for she had something to do with it. The chocha had to be good because you now you to have a change of heart."

"No, actually I had some of the widow Tucker King." Hernandez covers his mouth and slaps me five.

"Word. Wow, man that's all right. He wasn't hitting it right?"

"No disrespect to the dead but nah. I took care of that though." We laugh.

"Now back to the case seriously. I want to check out this Dena McMillan and what's her affiliation with Patricia."

"I had an officer pick her up for questioning she should be here in about fifteen. She had an altercation with another chick and wanted for a warrant on a felony for grand larceny. So she already has some charges pending. So she may be of help she needs this case to give her probation instead of time." Officer Cannon taps me on the shoulder.

"Your perp is a rowdy whore. She's in room two." Hernandez and I walk in.

"First off, I need to know why the fuck I'm up in here on some bullshit."

"I'm Detective Jones and this is Detective Hernandez. I have a couple of questions if you help me. I may be able to get what you call those bullshit charges to somehow go away." She sucks her teeth and rolls her eyes.

"I'm nobody's snitch. Pig, you can get up out my damn face with that needing me to be a snitch."

"Well since you're no snitch let me tell you what you're facing some serious charges. Multiple murder charges for not only killing Markel King but also a host of other murders going down in Buffalo and Rochester. Among other charges assault with a deadly weapon and if convicted your looking at a life sentence at Bedford Correctional Facility. You can talk now or with the DA ready to fry the bird bitch that's the Fat Girl Vigilante. Right now the vehicles you rented are all in your name. There is a murder in Rochester and the dude gave your name Dena McMillan" Hernandez and I walk to the door.

"I didn't kill him or no fucking body else. What the fuck are you talking about? The night he was killed I was with my cousin Rachel and Mika up in Syracuse. I don't have any friends in the Rochester. This is some ole fuckery." I shake my head and sit on the chair backwards. Hernandez said,

"So you admit you had a beef with him that day of November 14th?" She pats her weave and sucks her teeth.

"This some bullshit right here? You pigs are trying to set a bitch up. He and I were fucking. He put me up in an apartment. His wife Tucker one day came through my crib and caught us. A week later I get served with eviction papers. So yeah, I was pissed off. All I did was bust the windows and pull some wires out the wall that's it. That bastard deserve to die but I never killed him and anyway all he did was move another bitch up in there? You pressing me but not the fact that nigga and his goons was running whore houses along with his wife Tucker."

INSANITY AT ITS FINEST!

"No, honey I'm trying to get to the truth. As far as the whore houses and prostitution ring in Niagara Falls it is out of my jurisdiction. If you're innocent then talk." She rolls her eyes and bang on the table.

"Ay Yo listen I want the shit with Moesha erased, feel me?"

"Erased! Now talk. According to Rent a Wreck it shows that on the same dates the murders occurred you rented a Toyota Corolla and had it for week."

"Yeah, I did rent a car but for this chick with funny colored eyes and a pink wig. She came up to me and offers me $500 dollars to rent the car for her. So I did it?"

"Do you know her name?"

"She called herself Sarge." I look at Hernandez and he speaks,

"One more question. Was she older or younger lady?"

"She was older."

"When did she ask you to rent the car?"

She answered, "Shit, I don't know maybe four or five times. I've been doing this for two years now. She was my side hustle. How I keep my nails and hair did. I stand up and say,

"Deana how did this woman know you? I mean why would she pick you out of everybody?"

"She know my cousin, Shayla. See my cousin had said she runs this bootleg ass fat camp for women on the West Side"

"Okay what is call the bootleg fat camp?"

"Fat Girl Revolution."

I look at Hernandez think back to what Miyama said. It made perfect sense to me know everything Miyama was saying. Michelle mother is Serpent of Arms. I want to jump and down and scream.

"So can I go? Are you two through with me?"

"Where through but some other detectives want to talk about another case."

"Dirty ass cops you played a bitch." She screams kicking the table.

"I didn't lie about erasing the situation with Moesha. It's consider erase but you have a warrant dealing with some grand larceny charges."

We walk out the room and let the door close instruct the other detectives to talk to her. I see CSU investigator comes in and said.

INSANITY AT ITS FINEST!

We have a DNA but nothing matches the database. Whoever this is you need to get a match.

The cup, the fork and spoon didn't match the DNA on file either. It was found in the basement on a piece of wood she must have cut herself but it doesn't match the one on file. My mind is spinning a thousand miles an hour. I'm so close I can taste it. She is one slick bitch. Michelle is the only answer I have. She has to break and tell me something. I sit at my laptop and type in a florist. I find a florist order two dozens of Red, yellow and white roses and a teddy bear. I give the address to her job.

I do like her and my feelings are genuine but I also have a job to do. I enter my credit card number and enter her job address. I need to get her Mom off the street. My gut tells me that Patricia is the one but another part of me keeps in the back of my mind that Michelle is in deeper than I want to believe.

INSANITY AT ITS FINEST!

PATRICIA

I stretch out each muscle after my workout. I love it the way I can in my fifties exercise the way I do and how flexible my body is. I love to stretch naked in front of the mirror, admiring my beauty. My body built like the Goddess I am I notice my child hasn't been home in a few days. That dude must be dicking her down real good for her to forget to come home. I refuse to worry about her and how he will screw her over. She'll run back to Mama and it'll be alright

The cell is ringing and I answer. It's Shayla.

"How can I help you Mutt?"

"Um, you remember when I had my cousin Dena rent that Toyota Corolla for you those few times? I stand up and look out the window. The old white man has his afternoon peek of my body. I place my breasts against the window. I lick my lips seductively; I lift my leg up and let him get to see a peek of my hairless pussy. I turn my attention back to the conversation.

"Yes, what about it?"

"The police question her about it today and I'm afraid she kind of gave up the information that you was the one who pay her to rent the car. Now they're coming over my house questioning me and I don't need any problems. I'm trying to get my life back together. I have…."

I walk away from the window and throw on my olive green sweats and sweatshirt. Slip on my sneakers.

"Did they leave, honey? It is okay, Shayla don't panic?"

"I'm scared. I could lose my kids and I can't afford that. Why would they question her about some murders?"

"Mutt, I said it will be okay. I'll take care of it."

I disconnect the call, grab a bottle of water and drink it down, I walk back to the window and look at the Grey Saturn parked across the street for about two hours. I look up at the window and the old white man is staring at me. I love the police, they think I will just up and let them catch me. Now I have that feeling the Hispanic guy who follow me was trying to bust me that night. My intuition never lies they want to catch a killer. They want to play games. I love games and the wonderful part is I'll win.

I look around and realize Dena and Shayla has to die. I'll turn myself in after my mission is complete not them catching me. I'll walk in naked and in high heels sit in front of them and say,

My name is Patricia Sargent and I'm the bitch that put fear in hundreds of men and women hearts. Yeah, that's what I'll say. Shayla is chattering away and I hang up on her.

I decide to dial my daughter's cell after four rings it goes straight to her voicemail. I'll make an appearance at her job. I'm suspicious of that Cat, Bishop. I know he is up to some shit. I don't know what? He is really close to Michelle. I need to get rid of his ass. I don't trust him. He may give my child the sense she is safe with him. He's setting her up for failure because no one can take what was rip from my wound.

I call her again while I'm in the car still no answer. I pull up to the St. John's home and walk in; she's sitting at the desk with this large floral arrangement of roses and brown teddy bear. I look at the flowers and her eyes are on me.

"So now you get some dick and flowers you can't call me to let me know you are alive." She is typing on the keyboard and looks up at me.

"I've been busy, Mama. Why do you care whether I'm alive?" My first reaction is to spit on her. I hold my composure and clench my teeth.

"See me outside now, Michelle." I stomp out and she follows me.

"I think you recognize what I'm capable of. If I think your trying to set me up to get caught I will cut your tits off and leave you burning at the Delevan train station. As for your man I will slice his dick and mail it to his mother. Am I understood? Please take me seriously and understand what a bitch like me is capable of." I grab her jaw and squeeze it. Her eyes are filled with tears. I let her face go.

"Clean your face wouldn't want your man to see you looking a mess. Now would we? Those roses are beautiful. Tell playboy I said that." I walk off and step in the car. I see the Grey Saturn again there following me. I need to stay low and watch my step. Watch my

INSANITY AT ITS FINEST!

surroundings, I drive off and Michelle is already inside. I watch the Grey Saturn go up Main Street. They're on to me.

Bishop

I cut down Main Street and stop at McDonald's and go through the drive-thru. I order my usual of a quarter pounder meal and Sweet Tea. I saw everything that transpired between Michelle and her mother. It's clear that Michelle is afraid of her. I call her as I pulled into the parking area to eat. The phone rings three times and she answers,

"Hi, Bishop!"

"Hi Beautiful. Did you get the flowers?"

"Yes and thank you so much. They're so pretty. How are you?"

"Fine now that I heard your voice. I've been thinking about you all day. I thought now since you done put it down on a brother you was going to abandon me."

She laughs, "No Bishop! I had to finish up payroll and some other projects. Can I stay at your house tonight please?"

"Why, what's wrong?" She sighs.

"It's my Mama she came to my job. She is just not the person I want to stay around. I think I should look for an apartment." I bite into my sandwich not knowing when the opportunity would present itself for me to sit and eat without being on the run.

"You're more than welcome to stay. I'll pick you up! What time do you get off?"

"I get off at six thirty. I'm staying late to finish up these reports."

"Did you think about my question? You thought I forgot?"

"Yes. I have and I'm worth being loved, being treated with respect and most of I have to know my worth to myself."

"Good answer. We'll talk more lately."

I hang up the phone and at that moment I feel conflicted with the new feelings that I have develop for her and feelings as if I am taking this too far. I went a step beyond the call of duty by sleeping with her. I didn't take into consideration what she may have knew or if I was going to be her next victim. I was being careless but it was something about her that made me want to be close to her. Yet, when I'm around her I don't feel endanger.

She is a breathtaking and sensitive, wounded woman looking for the right person to care for her. The way her mother treats her makes no sense. She never given her the nurturing she deserves. My thoughts

INSANITY AT ITS FINEST!

are broken up with the ring of my cell. I look and it's Tucker, let me answer this call this chick has been calling me non-stop.

"What up Tucker?

"I'm fine Detective. I see you're too busy to answer my calls."

"Very busy Tucker what is that I can help you with?" She laughs and snorts a little.

"I called you because I want some more dick. It was good and rough like I want it. So what time are you coming to my place?"

"Not tonight. I told you I'm busy."

"You're too busy for me, Mrs. Tucker King. I can get quality dick anywhere but I choose you. So this isn't a request but a demand. Or I slip and tell your superior how you took advantage of me."

Trifling bitch now I can understand how her husband went outside of the marriage. She is too cocky for her own damn good. To think she can tell me what to do, without the ability to show me a birth certificate that produces her name as my parent. I clear my throat, "Now Mrs. King let me advise you that I have never take kindly to threats. Those messages you left on my phone will prove you are harassing me. What we had was a brief sexual encounter. Maybe, just maybe I didn't call you again because the sexual experience was not all that good. If you want raw truth your sex game was wacky. Now I am trying to be a gentleman about this whole matter but if you want me to call you out. I will do it without hesitation, you decide but that weak ass threat could never put fear in my heart."

"You know what go fuck and suck yourself, Bishop!" I hang up and finish my lunch.

I pull out and I go over to headquarters to meet with Shayla. I walk in and take the elevator. I watch her walk into the room. She's the one in the interrogation room 2. Hernandez walks up to me.

"Hey Bishop! I took the liberty to pull up her file. She has two priors' misdemeanors. "

"You think she'll give us what we need?"

"I don't know. Let's find out."

He and I walk in the room. Shayla legs are shaking and she is chewing on her nails. I sit right across from her and Hernandez sits next to her. Shayla mouth drops open and looks at me

"Hello, Shayla. My name is Detective Jones." Hernandez introduces his self.

"I'm Detective Hernandez." She's biting on her nails and her leg is shaking.

"Shayla, you've done nothing wrong. We asked you down here to verify some information. Where not here to arrest you so take a deep breath and calm down." Hernandez go and get her something to drink. You want coffee, tea or a soda."

"Water, please!" Hernandez walks out the room to get her a soda.

"So is Dena Macmillan your cousin. Now I talk to her today and she stated that you bought this woman to her to help her rent a car .Is that true? She's shaking her leg and biting her nail.

"Yes. She paid both of us. Aren't you Michelle's boyfriend? " I pull my ear.

"That's irrelevant and right now I'm asking the questions. How much?"

"She gave me 100 dollars and my cousin who rented the car for her gave Deana $500 for renting the car." Hernandez ask,

"How come you didn't rent the car for this woman?"

"I don't have a license."

"So how well do you know this woman?"

"I don't know her well. I met her through a mutual friend who ask me if I knew anyone who could rent a car." I ask the next question,

"What the name of the woman who asked you to rent the car?"

"Her name is Amy." I blow out air.

"Amy is the mutual friend of yours name? I need to know the person's name who rented the car?"

"No, the woman who my cousin rented the car for. The mutual friend I didn't know by name we just went to group together" I look and Hernandez and he look at me. I lean forward and fold my hands. I smirk and lick my lips.

"Shayla, what you're telling me makes no fucking sense at all. Now let me make sure my partner and I are hearing you clearly. This mutual friend or acquaintance whichever he or she is you have no clued what name this person may go by? You say the woman's name is Amy and you know that I know your lying to us. I don't appreciate being lied to. Your cousin as trifling as she is gave me the truth. Right now I'm aggravated, let me give it to straight from the gut. The

INSANITY AT ITS FINEST!

person you covering for don't give two shits about you. I know your situation and that your husband had custody of your children. You mean to tell me you would risk ever having custody of your children again? I don't get that. So you have a choice, you can sit here and give me what I need which is her actual name and what you know. Or go to jail for obstructing justice."

"I told you her name? I did nothing so why are you treating me like a criminal? She told me that was her name. I don't know anything else."

"Your cousin story is totally different from yours. She gave me a name of Sarge." She knocks over the water."

"I don't know her by any name but Amy, Honestly. I want to go home now."

"Describe this Amy broad to us, Shayla." Hernandez ask.

"She's, she's a white woman, tall, had tattoos and…" I cut her off.

"You going to lie to us again after we had a conversation. You know goddamn well she isn't white." I yell.

I rub my hands over my face and realize I need a cigarette and a headache has come from out of nowhere. I look at my watch it's 5:30. I'm supposed to pick up Michelle at 6:30. I look at her. She's covering for her because she's threatened her. She has given me a headache. I rub my temples and stand up.

"I want you to understand if I catch you in a lie. Which I'm sure I have, I will have a warrant for your arrest for obstructing justice. I promise you that! Michelle better not hear about this conversation." I escort her out.

The pain has taken over and I sit down at my desk. I look in the drawer and pull out the Tylenol pop two in my mouth. I sip on the now watery Sweet Tea. I listen to my messages and nothing of importance. I look through all the clues and it the minimalism of nothing. I need something and it's frustrating that this chick is Ms. Fucking untouchable. I put all my eggs in one basket that this bitch has threatened her to keep quiet. My only hope is Michelle confiding in me.

INSANITY AT ITS FINEST!

I walk out the door and I get in my truck this headache is still here. I call Michelle and she answer,

"I'm on my way. I was stuck at work."

"It's okay. I'm just finishing up. You don't sound good. I have a headache."

"Oh, did you take something for it?"

"Yes, but it's throbbing. I had a stressful day. So I'll see you in a few."

I turn down my CD player down what usually sounds good sound like jackhammers hitting the streets. I don't even want to think or talk to anyone, I need to feed my dog, let him out to shit and piss. Turn off the light s and let this headache simmer. I pull up to Michelle job and she was standing outside.

She has her teddy bear in hand opening the door. She squeezes it close to her and speaks,

"Aww you poor baby. You're in a lot of pain?" I kiss her hand and lips.

"This headache is kicking my ass."

"Do you want me drive, Bishop?" I get out and switch sides, and takes the teddy bear and let her drive. I want to ball up and cry because this is past a headache this is a migraine. I look over at her and she is concentrating on the road until she reaches my block. She walks out the car and opens the door for me, she unbuckles my seat belt, extend her hand out to me. I take it and step out. I close the door. My head still feeling like

there is a jackhammer drilling through my skull. I open the door and Bullet greets us by wagging his tail. I bend down and rub him. He licks my face. I open the back door and let him run out. Michelle washes her hands and prepares his water and food. He runs in and eats.

"You didn't have to do that?"

"I wanted to you don't feel well. I'm just trying to help."

I walk into my bathroom lock up my gun and badge. The shower water I turn on is steaming hot, I step in and it massages each aching muscle, the scent of peppermint clears my head of thoughts. I stand there and soap up one more time. I step out and dry off, Michelle is

INSANITY AT ITS FINEST!

standing in the doorway with a bottle of warm oil in her hand. She takes my hand and leads me to the bed.

"Would you like a massage? It might help your headache?" I lay on my stomach and realize how good it feels at 7:30 in the evening to lie down and just relax. She sits on her knees the warm oil and the heat of fingers massaging my shoulders have my head sink deeper into the pillow. The way her small fingers are touching me wakes up every nerve in my body. Her fingers are now on my temple and all I muster up and say is, "Baby that feels good."

Her fingers are now on my lower back. I feel so relax as if I been pamper like this all my life. She massages my butt, my legs and feet. I'm having a feminine moment because I want to cry out.

"Can you turn on your back?" I answer her question by following directions. My erection is reveal. She starts all over again touching, and massaging every limb on my body. She never touches my erection, I watch her and she bend over and whisper in my ear. "Is your headache any better?

"It's disappeared."

She lifts up and I wrap my arms around her and pull her close to me. Here I go breaking my rule again. I kiss her passionately, I open up her buttons on her dress and with each button open I kiss what I reveal. She cries out my name. I release her swollen breasts from her bra push them together I allow my lips to suck on each of them. Her eyes closed and she sings my name. She kisses every place she has touched, take my fingers and sucks on each of them. I remove her dress, her bra and panties. An urgency to be inside of her. Instead she takes control by saying,

"Bishop, it's my turn to make you feel good."

She licks her full lips her grin sinfully dangerous and my erection grows an inch longer calling for her lips to taste me.

She and I kiss hungrily; she then takes her tongue and trace over my body until she gets to my waist. Her hands stroke the length of my erection; her red hair rubs on my stomach. I grab two hands full guiding her to taste me. She knew what I wanted and took all of me in her mouth. I moan out, "Oh shit that feels good." I open my eyes and try to figure out who taught her to deep throat. I pull her hair harder and she does that swallowing thing that makes my toes curl. I find myself thrusting her mouth this feel so good,

"Michelle, Michelle damn Mommy don't stop." She looks up at me and her green eyes are watching me as the pleasure takes over every bit of commonsense and right mind thinking. She releases me and run her tongue up and down my shaft.

"Bishop, your headache am I making it better?" She does it again and runs her tongue up to the head. I pull her body up to me

"I need to be inside you, now" I growl.

"You don't have…"

Before she can finish her sentence I've entered inside of her. The sound of our moans and the bed creaking is the choice music. She cries out and so do I. She lies on top of me. I feel like I've touch heaven. I want to smoke a cigarette, my fingers tracing her spine. I come down from the sexual high; I look down at her and kiss her forehead.

She is breathing heavy and I feel her tears on my chest. I look down and lift her face.

"What wrong, baby?" She looks at me and she said.

"I'm scared, Bishop!" I slide up and she looks way.

"Of what? What's going on?" She puts her hand in her face.

"That I'm dreaming. I mean you make me feel so beautiful and wanted. I've been waiting for this feeling all my life. Do you really care for me? I'm not asking you to love me because that feeling is something that takes a long time for someone to feel. I just want to know you care about me. I have feelings for you and I just don't want to get hurt anymore.

I kiss her forehead and pull her close to me. I look her in her eyes. I take my thumb and wipe her tears before I speak.

"I told you before I care for you. I mean that and it's sad because you are so use to not having someone show you or even tell you they care. I can say it, I can show it but if you don't recognize it there is nothing else I can do to show you I'm genuine about you. Michelle I'm falling for you."

She kisses me again and at that moment I realize what I said was the truth. It wasn't about solving this case, I thought of the consequences that came after the truth reared its ugly head of me

INSANITY AT ITS FINEST!

deceiving her. The fact I was a detective investigating Michelle and her mother. The fact that if she did murder Markel King I would have to put what I'm feeling on the side and do my job. The thought has me hold her tighter.

I clear my throat, ". Lately I've been thinking about you?'

She lies across my lap; I hold her hand and kiss each of her fingers.

"Bishop, if I did something terrible, would you still feel the same about me?" I turn her face towards me. She is crying again.

"Yes, I would still feel the same about you? You can trust me." She stares at the ceiling and takes a deep breath

"My childhood was normal until my Dad left. One day my Daddy took me in the room and he told me that Mommy and him were not getting along and that he was leaving but he loved me very much. That changed my whole life. I remember begging him to stay but he didn't. He was the first man to break my heart. I've been chasing that love he gave me. I need that love. The minute my father left I believe once my Mama lost love it changed her, made her cold and bitter because she get it from my father. She used to be overweight and she believes that why he left her. She went back to school and got her Degree in Nutrition and Physical education. After the weight loss she thought that Daddy would come back. He never did and that's when she…. ." Fuck, I think close but no cigar.

"She what?" She sits up and looks at me.

"Bishop, you can't tell no one I told you this. I hold her hand and begin my path of deceit."

"I won't." She takes a deep breath and speaks again.

"Two men didn't kill my father someone else did and I should have told a long time ago but I was scared. That makes me a bad person because I never told that person made me watch her cut off my father's dick. She torture him Bishop for hours, then she cover him with gasoline and… I could have saved him. The last word my father said, 'help me baby and I love you Bunny.'

I feel so guilty; I was so scared and confused. I was just a little girl. I should have stopped her" She sobbing and can't catch her breath. I comfort her and the pain shooting through my heart let me know

INSANITY AT ITS FINEST!

this was love cutting through me. It was love saying that I would go to the end of earth to protect her.

"It is okay baby I need you to take deep breaths. I'm so sorry you had to witness your father's death."

I go get her some water, my stomach and mind in turmoil. I want to ask if her mother did this. When I walk back in the room she holding the pillow, rocking back and forth. I hand her the water.

"Drink this and take deep slow breaths." She sips the water and inhales and exhales. She lays her head on my shoulder.

"I'm….." I cover her lips with my finger.

"Catch your breath, baby nice and slow. No more apologies it wasn't your fault." I rub her back so she can calm down.

She didn't have to tell me no more. She didn't have to say her mother's name to assure me of what her mother was capable of doing. I knew what I had in front of me was a psychopath who had no conscience. She tormented her child by making her watch the massacre of her father. What else had Patricia made her see? Was she frozen by the fear the woman who brought her into this world could take her out? I rub her back, pull her closer to me I knew she wasn't safe.

THE FIGHT OF HER LIFE

It's 6:06 am and Bishop is sleeping sound and Bullet is lying at the foot of the bed. I snuggle close to him. I wanted to tell him about my mother but fear stole my words. My phone rings and I am afraid to answer because it might be Mama. Shayla name flashes and I hit ignore when Bishop wraps his arms around me and pulls me close and kisses me.

"Is everything okay, Michelle?" He yawns and stretches.

"Yes, a friend of mines calling me I'll call her later." He sits up and lights a cigarette. He walks in the bathroom, I hear the shower running and my phone beeps again. The alert goes off three times on my phone want to ignore it but it has to be urgent for Shayla to call me back to back. I open my phone and the text reads," your

INSANITY AT ITS FINEST!

boyfriend did you know he was a cop? He called me in for questioning about your mother? Please call me ASAP. I need your help."

I sit up and it hits me him showing up everywhere I am. The questions about my past, another man pretending to care about me. I gasp for air, my heart pounds in my chest, I feel nauseous and dizzy. "Bishop, are you a cop?"
His startle look on his face told the truth. I throw on my dress and shoes run down the stairs.
"Michelle wait!" He blocks the door.
"You lied to me, Bishop? Everything you said to me was all lies to get information about my mother? You said you weren't going to hurt me?"
I try my hardest not to cry I can't look at him. He tries to console me, he wraps his arms around me and push him off me. I don't want him to touch me. I step back and all of sudden he doesn't look good anymore. He is like the rest of the men I've had relationship with "Are you going to listen to me, Michelle?"
"Are you going tell me the truth? Are you investigating me and mother? Is that the only reason you are around me?" Our eyes lock and the guilt is written all over his face. He runs his hand over his face and he bites his bottom lip.
His towel falls to the floor and all of his business showing. His expression on his face answers the question.

"Michelle, I'm sorry. Let me talk to you…" I smack him in the face. "Thank you, Bishop for being another man who has rip my heart to shreds. You must feel good about yourself right now."
I try to walk out the door but he blocks me. I begin crying, gasping for air, my body is hot and my mind is foggy. Mama's words playing in the back of my head that no man wanted a fat girl like me. He was playing me. Mama words pounding in my head over and over again. "You don't care about me, Bishop! You didn't have to pretend to like me. You just felt sorry for me."
Please, just listen." He pleads over and over again.

INSANITY AT ITS FINEST!

"Bishop, it's okay. Do your job ask me if I killed anyone? Asked me Bishop did I cut off a man's dick and set him on fire? Or is my crazy ass mother a murderer?" He tries to hug me, I push him away from me.

"Please just ask me, Bishop. Am I free to go, Officer?"

"Michelle, I'm sorry. I never…" I put my hands on his lips and stop him from speaking.

"That seems to be the song of my life sung to me. I've never meant to hurt you. Am I free to go, Bishop" He opens the door and I turn around.

"Yes, you're free to go. Michelle please let me help you."

This time the pain was too much to bear. I walk all the way home. Bishop follows me and I ignore him. My hair is drench with snow, my face is numb and fingers are frozen.

Mama opens the door and the smile was her sign of yet another victory another man didn't want me. The sign I set myself up by giving my body to a man only to be a fool. I walk in and fall to the floor crying. Mama laughter cuts deep like the way the knife cut Daddy.

"Let me guess? Old lover boy played you for a fool? What she came over and pulled you out the bed? Or he told you it was all about the ass and deuces. You are so fucking stupid. How many times I have to tell you no man wants a fat ass girl like you. You are worthless and all you'll ever be good for is fucking nothing else!"

Those words sound as if Markel is in the room. I've used up every feeling in my body and now what is left is anger.

I heard Sarge say, "let me handle this bitch for you." I was to drain to handle her, as Michelle my emotion was dead as her. Sarge on the other hand was strong, good and angry. I stood up and I face her.

"Get the fuck out of face, Mama? You are fucking evil witch. You are happy to see me hurt how sick are you?"

"Oh, shit my child then grew some guts." She pauses and claps her hands.

"I have every right to laugh at your ass. How could you think a man as fine as him would want anything but you're raunchy pussy? What you thought he was going to marry you and live happily ever after. Fat girl fairy tales always lead to blues." I stand up and we are eye to eye with one another.

INSANITY AT ITS FINEST!

"I'm tired of you Mama. You have ruined everything for me. You took my daddy away from me. You are a murderer Mama and you kill all those men. Why? I refuse to turn out like you cold-hearted and a bitch. "

You beat on me and treat me like an animal. That's all I know, you never showed me love. What is it that I ever did to you for you to hate me, your own child? If you hated me so much why don't you just kill me? I want to die knowing my mother hates the ground I walk on. You never have to worry about me again. I'm out of here."

I walk up the stairs and grab a suitcase. I throw all my clothes in there and some toiletries. I had no clue where I was going my cell phone ringing non-stop and it was Bishop. Fuck him! I throw the dress down and it smells like him. I cry into my dress and try to compose myself. My mother stands in front of me with her arms folded and she runs her tongue across her teeth.

"Move, please!"

"Where you going? You have no friends and your so call boyfriend played you. Where you going?"

I push past her again this time trying to run down the stairs, she punches me in the face and I hit my head on the wall. I fall back on the stairs she jumps on top of me kicking me in the ribs, stomping her feet into my chest and stomach.

She yells,

"You hate me? I hate you more bitch! Your Daddy is the man who raped me. Every day you are a constant reminder of that motherfucker and I going to show you what he did to me you dumb bitch.

She grabs me by the legs and I scream. She drags me down the stairs hitting my head on each of the steps. I try to get her off me but she is stronger than I am. She takes me to the basement. I get her off me and run for the door but she has locked it. She hits me again and I fall to the floor. She goes to the box and pulls out the pink dildo.

"This is what that mother fucker did to me. When I shove this in your pussy I want you to scream Halle…" She lays on top of me, forcing my legs apart, rips my pants and panties away from me as she tries to rape me. I beg her for her mercy and I beg God to get her off

INSANITY AT ITS FINEST!

me. Her sweat drips in my mouth, her green is fill with fire and glowing. I muster up the strength to beg.

"Mama I'm sorry please don't kill me. Please don't kill me."

I break away from her and ball up in the fetal position, the blood running from my face. Her mouth drops and tears fall, she cover hers mouth and whispers the words, "Mommy's sorry for what she did to you."

She runs up the stairs and I hear the door close. I wanted to die down here because the pain was too much to bear. I heard my cell ringing over and over again. I saw the bright light flashing in my face.

"Please go away! Please leave. I'm sorry Mama I won't be a bad girl."

I hear the footstep and feel material on my body. I sob uncontrollably. Shayla puts her arms around me and holds

"Michelle, I saw everything that happen. Honey, you need help. I'll call your boyfriend"

She takes a cool rag and wipes my face I turned away. The blood soaks the rag. My phone still flashing, I feel dizzy and nauseous I vomit up blood.

"We need to get you to the hospital. Your face is pretty beat up. You're throwing up blood." I look at the mirror and my face is now two times its normal size. It burns to cry.

"I'm your friend and we need to get you the hospital. Please let me help you. I know you're scared but you need to talk to the authorities. I know your mother is the one killing all of those men and I know you're scared but she is going to kill you. You have to take back your life." I lean against her."

"Nobody loves me, Shayla. I don't even love myself so how do I expect someone else to. I have the worst luck in the world. Mama right no one wants me, girls like us, fat girls. Fat girls don't have a happily ever after. There is no knight and shining armor to save us."

She wipes her eyes and helps me up. I fall back down because the pain is shooting through me. She grabs my cell.

"Honey, you need an ambulance. You're bleeding pretty badly." I shake my head no.

"Please don't! I'll be fine. "She ignores my pleas and dial 911 on her cell phone...

"I promise I will stay with you. I can't let you bleed to death."

INSANITY AT ITS FINEST!

Tamyara Brown

She pulls the cover over me. She has my blood on her shirt. She holds me and everything seems dark, my body feels so cold. I hear the walkie-talkies and the see the flashlight flashing. I hear the paramedic ask what happen. I hear Shayla say," Her mother beat her up." I feel dizzy as voices and people are talking. I feel my body being moved and lifted by the paramedics. I feel a needle in my arm. I hear them ask me what happen and who did it but I can't respond. There are more voices coming from every direction. I hear Shayla voice talking to the men and I wish she wouldn't do that. I want to go sleep but people are hovering over me. I feel a mask covering my face and a gush of cold air blowing through. I wonder if I died if my Mama would come to my funeral. Would she miss my presence and stop killing people because the person she hates the most is no longer the burden or constant reminder of her rape.

Would Bishop come to the funeral and tell me that he really cared. Would I see my Daddy and Auntie in heaven? Would I be in heaven or hell for taking Markel's life? Would god forgive me for the sin I committed. I feel cold again. I want to talk but I can't.

Bishop

Shayla sits in the same room I had her in a couple of days ago. Hernandez and I walk in. She is drenched in blood and her eyes are red. She looks at me and wipes her nose on her sleeve. Her voice low she speaks,

"I lie to you yesterday about what I knew and I'm sorry. My friend Michelle is hurt very bad. Her mother killed all those men, I heard her say it but was too scared. Now my friend may die because of me" She sticks out her hand so I cuff her and read her Miranda rights. I feel my heart drop to my stomach, I feel my head spin as my mind plays back to this morning." I look at Hernandez, who said,

"Go check on Michelle, man I'll talk to Shayla." I hear Hernandez ask,

"What hospital is she in?"

"Erie County Medical Center."

INSANITY AT ITS FINEST!

I run out and down the stairs. I sit in my truck and bang on the steering wheel. I say to myself," I fuck up! I fuck up!" I start my engine and drive off. I have never cried over a woman looking through my CD player I need to play some Jay-z. I hit play and remember the last time I cried was at my grandma's funeral. I turn the music on high as I hit the 33 expressway. I let the song do it. I think back to holding her and kissing her, thinking back to the night she touch my body. My face is stone and has no expression. I'm sick. I inhale and breathe.

I curse and spit out the window, I do anything to not let one fall down my eye. I visualize her tears of pain and then the tears of pleasure. She had showed me all of her emotion. She told me all of her hurt and I was using her and the end result of losing another person I love. She could die because of me. It's my fault and the thought sickens me. I pull over on the side of the road. Shit, replaying of me wiping tears from the little girl who died in my arms the very last emotion I saw was that one tear. I'm not letting them come down it's a sign of weakness.

Pride and my father told me real men don't let them touch their cheeks, cops don't let tears faze them. I pull out a cigarette to wash away the salty taste in my throat. Wash away the thought of letting that emotion show

I pull into the emergency area where I park. I flash my badge and I ask for her by name. I walk up the stairs no need to prepare myself because this is nothing new. I've seen bodies burned and men's dick cut off. I had a little girl die in my arms. I'm no stranger to death nor its smell. I'm no stranger to seeing someone battered and abuse. I stand outside of her room. Hear the sound of the heart monitor beeping, her face cover with the oxygen the taste of salt and vinegar is in my throat and my stomach churning. I need to walk in that room so I inhale. I exhale again and I open the door.

I stand there and her face black and blue. I rub my hands over my face, I walk closer and pull up the chair near her and I'm not a praying man but today I pray for her. Pray that God doesn't take her away I pray for me. I take her hand and bring her fingers to my lips and kiss it. I say,

"Baby, I care about you. I love you. Please don't die."

INSANITY AT ITS FINEST!

I kiss her fingers, rub my thumb on her cheek and say a silent prayer.
I look up and it's Hernandez his hand on my shoulder.
"Bishop, are you alright, man?" I kiss her hand one more time. I
stand up and kiss her forehead. I use the word I've hidden and I say,
"I love you Michelle."
I walk out the room; I look back hoping she opens her eyes whisper
for me to come hold her. I stood there, no words and her eyes still
close. The monitor beeps letting me know she still fighting for life.
Once I close the door I was the officer of the law. The place I always
seem to travel to.
I watch Crime scene unit take pictures of her body. I watch them
clean for tissue in her nails. I watch them do there preliminary
investigation. I turn off that feeling that's inside of me. I need a
cigarette.
"I'm fine Hernandez. What did she say happen?"
"Look, maybe you need to take breather before I go into this." I yell.
"I said I'm fucking fine. Okay, I'm good! Just tell me what happen"
I lean against the wall and slide to the floor. This case, this situation
was causing me to overdose like an addict. My addiction is catching
Patricia Sargent and placing the cuffs on her. Listening to the judge
give her life imprisonment I sitting there watching the liquid flow
through her veins for afflicting so much pain on her own child and
the men she brutally massacred.
Hernandez sat next to me and he read my thoughts. We saw this shit
every day. I lost more than one and I love this career more than I do
myself. I am an addict to the motto of serving and protecting. Being
an officer of the law and when you see dead bodies and the innocent
not protected, the guilty go free on a technicality.

It means I've failed to live up to the motto. That salty feeling in my
throat again, I swallow it back. Wonder if what I taste was my tears
inside me? It was this one bitch making me rethink my career steps I
chosen at the age of three. Hernandez breaks my concentration.
"Bishop, we've been on the beat for a long time, man. I know where
your head is? I know you care about Michelle. I saw it and I know
you too are closer than you admitted to me. She is more than some

perp or a female you sexed. Your heart is in it. I just don't want you to lose your head and take the law in your own hands. Lose your career and freedom. The DA is pressing charges on her mother for assault on Michelle. We have a warrant to search the premises. CSU will find her DNA and it's over Bishop. We catch that bitch and we watch her die. I need your head in the right place, Amigo." I marinate on the words. I clear my throat.

"Hernandez you warned me, man not to fuck around and fall in love with her. I fucked up. Now I'm in so deep I don't want to let go. I love her."

"You into music man remember that song by Baby face and Pebbles. Love make things happen."

"Amigo, you ain't never lied. That shit came in the door and I wasn't looking for it."

We stand up and I smoke two cigarettes back to back. Hernandez talks on the cell phone while I gather myself. My stomach growls and I rub it. My cell rings again and the name flashes Tucker. I forgot I told her I would meet her yesterday. I spit up phlegm and cough. I look at the people standing at the bus stop, look around if I see Patricia might pop up at the hospital. I have Michelle on guarded status so if she tries to show up I have the whole hospital and officers on the premises.

Hernandez walk over to me and said,

"You ready? We just got the warrant to search their house?"

"Yeah, ready as I'll ever be." I said.

We put on our bulletproof vests, my blue BPD hats, guns in our holster locked and loaded. I say to myself the prayer my grandma taught me. I jump in my truck ready to see what fact is and what fiction is. I drive down Girder Avenue and my thoughts wander to Michelle. Wander to the fact that if I find anything incriminating it would put me in a position to honor the motto and oath I took. My heart wants to believe the woman I have fallen for is a good girl caught in a world she felt she had no way out of.

The house is surrounded by SWAT; ten other blue and white cars cover the block. Hernandez and I walk out with our guns drawn. On the other side of the street is the camera crew from all of the television networks. Our weapons drawn and the house are surrounded. I walk in and on the stairs is dried blood. I look around

INSANITY AT ITS FINEST!

the living room and nothing is there. I open the closet and there is a weight station with different size hand weights. Hernandez and I go in the basement large amount of blood and a pink dildo lies on the floor. As we move closer in the back area is a box with about twenty pink dildos in there. I look at Hernandez and shake my head. "Okay! She was always sexually satisfied. I mean damn a whole case full. Hernandez said. I open the closet and the mother lode of jackpots a glock 19 with trijicon nite sights and a snub nosed .38. I bag it and hand it to Hernandez. Two bloody hunter's knives and a box of latex black gloves.

"This bitch has just wrote her ass a ticket for incarceration."

I look further and find a bloody Hunter's knife wrapped in a plastic bag." Hernandez goes into Michelle room and searches through her things.

I look through her book collection, through her drawers and nothing. Hernandez flips her mattress and finds pictures of her overweight. Each one is marked in red marker with the words, ugly, fat, disgusting. I look at the picture of her and her older guy who must have been her father. I pick up her diary and put it in my back pocket. I look through a box and open it. It's letter from a Richard Edwards. Different kinds of cards and letters she receives from him. Hernandez called me over and my stomach is nervous from the thought he found she was committing a crime. I walk over, "Here's our evidence Patricia been doing the killing." He hands me the letter Michelle wrote. I read and it said,

DEAR MAMA,

I am writing you because I am scared. I miss daddy so much. I know you hated him but did he have to die? Why did you kill him in front of me? Mama I hate you for what you did to me. Mama I'm confused. You won't listen. Michelle."
The letter was dated February 15, 1990.

We go through her room and allow CSU finish up with pictures and go to the last room. The door to the next room is lock; I hear the birthday song playing over and over again. Hernandez on one side, I

INSANITY AT ITS FINEST!

draw my gun and so does Hernandez. I radio for other officer to come up stairs. The door is covered. I kick open the door and the sight we see of an Caucasian elderly man hung on the ceiling fan with his dick in his mouth blood spilling from where his genitals where and a strap on dick around his waist. In what I suspect is his blood saying, **"YOU CAN ONLY CATCH THE FAT GIRL WHEN I SAY SO. OFFICER BISHOP YOUR NEXT, YOUR DICK I'LL SERVE TO MY DAUGHTER ON A PLATTER!"**

I look out the open window and no one is there. She was here she set this whole shit up. I'll play chicken but she'll be the bitch on the way to the slaughterhouse. I called CSU and the coroner. She is fucking sick. Hernandez, "she's slipping on purpose she even left footprints. Listen Bishop you need to lay low for a minute."

"No, if I didn't run from the Bloods and Crips what makes you think I'll run from a crazy Bitch. I was never built like that. I have a job to do and at the end of the day the risk to this job is death. I'm not running from her. I'm running towards her watch and see. I couldn't do that to her instead I should've bash her heads in the cement watching it crack open.

THIS MOTHERFUCKER IS A COP

This motherfucker is a cop! A fucking idiot of the Buffalo Police Department fucking my daughter. She was feeding him information about me all along. I should have killed that bitch when I had her in the basement. The only thing that stops me was her looking like me as a child.

The scene repeated itself in my head my fat body balled up in the corner of the shed blood leaking from my bowels, which had been ripped open. Watching them screw one another, watching them kiss and disregard me as a child. Their aphrodisiacs of molesting and praying for her soul got their cocks hard and my friend Thomas the victim of their sick game.

I begged those heartless bastards to stop and listen to my cries, I realize that day crying don't do shit but make your eyes red and swollen. Tears represent fear and animals like the Pastor and Deacon

INSANITY AT ITS FINEST!

drink it and get drunk off it. In my case it save Michelle. I turned into those animals that raped me. Shit, I need gas. I pull over into the Delta Sonic on Main Street and Utica. I throw on my wool overcoat and swipe my credit card to pay for the services.

I look around and realize that I've had nothing to eat and whether my child is alive or dead. I go inside and grab a salad and soup. I look at the news and a picture of my face is plastered on the screen. I look at the woman at the register and she shaking. I smile at her because what I feed off the most too is fear.

"You are so pretty, hon." I wink at her and touch her cheek.

She hands me my receipt everyone wants to say something. Their eyes shifting to the phone. I say to the girl,

"I'm famous now and if any one of you bitches touch your cell or phone. I will blow this pretty little lady brain to pieces."

The gun in her face as she rings up my order. She bags it and her tear falls on my gun. I stick out my tongue and lick it off. I sashay out in the cold let the wind blow my red hair in my face, let the snowflakes glisten my body. I look back in the store and point the gun. I point to the lady and make a shooting gesture and blow on my index finger. I laugh out loud the people pull in looking at me. I see a lady pick up her cell phone and dial while I get in the car.

She gets out and has the nerve to walk towards my car to get my license plate number. Did she not hear the chief of Police say, I'm armed and dangerous? I'm that bitch Satan's afraid of. She brings a friend how sweet of her to bring a friend to die with. I love it. What's real cute is neither one of them are paying attention to the fact that I have a .38 special in my hand? That while there on the phone with the police I put a bullet in her friend's head for just being stupid and then the bitch with the phone in her ear talking to the 911 operator ends her call with the phone dropping. She has the look of fear in her face but I erase it with the bullet. Simultaneously they drop to the floor and the blood colors the snow covered concrete

INSANITY AT ITS FINEST!

red. I get in my car and back up over the women's legs. I pull out and the police again are two steps, a day late and a dollar short of me. I left them the pleasure of my coat, my fingerprints on the smoking gun.

I feel that fire inside my loins after every killing burning up; I squeeze my legs and hold on to the lust ready to be released. Now I need to get out of the city. I need a place to hide and think, my mind is clutter and I'm making careless moves, playing a blind hand without a clue to what my next move should be.

I just need to lay low place where I can regroup for a while. My business in Buffalo is unfinished; this city will get some rest for now but I' be back. I drive the back roads and the snow is heavy now. I pull over and eat the salad. I eat it until it is fully gone, never realize how hungry I was. I grab two bottles water and drink both of them down. I feel refreshed but now I wish I wouldn't have left my coat. I look in my gym bag and thank god I left my velour gym suit, I throw it on. I look and find my black wig and makeup in the bag. I have hygiene products to hold me over until I get into another state. I pull up to the drive-up ATM and pull out $500 in cash out of my account. I also get a cash advance of $500 off my credit card. I have an enough gas to ride out.

At this moment I wish I had a friend to take advantage of and hide out in their house. I wonder how my child is doing. Did I kill her? As much as I want to forget the look in her eyes, the way she was in the fetal position crying and rocking I can't. To hear her say after what I inflicted on her she still loves me but hated me too. I look back on my life with no music, just dark roads cover with snow and road kill. May be I should have made her my ally instead of my enemy, no need to cry over spilled milk. What's done is done. I pick up the phone and call ECMC the only hospital that accepts trauma patients. The woman answers,

"ECMC. How can I help you?"

"Michelle Sargent. I am her grandmother and would like to talk to her." I hear her type in her name.

"I'm sorry I have no information on a Michelle Sargent."

"What the fuck you mean you have no information on her. She's my granddaughter, I demand you tell me if she alive and living." The rude bitch hangs up on me.

INSANITY AT ITS FINEST!

Tamyara Brown

It's cold and the snow is heavier than before. I feel my eyes getting heavy and I need to rest. I pull up to an old country mom and pop hotel. The last exit I past was exit 56 unsure of where exactly it didn't matter I needed to sleep.

Next door is a restaurant and a 24 hour Rite Aid. I walk in and purchase some hygiene products, food and four cases of water for the road. I load up on tampons, soap, wet wipes and toilet paper. I pack up on food. I swipe my credit card and pack up. The white man with the glasses hanging on his nose looks at me.

He said, "Long trip, Ma'am"

"Yes sir." He looks at me and clears his throat.

"My wife and I own that motel right across there if you need to rest your head young lady?" I look over and think of the option. I am tired right now and I need to sleep.

"How much is it a night?"

"With tax 44.25."

"Do you want me to pay you or your wife?"

"Pay her she run that there. You get yourself some rest. You look tired."

"Thank you, sir!" I load up my things I bought and pull up to the motel. The old woman with Grey hair is dress in her flannel nightgown and slippers.

"Hon, what can I do for you?" My voice is sweet and innocent.

"Good morning, Ma'am. My name is Harriet Monroe and I was wondering if I could rent a room? She looked me up and down.

"$44.25 and I don't want no men's running in and out my establishment. I don't deal with no heathens in here." I chuckle.

"Ma'am I'm traveling to my Auntie's funeral and just needed to rest that all. I'll be gone by morning."

"Hmm. 44.25 please."

I pay her in cash she looks at me under her glasses as she hands me the key and receipt she hand writes. I walk to the room and when I open it. It's actually clean and nice in here. It smells of Febreeze, I strip down and go the bathroom shower. I have no clue why my child is on my mind. I run my head under the water and images of her face flash before me. Images of Miyama, my daddy, my mama and my husband.

I step out and crawl under the cover and pray those images won't plague my sleep.

INSANITY AT ITS FINEST!

Four weeks later

SUSPECT OR VICTIM

The tight squeeze of the blood pressure cuff on my arm wakes me. My face is so sore and my eyes I can barely open. A large woman with pink ribbons on her scrubs smile at me while sticking the thermometer in my mouth

"Good morning, Hon? Glad to see you awake. Do you know where you're at?" I look around and the room is white and bright. The IV pole has one bag with clear stuff in it and another with milk looking stuff in a bag. I force my mouth to open but it hurts

"The hospital."

She prints the numbers on the blood pressure machine and takes the thermometer out my mouth pop off he plastic cover in the trash.

"Yes Hon you are. Do you know what today's date is? Do you feel any pain?"

"Yes. All over and I'm not sure what you want."

"You took a bad beating Hon. I'll get you some medication for the pain. Also, you still have a fever so looks like you'll be here for a while. The doctors and the police will be in to talk to you." She touches my hand.

"The police what did my Mama do?" she pats my hand and said,

"A lot to you honey and everybody don't worry about that we just need you to get better. I bought you some Ensure and applesauce so we can take you off the IV fluids and feedings." I try to sit up and the pain pierces through me. I exhale and try to replay the events with Mama and Bishop. I look and a balding man with a white coat walks in with two other men are staring at me.

"Hi, Michelle my name is Doctor Spinks and I'm taking care of you. These are two of my students who are residents Dr. Patel and Dr. Rashad. How do you feel today?"

"I'm hurting. Why is um…?" I look away because from the look on their face. I'm beat up pretty bad."

Dr.Patel begins explaining what wrong with me.

"Ms. Sargent suffers from a concussion, four broken ribs and busted. She has been in a coma for four weeks. She began responding to light and sound
She is currently four weeks pregnant." I listen and say,

"Stop, what did you say?"

"Your four weeks pregnant." My mind is all over the place. Bishop's and I are having a baby both times we use no protection. I'm pregnant is all I keep repeating to myself. The doctor exams me and I notice that a fetal monitor is on my stomach.

"Is my baby okay. Dr.Spinks?"

"Yes, so far the fetus is doing well. You do have a low-grade fever but nothing serious because of an infection. We are just glad you're awake and responsive."

The pain in me is more emotional; I'm now carrying the child of a man who has made a fool of me. Better yet I made a fool of myself I touch my stomach and I rub it. A child to love me maybe that's the gift Miyama was talking about. I don't know anymore. My mind thinks to the day Mama and I got into it, she hates me etch a sketch in my mind to stop loving what doesn't love me back. Those people who have abused me couldn't have loved me, right?

I gave my body to Bishop and I believed he loved me and once again the woman who was prettier got him. I'm used to losing and I guess it was in the cards for me to fail. The whole time I was just some pawn in his game to catch Mama. I hear a tap on the door, which interrupts my thoughts. Shayla walks in and she looks real pretty dressed in a blue pants suit and heels. She walks over to me and hands me flowers and kisses my forehead.

"Hi Sweetie! How are you?"

"Not so good. I don't know seems like I've been gone forever and the doctors said I was in a coma for four weeks. Then I find out four weeks pregnant. What am I going to do?" She rubs my hair.

"That officer is the father isn't he? He has been here every day by your side, talking to you and holding your hand. I went on an interview today."

"He was."

INSANITY AT ITS FINEST!

"Yes all these flowers he bought them in. I'd be coming in and he'd be leaving."

"So you have a job'

"Capital Management the collection agency. It's a start it pays 9.75an hour. I'm piecing together my life. I hope real soon I'll have my kids back." I squeeze her hand.

"The police they know everything my Mama did don't they? Did they catch her?"

"No Michelle actually they haven't she on the run. It's like she disappeared from the face of the earth. The detectives are going to question you." I take in a deep breath and blow out the stress.

"I know. I'm ready to tell? Are they going to arrest me for knowing and not telling? I was scared, I wanted to tell but she would have kill me." Her eyes sympathetic for me as tears spill. It now hurts to cry. I look at my arm with the bandages.

My side aching because all they've given me was a Tylenol 500. Which isn't working. I stand up because I have the urge to go the bathroom and pee on my own. My legs are wobbly and shaky so I fall back in bed

"Michelle they have a bedpan for you to use. I don't think it's a good idea to stand your weak right now."

I follow orders and use the pan. I'm embarrassed by the fact she sees me pissing in a pan. When I look up again Bishop is in all blue and the badge around his neck rips makes me lose my breath. His hat read BPD and the turtleneck with the same letters. Our eyes lock on one another he licks his lips, runs his hand through his beard. I turn away from him because once again another man seeing me at my weakest.

Now it all comes clear to me he was using me to get to my Mama. Or did he think I did all those killings? Does he know I killed Markel? Thoughts are clouding my head and tears from my already swollen eyes are running. I hear him say to Shayla,

"Can you give Michelle and me a moment alone?" she walks over to me and kisses my forehead.

INSANITY AT ITS FINEST!

"Michelle, I'm here if you need me. You take care of yourself, you have another person who needs you." She walks out and he watches the door close. He pulls the chair close to me and he looks at me. His bedroom eyes weaken the fact he has lied to me. He weakens me when he takes my hand in his and brings it to his lips. I finally get the strength to break from his handsome face and say,

"You're a detective. That's why you got close to me to get to my Mama. Or did you think I killed all those men? I mean the truth is evident you really didn't..." He stands up and his lips covers mine and he kisses away every angry thought. He swallows every angry word coming out of my mouth.

He answers my question.

"Yes, I am detective and I've been investigating this case for two years. I got close to you partially for that reason. I also got close to you because you have stolen my heart and I care for you. Did I believe you were a suspect, yes? I did not know you and I needed truth. "He bites his bottom lip, rubs his hand through my hair'

"So you was using me? Bishop after everything you knew about me didn't you think it would hurt me."

"Yes, I was in the beginning I got to know you and my feelings change, I begin to feel for you in every way imaginable. The next thing I knew I begin to like you more, care for you. I fell in love" I try to raise my hand to smack him but I'm too weak. Tears dribble from my eyes. His breath smelling like cigarettes kisses them away look at his eyes trying to find the lie but in them I see sincerity and love. I'm easily fooled but why am I allowing my heart to believe him.

"Why did you lie to me in the beginning?"

"Would you have told me the truth?"

"Yes, because I had lived with this for majority of my life, maybe I would of. You never gave me a chance

"No. I need you tell me everything you know about the murders. If you refuse to cooperate then yes I will have to arrest you for obstructing justice and hindering a police investigation." I touch my stomach and wonder if the doctor told him I was pregnant. I try to sit up but the pain shoots me back down. I whimper from the pain. He adjusts my pillow and helps me sit up,

"Relax okay."

INSANITY AT ITS FINEST!

"Bishop, she'll kill me and you." Bishop kisses and away my tears. "I'll protect you. I know my word hasn't been my bond with you lately but I swear on my grandma's grave I will not let nothing happen to you."

"If something does Bishop will you take care of our baby?" His eyes opens wide and he sits up straight. I continue

"I'm pregnant Bishop."

He doesn't say anything. He instead removes the cover and lift up my hospital gown. He kisses my belly and places his hand on top of the monitor.

"I'm going to be a father?" I shake my head yes.

He closes his eyes and leans his head back and laughs.

"Wow! I swear your Auntie Miyama predicted this to the letter." He kicks off his boots and he helps me move over, he gets in the bed with me and wraps his arm around my shoulder.

"I'm sorry for not being honest with you Michelle. I know she is your mother but she has to be stopped. It's not about just those other people; it's about the years of abuse you've gone through. You didn't and you don't deserve that. Now that you are carry my child nothing in the world will stop me from protecting you. Do you understand that?" His fingers wipe my eyes and his lips kiss me again.

"Did she kill anyone else?" He pulls his ear and removes his hat.

"Yes, she killed an elderly gentleman and two women at a gas station. We comb Buffalo and even had Rochester PD looking for her. Where else would she go Michelle? Does she have any friends or relatives she can hide out at?"

"Mama has no friends. She could have gone back to Brooklyn. It's where from?"

I watch as he stands up and put on his boots and hat back on.

"I have the police on a look out there too. This is national news now. The hospital has kept the reporters away but they want to talk to you. We still have them believing you're in a coma. Your mother did do one good deed. The Pastor and Deacon of New Deaconess Baptist Church since the report over twenty five people have come forward about what they have done to them as children. Did you know this happen to your mother?"

"She never told me until after she killed them. She said that my Auntie Miyama knew what they were doing to her. She said she stood outside the door playing as this happen and it's crazy. How could she do that to her?"

"Do you know her motive for killing? Her DNA matches in Rochester linked to a woman named Camilla Wright, also in the William Johnston murder. Who is this woman Camilla Wright?"

". She killed Camilla because she slept with my daddy. Mama is a jealous woman and she hates to lose. You have got to be careful." He stands against the wall.

"And Markel because he hurt you. Right? They found he had a prostitution ring in Niagara Falls."

It's easier to tell a lie when you're at the risk of losing everything. I need to be a good mama for our unborn child. I need to be here and I can't go to jail so the lie rolls off my tongue. He stands up and slips back on his boots. He pulls the cover back over me.

"Right. I guess it was her way of protecting me. I don't know."

His face-harden and his partner Hernandez walks in and to say that my heart skip a beat is short of the word.

"Michelle as much as I love you and care about you. I have to treat you like any suspect because I'm baffled. Markel King was killed at an estimate time of 12:45 am but if your mother killed Camilla at estimated time of let say according to the reports 3:00 a.m... It doesn't add up to me." He hits his hands and continues,

"I know that he beat you, belittle you so love you have every right to be angry and even want to stop him. Maybe just maybe you two got back up again to sleep together because he kick game to you, promise to never hurt you again. You decided you know what I'm going to end this nigger's life"

"I wasn't I was at home. I can't kill." He sits close to me and holds my hand; I pull it back because he is confusing me now. A moment ago he was telling me his feelings and now he treating me like a low class criminal.

INSANITY AT ITS FINEST!

"I want to believe you my heart said the woman I am in love with wouldn't kill. I also know this man hurt you and your Mama's motive as you describe is to get back at those who hurt her. She hated you and she seems and again I'm speculating, okay. Why, why would she kill him if she didn't care if you lived or die? I mean she was beating on you so it wouldn't matter if he did the same to you. So…" I feel Sarge take over me her voice said play this dude like he played you. "You think I killed him don't you? Investigate me, I don't have an alibi. I went to work and then after that I went home to work out. I never left my house after that so it works against me. I know that My Mama came in at about 5:00am that morning when I got up to exercise and prepare for work.

 I cared about Markel even after all he did to me. Hell, the mistreatment and beatings from my Mama where worst and she still alive. I know because she is a killer doesn't mean I have that instinct. Markel isn't the first man who has hurt me. I dated Richard Edwards previously before that and Jerrell Mitchell. I never did anything to them but ask them what my Mama did to them. I'm a suspect fine, once you find your proof. Do me a big favor and stay out of my life. I don't need this I have a baby inside of me who needs me. So do whatever you need to do." I turn away from him; I hear Hernandez thick accent speak up,

"One more question I know you've been traumatized and hurt. So answer us this why should we let this notion go that you did not kill Markel? He was your man and he dumps you out in the cold with no clothes on. He ripped your pride away, humiliated you so why shouldn't we believe you don't have the motive to kill." I look him in the eye so my lie would sit pretty. Let Sarge answer the question the only way she would."

"I never ever wanted to turn into my mother.
She killed my father right in front of me. Even if the thought cross my mind I would have saw my father's face." I continue to look at him ignoring Bishop. They both look at one another.

"Michelle, I'll get back with you. Don't let me find out that you're lying to me, no matter what I feel for you. If you are I will do my job and arrest you. So you have the opportunity to tell me the truth don't wait until it's too late for me to help you."

He rubs his hand through his beard, looks at his watch and his sea blue eyes are on me. He walks close to me.

"Bishop, you want me to be the one who killed Markel. If you believe this then arrest me, all I ask is you don't let our child go to foster care. I didn't kill him and I have no clue how to make you believe that so I won't. "I stick my wrist out for him to handcuff me. He pushing them away, they walk out. I don't know if he believes me but at this point it's not about me. It's about the baby inside of me. I touch my belly again. I say out loud a personal promise to her or him.

"I will never mistreat you. I will value your life and be the best mommy I can be. I promise you." In eight months I will have someone who will love me and I love him or her back

INSANITY AT ITS FINEST!

CONFUSED

I listen to her say the words to our unborn child. Hernandez looks at me as we go down the elevator. I stop at Tim Horton's and grab a triple triple coffee and buy Hernandez the same. We grab a seat and sit down. He sips his coffee and clears his throat.

"You're the father of her baby aren't you?" I look away from him and lean back.

"I tried to avoid the feelings I was developing and one night we and then." I pull my ear and cough.

"I knew your ass was going to fuck around and fall in love with the perp. I mean she is beautiful but she's still a suspect Bishop. I can't figure her out and I want to check into those two dudes see if her story checks out. Her mindset when they broke up."

"I know my job and I pull no punches on her Hernandez. If she killed Markel I will arrest her but something she said makes me think she couldn't have done it. I also thought about what the woman said her aunt and even Shayla. She never put her hands on her mother. All those times she could have fought back she didn't. If she had this nature she would have kill or at least attack her mother. That part makes me no sense to me." I have an urge for a cigarette but promise myself I would cut back.

"How do you feel? I mean this is your first child, Right? I sigh and answer,

"I always wanted to be a father. I wish it wasn't under the circumstances she was a suspect of a murder and her mother was a serial killer. It is what it is and I'm going to be a good father to my child." He and I look at our watches.

"One more question what happen to Tucker King or was that a cover for Ms. Michelle?" I laugh.

"No, that was actual fact of me sexing Tucker. What happen with Michelle happen afterwards?"

"So I mean Michelle is fine but Tucker seems more your speed, your type. I don't know, AMIGO!"

"She is that type of woman you see in L.A they have the body and come to find out that everything including her ass cheeks is unreal and their attitude sucks. I mean and she in my opinion doesn't know how to satisfy me in that department. I don't know then she was arrogant and demanding. I don't like that shit." We laugh.

"And Michelle? Yes Amigo I want to know."

"Hmm, she was damn good left a brother sucking his thumb. I mean she felt right and I enjoy her company, I do like her a lot."

'So much skill she made you forgets the condom."

"You got jokes, let's go check out Michelle's story. See where the truth lies. We walk out to leave and get in my truck." We drive back to the station and a pull up a report of last know addresses on Richard Edwards he lives on 473 Grant Street and it list a number. Jerrell Mitchell is residing in Attica Correctional Facility doing a bid of fifteen to life.

"So we check out the dude Richard on Grant and then the inmate Jerrell at Attica after that." Tucker name flashes on my cell. I hit the ignore button then shortly after she text me, before I delete it I show Hernandez the text.

"She back in Buffalo or she prepping to put fear in your heart."

"Never that. Anyway we're in front of this dude house."

I had two officers on twenty-four watches for her. I step out and of force of habit I look around. I walk up and knock on the door. The dude answers,

"Who the fuck banging on my door like that. What's on your membrane, son?"

"It's the police we need to talk with you for a moment." His face tight and he looks us up and down.

"Yo. Let me see your credentials." We flash him our badges and he opens the door motions for us to come in. His apartment is clean and tidy.

"Okay, so what the fuck you accusing me of, I did nothing I go to parole, I work and been off the streets. So what you want from me?"

"I show him a picture of Michelle and her mother Patricia.

"You know them Richard?" I study his facial expression as He looks at the pictures.

INSANITY AT ITS FINEST!

"Crazy bitch her mother is she the bitch that's going around cutting off nigger's dicks and shit, I'm not surprise." He throws her picture down but holds on to Michelle. He looks at it and touches her face. "Michelle you lost a lot of weight. If her mother would have mind her business she would have been my wife. Even though she was overweight she had a beautiful heart and the pussy was all that. I never wanted to hurt her but her mother she was causing mad trouble." I look on the mantel piece and Michelle picture sits there her face was fuller but she still was pretty.

"So what kind of trouble did she start?" Hernandez asked. He rolls up his sleeve and show the long cut on his arm.

"She came up and cut me telling me I was no fucking good for her daughter to stay away from her. She cause some beef between me and some dudes on the block. One time she threw fucking hot water on me another time blew out my tires when I tried to take Michelle out. So after she cut me I broke it off with Michelle. I would have been in jail a convicted murderer." I look at the pictures of his children and another woman. I ask,

"So how did Michelle react when you broke things off?" He stands up next to me by the mantel piece.

"Real talk she took it light. I mean she cried and shit but she wasn't crazy with it. She kept saying it was because she was overweight and ugly. I tried to explain to her it was her Mama and she was beautiful." I look over at Hernandez and he asks,

"Does she have the mentality to hurt anyone?" Richard looks around and sucks his teeth.

"Hell no, she real soft and you know nice. She was different then her mother and I never wanted to leave her. I still love her and care about her. Is she in trouble?" I felt a tinge of jealousy inside me to hear he still cared about her but the feeling of knowing she told me the truth gave me an inch of faith she may be innocent.

"Has she ever show behavior out of her character?"

"No not really. What trip me out was that her mother would beat her up and she would never hit her back. That was another reason I would like want to get away from her. I know you suppose to honor

your mother and father but I would have fuck that bitch up for real."
I look at the picture again.
"Thank you, Richard. She'll be all right. I'll let her know you ask about her."
We walk out the door and I feel relieved that he confirmed Michelle story.
"Before we go anywhere Bishop. I need to stop over here for some food. I'm starving you can go all day without eating but I can't. I'm hitting up this Spanish restaurant and having some food and you too. You are about to be a Papa in a few months. You need to eat?"
We walk in and I order the con arroz pollo and plantains. He orders the same. We sit in the car and eat. I didn't realize how hungry I was until the Styrofoam's empty. I lean back and burp.
"Damn, that was good."
 I want to call Michelle and check on her and see how she feeling. Tell her that I really want to believe her but the detective in me advises me to investigate every angle of this homicide. I turn on my CD and prepare for the ride to Attica. K-CI and JOJO life appropriate for the place we're going.
Hernandez driving there he takes the back roads. The last time we took this road was to investigate Big Willie murder now that we know for sure she is the one who did it. Now I need to have her behind prison bars. R. Kelly playing "I wish" in the background and both bopping our head to the song. I put my official police business sign in the window. K-CI and JOJO life appropriate for the place we're going I walk in and show my badge. They were aware I was coming to visit the inmate Jerrell Wright.
I Look at the women sitting waiting to visit the man they loved, go through checkpoints to see whether they had any contraband. The dehumanize part of visiting the one they love willing to sacrifice their pride just so he who committed the crime can feel loved and wanted. Some of them are putting money on their books and bags of groceries. I hate that shit bringing their sons to a place reminding them it was a fake ass badge of honor to be a thug without a cause. Fucked up world when it's where little boys and girls are visiting their daddies and mommies. I think of Michelle and hope I won't have to bring our child to see her in a place like that.
A prisoner who I put in here stares me down and I smirk.
INSANITY AT ITS FINEST!

"Like your new residence, bitch! You know the bars, the greens and the nasty ass pig slop. Is that your boyfriend?" His face is frown up and he whispers,

"Fuck you, pig?' Hernandez and I laugh at him. This bastard shot his wife in the head and threw her in the river after taking him in while he was sick was cancer. The smug bastard killed her and threw her body over the bridge as a way of saying thank you.

"You should have gotten the chair scum." I spit at him and stand toe to toe with him. The guard looks on in hopes he lays a hand on me so tonight they can beat his ass for shit his wife and kids did to piss him off. I hear the guard say,

"Maggots, keep it moving." He walks pass Hernandez and I. I walk in the interrogation room and Hernandez and I sit. Prisons have this stale smell of ass, feet and strong ass ammonia. Jerrell walks in a few minutes later. He's had a cut on his left cheek from his eye to his chin. He sits down.

"My name is Detective Jones and this is my partner Detective Hernandez. I'm here because I need to ask you some questions. We hope you will cooperate?" he folds his hands and sucks his teeth, he leans back and grabs his dick.

" Is that going to get me time off my sentence up in this mother fucker. Am I going to have some money put on my books? If not I don't have shit to say to you?"

I shake my head and run my tongue over my teeth. I crack my knuckles; the agitation sitting in the place I put majority of these cocks suckers in flares me up. I say,

"Hernandez holla at this dude because I'm not in the mood." I stand up and stand by the door. Hernandez goes at a different approach.

"I can put some change on your books. Let say 40.00. I need some information so you help me I. I help you with money on your books. This offer is not up for negotiation or discussion. Take it or leave it." He adjusts in his seat and asks.

"What do you want to know?" Hernandez asks,

"Do you know of a Michelle Sergeant?" He shakes his head.

"Yeah she was this female I use to date back in high school." I show him the picture of her both small and overweight.

"Yo! Michelle than lost mad weight, Damn she look good. Yo!" He starts laughing. He ogles her picture holding on to it.

"How was your relationship with her" I ask him and he answers,

"Yo, Hernandez I don't like your partner over there but this is about putting some gas in my tank. Michelle and I was you know cool. Real talk she was cute in the face but huge in the waist. Shit she wasn't my type; she was soft letting people run all over her. I can't stand a weak bitch. I was straight using her to pass my damn math class. I took her virginity back on senior ditch day and then I dumped her." The anger wells up but I keep my composure.

"Okay how did she react when you left her?"

"That bitch was crying but if you mean she got violent she knew better. It isn't in her nature she uses to let mad chicks clown her and she ain't do nothing. She was soft she had no spine, her mother came up and fought her battles. Her mom's on the other hand came after me and killed my dog. She hit Boomer with her car and cut off his nuts and handed it to me. That sick bitch had the nerve to laugh. That shit fucked me up when I went after her I ain't gone front she kicked my ass."

"That's all we needed from you. I'll go out and put the cash on your books." We walk out and I reach for the picture.

"Yo, tell Michelle hit me up in here and write a nigger. She looking damn good." I hit on the door and the guard lets us out. I walk through the halls my mind at ease.

"Yo, you may be right everyone we talk to said she doesn't have the heart to kill. So maybe Patricia did kill both people." I think of the time line the detective in Rochester gave and the time they found Markel dead he was dead way before the fire started. The old woman said she saw him arrive around 7:30pm the fire department was called around 8:30pm which could have place either of them at the scene. The time frame would have given Patricia time enough to travel the hour and twenty-five minutes it would have took to get to Mrs. Wright house torture and kill her. My gut clinches and I think

INSANITY AT ITS FINEST!

that maybe she didn't do it. I let it ride and put it on Patricia. The feeling doesn't go away that Michelle may have killed Markel. Why?

MICHELLE

After weeks of physical therapy and regaining my balance to walk without feeling like I was going to tip over. I'm walking shortly after the visit from Bishop because I'm pregnant they have transfer me to Women's and Children's hospital. I like it here better and I get the opportunity to look at all the newborn babies. The nurses treat you better.

I'm now fifteen weeks and sooner than I like they will release me. The hospital has been protecting me from the media and the two female officers who stand guard occasionally check on me. The nurses and Shayla keep me company. I haven't seen or heard from Bishop, which means he has let me go.

I just finish physical therapy and a light tap is on the door. When he walks in if I could I would allow my jaw to drop. Richard Edward's dreads touches his shoulders. I could smell his signature oil. He smiles and dimples appears. When he came close to me and kisses me on the cheek. A million memories flooded my head of our time together.

"What's good with you?" I can remember him hating the hospitals and now he dressed in a Healing health blue shirt and slacks.

"I'm okay. How are you, so you working here now as a janitor?"

"I'm good you know working, living life, staying off the streets and away from my old life. I needed to see you and know what's going on?"

"I know the news has said a mouthful." He sits down and slouches in the chair he continues,

"Chelle, this is me okay and when detectives show up at my door asking questions it's more, be real with me." I take a breath and I feel secure to tell him what going on.

"They think I killed Markel King?" He sits and folds his hands. My memory plays back to the time Leontaye Saxton a.k.a. Black Ice had the gun to Richard's head ready to kill him over his money being short. Sarge felt the need to protect him. The time the cab driver

INSANITY AT ITS FINEST!

tried to rape her and Sarge killed him to protect her. Yes, he knew about Sarge. He knew I was capable of killing someone when I became the other woman. He knew her secret but she saved his life, she had payback many of his debts when he was getting high. He would protect her with his life.

To make the murder look like it was my Mama by writing FAT GIRL Vigilante on the floor. He looks at the door and he read my facial expression and let a deep breath.

"I know the answer, Michelle. I worry about you."

"I know." My head is low. He reaches over and lifts my chin.

"I left because of your mother not you. I just want you to believe it wasn't about you." I look away from him.

"You left because of me, my weight and."

"Your insecurities about yourself. I love big girls and you know for a fact that was never a problem. So don't go there with me about weight bull shit." I want to scream but control my composure.

"I deserved for you to stay. Didn't I deserve that from you? I loved you and did what you expected of me yet you left."

I'm crying as usual and his hands wipe my eyes.

"At the time I was fucking around with them drugs. I was in the streets doing a lot of foul shit. I love the hell out of you. You couldn't see that because you held on to everybody opinion except the one that was most important, yours! Real talk I wanted to marry you and make you my wife." His eyes soften as he looks at me I touch his dreads run my fingers through them.

"Marry me as messed up as I am?" He pushes my hand away and said,

"See what I'm talking about? Baby, listen I never saw you as no messed up chick. You're beautiful, smart and the loving was damn good. You have wifely qualities but you beat down on yourself. If you were a fucked up individual, real talk I would have never asked you to be my wife. Feel me?' I shake my head and he kisses me this time softly on my lips and I respond back. We break apart and I decide to tell him.

"I'm pregnant, Richard." No expression is on his face.

"By who?"

"A cop the detective who came to see you?"

"Which one the nigger with the blues eyes or the Spanish dude?'

"The one with the blues eyes." He stands up and looks out the window.

"A fucking Pig of all people. The one who is investigating you and trying to arrest you. He using you."

"He could have really like me. See, one minute you build me up and then tear me down." I suck my teeth and look in the air.

"I'm not tearing you down. This was all about catching you or your mother, Ma nothing else. He may of caught you know a little feeling for you. Needed to get his dick wet but real talk it was all about a conviction. I know a cop like I know the back of my ass and as sure as my name is Richard Edwards, he was playing you. So is he going to take care of his seed?" he sits on the bed and touch my stomach. His hands feel good against my stomach

"He said he was?"

"Should have been my baby? You love this pig?" He kisses me again this time a little longer. He brings back old memories and feelings I thought die a long time ago.

"Yes but..." He cuts me off

"You still have love for me because you wouldn't have let me kiss you. If he not there for you and the baby call me. I got your back because you always had mine. I could have been gone from here. You gave me a second chance at life and I will never stop loving you for that. I'll take that shit to the grave with me. Feel me? It was good seeing you but I have to go. Here's my numbers and address." He hands me the paper and kisses me once more and I hug him.

"Before you go how you did get pass the guards?"

"Come on now nothing for me is impossible when it comes to getting to you." He winks and I smiled.

Maybe Richard was right about Bishop maybe all I was a suspect. Maybe he knew about my alter ego Sarge and the fact that I not only kill Markel King but also Black Ice. I won't let him take me away from my baby even if I have to I'll kill him too.

A plus size woman enters my room she has a legal yellow pad and pen. She is dressed in a black suit with a butterfly color. She greets me,

INSANITY AT ITS FINEST!

Tamyara Brown

"Hello Michelle, How are you? My name is Mrs. Randall and I am a clinical psychologist and they have suggested we just have a few sessions. You have been through a traumatic ordeal. If you like we can sit and talk!"

"Okay!" I answered; I studied her as she sat close to me in the chair. She began by going over the HIPAA and confidentiality rules. She explains that she would only contact authorities if I stated I wanted to harm or hurt someone else or myself. I signed on the dotted lines as requested.

"So Michelle are you going to talk to me today about whatever?" I look in her eyes and say,

"I'm afraid of never being loved. I'm afraid that I'm not meant to be happy and that I am cursed." She scribbles on her pad and she crossed her legs. I lean back on the pillow because those words are what have been and still are weighing me down.

"Okay and I'm sorry you feel that way. Why do you feel that you're cursed?"

"I have had a lot traumatic life experiences around me. I watched my mother beat, castrate and burn my father alive. You know the funny thing is I wish he had told he would have said he loved her and not me. No one person should have to endure so much pain not even my mother."

She writes some more and pauses. She scratches her head and her wig shifts to the left.

"Do you feel sorry for your mother?"

"Yes. One or two people began a saga of which she has become. Mrs. Randall if you don't mind I'm tired and I don't want to talk. "She stands up and fixes her clothes. She washes her hands.

"Can I talk some more with you tomorrow? I just want to help but I won't push. On your time and when you want to talk."

"Yes! Have a good day?"

INSANITY AT ITS FINEST!

Bishop

SEEKING TRUTH.

The truth is what I'm still seeking in what happen to Markel King. A riddle to the saga of who took his life. I shouldn't care because Markel was a fucking dog. My gut feeling has had me sick for the past couple of days because I know that the woman I love may have been the one who killed Markel. The problem is I don't have proof. Richard knows something and I plan to press him until he talks. I playback the recording of their conversation and he said she save his life. How?

I look back into my cases in the past two years. It hits me Leontaye Saxton AKA Black Ice was beheaded and castrated on July 11, 2006. He too was killed on his birthday. I decide to ruffle Richard feathers and see what I get out of him something wasn't right. I read the report and pull up Richard Edward's record he was a former petty drug dealer who worked with Leontaye Saxton AKA Black Ice. Bingo! He was link to him. I tap the table going throughout the file and I arrested a Sylvester Stone but was later released because he had a tight alibi.

This case had the Fat Girl Vigilante signature but it was written on the floor. I pull out the photos and I examine each of them and the handwriting is different. I pull out Markel King and the handwriting matches both of these are written in cursive but the other murders associated with them are in block letters. I look at both pictures. Michelle did it!

The ride to Richard's house was one I needed to take alone without interference. I pull into his driveway and park. He's looking out the window. I walk up the stairs,

"We need to talk, now?" He and I are eye to eye.

"Man, here we go. What the fuck are you harassing me for now?"

"You can do this the easy way or the hard way. If you have nothing to hide then it should be no problem talking to me." He smiles,

INSANITY AT ITS FINEST!

"On some real shit, I know my rights and because you have no warrant. You can't do shit to me but jump in your truck and run off with your tail in between your legs."

"Your right Richard but this is casual talk. No harm no fowl. Look, I learn some things about you. I know and you know you're protecting Michelle. I love her and all I want to do is help her. She's the mother of my unborn child and I want the truth. I'm going to get the truth." He folds his arms and asks,

"You love her or was she one of your pawns in a game to catch a killer. Her mom's did that shit man. Michelle's been through enough with all the shit her mother has done to her. Let this die, man worry about your seed, Officer."

"To answer your question yes I love her and you still love her. We are two men in the position to save her from spending the rest of her life in prison. Hiding the truth is going to hinder her man. Answer me this and after that I'll leave you alone. What happened to Black Ice the night he was murdered?

"Man, I ain't killed him." He folds his arms looks at the car passing by.

"You know who killed Black Ice. I am aware that someone saw you walk out with a heavyset woman. Did you smoke up his shit, now that was gone and you didn't have his money. I know from the block he was after you. He was ready to murder your ass. Then on his birthday he turns up dead, head and dick cut off. The coincidence is you and Michelle running out. No, I'm sorry a heavyset woman.

"Like I said, Officer I don't know how he got murdered." Richard's eyes shift. I sit on the steps and I think through the pattern. I light up a cigarette take a puff and exhale.

"You know Richard what I discovered about you. You're loyal even when you were hit with a bid. You had the opportunity to squeal on your enemy and you didn't. I can respect that even did time in Collins correctional Facility for five years behind loyalty. This is different because this time along with your loyalty is love. You and her shared time together. Michelle is sweet, kind and beautiful but you see she has never seen that because her mother poisoned her mind, maybe even poison her mind to kill. If that the case she is then innocent. You know more about Michelle than I do. She's been through hell and back but she held on to her mother's secrets for years. Loyal she is to those she loves. She was loyal to you. Maybe he was trying to hurt you and she needed to protect you. The only way she knew how was by doing what her mother has done. Kill him. I could be wrong, Richard just a theory, you know. If you love her help her by telling me so I can get around this." I hand him my card and add on.

"I love her too and the last thing Richard I want to do is see her away from our child. I'll be seeing you. Think about what I said, man."
I stand up and wipe the back of my jeans off. I get in my truck and back out, Richard's still holding my card and walks in the house. I hit a nerve now it's time to see the mother of my child. My cell rings and it flashes DAD. I answer,

"What up old man?"
"Your old man still look good for sixty-five. How are you, Son?"
"I don't know I still haven't caught the woman killing all those people and to add insult to injury. I think my baby mama's a killer too. So to sum it up it sucks to hell to be me right now." I pull out a cigarette and light it. Take two puffs because I'm stressed.
"Okay, so what are you going to do? You told me the situation now what's your resolve?"
"I have no clue. I'm stuck."
"This serial killer has a pattern and after she murders them does she leave her mark, right?"
"Yes she writes her signature in her victim's blood. She burns and castrates them. She changed up her pattern by shooting a couple of people."
"Alright son so now what I see is she wants attention, she wants to get caught because most likely she has nothing to lose. So you bring attention to her. So she can come to you?"
"Okay, I've got that. What about Michelle?" A pause and simultaneously.
"Michelle and her mother pattern is not the same. I've always taught you in the cop world there are murderers and killers. Murderers plan an execution. Killers are careless and act on emotion. Patricia is a

INSANITY AT ITS FINEST!

murderer and Michelle is a killer if indeed she has killed Markel. I say that because she has been hurt numerous occasions and never killed but when she losing something or a person she loves is threatened that's when she attacks, right?"

"Yes."

"She had to be protecting someone, she's loyal and maybe because she couldn't protect her father. She is protecting the one's she loves or lost by killing them. I'm playing around with theory. Women serial killers have a reason and a motive."

"Patricia is out of being molested and hurt by people. Michelle is out of losing something or endangering someone she loves like a man. She making up for not protecting her own father."

"Exactly, when you're dealing with the human being you have to go deeper than facts but their make-up. How they think, how they act. Michelle is scared out of her mind right now and she doesn't want to lose neither her child nor you. Which can work to your advantage. Let her confide in you, trust you again."

"I don't know if that's going to work. I press her ex."

"I don't know Dad."

"You love her?" I smashed the cigarette in the ashtray and pull in the parking lot.

"I do but it scares the shit out of me? Worrying about having my child born in a prison cell. I could let Patricia take the fall because no matter what she's going to die in jail. I know what her Mom's put her through but it that a legitimate excuse to let her get away with murder and rest at night! What if she feels like following in her mother's footsteps?"

"Son, this is a tough call. If she is incarcerated would you take full custody of your child?'

"Of course I would Dad? He or she is a part of me?"

"I raised you right, son to be a man and take responsibility no matter how bad situations may be. That's apart of us and your mother and I will help you to raise that child. Understand?'

"Yes Dad I do. I'm at the hospital let me see Michelle."

INSANITY AT ITS FINEST!

Patricia

FACING YOUR LIFE

The child you birth from your womb turns against you and maybe it's payback for me turning on my mother. Hating her for not fighting for my father. I fought for Michael and he left. I fought for Michelle and she chose some cop over her mother. The motel room where I rest and I have been in deep thought about this situation. My reaction would normally be to kill her ass and set her on fire but since I've been in the woods I need to tell her some things. The knock on the door breaks me out of my deep thought. I put on my wig and glasses.

"Yes Ma'am."

"Good morning Sunshine?' the elderly lady said as she hands me the towels. I wait until she finishes her cleaning and she humming amazing grace. She leaves and I pick up the phone and dial Michelle's number. It rings twice.

"Michelle, it's me..." The phone hangs up on me the fury of anger rings through me. I dial her number again.

"Yes! What do you want?'

"I want to talk?"

"About what, Ma'am?"

"I'm..."

"Don't say that word because you don't mean it. Mama that's not a part of your vocabulary."

"Michelle, did you turn me in?" I take a deep breath.

"You have no clue who I am? I've protected you for twenty- six years. I was loyal to you kept your secrets of all you did to people. For what? You took every person who ever loved me away, including yourself. I needed you to love me, be my mother not my enemy but instead you chose to abuse me, denounce me as a human being. Now, you need me for something. Who's my father, Mama?"

I play back the day I found out I was pregnant with Michelle, the flood of the truth the man I love didn't create the blessing. My

INSANITY AT ITS FINEST!

unborn child was supposed to be his gift and the seal of keeping him with me. Instead the Deacon seed had curse my womb. I hated myself because after being an adult I went back. The Deacon promise he'd tell my father the truth. At the time I was in Buffalo to see Daddy who was sick in the hospital he'd called me a liar and evil woman. I went to the church begging the Deacon to tell him what had happen. He said only if I slept with him again would he tell the truth. The deacon words echoed in my ears,

"I need to touch you one more time." His hands ran through my red hair and his lips kissed me. As disgusted as I felt all I wanted was for my father to know the truth I wasn't a whore. After all those years he still had power over me. I needed my Daddy to not die hating me. I needed him to know the truth. That day he took me back in the same shed and this time the sex was consensual. He never kept his promise and my father died believing a lie about me.

Six weeks later I turned up pregnant. I told Steven he would be a father and he married me. I didn't want to lose him so I never told him what happen to me. Never confirmed his or anyone's suspicions that Michelle wasn't his child. He would years later find out by that deceitful bastard would tell his son his daughter was in fact his sister. I never knew the Deacon was the father of Michael until that day after she was born and he came to see her. It was the reason Michelle favored him. It was the reason I hated her so much.

"Your father is the Deacon and Michael is your brother."

The sound of the dial tone let me further know that she was through which fuel me to want to kill her even more. She screws herself with no lube because as of right now there would be no peace in Buffalo. I'm coming home with venom so deep in me to kill Michelle and kill Detective Bishop. Anyone along the way is just causality to the war. The old woman knocks on the door and I answer,

"Yes."

"Breakfast is hot and ready. Found some of that steel cut oatmeal you like and fresh berries on the side."

"Thanks. I'll be out to eat in a minute."

For the first time in history I met someone who is genuinely nice to me. I have to say it's the only reason I've let them live. I turn on the

TV and they are trying to analyze a female serial killer. The renowned Dr. Drew who is trying to put a theory on my madness turn every channel and someone is talking about the Fat Girl Vigilante. My picture is all over the place. The wonder if my daughter was my side kick. I'm a one woman show and need no side kick. I'm described as a maniac but I preferred to be called a Psychotic Beauty on a Rampage. I turn the channel and I'm everywhere.

I yell out, "I'm national, Mom!"

Wow, they have a forensic mental health analysis trying to figure me out. I'm headlining the national news. Shit, I'm even being profile on Nancy Grace. I put on my wig and glasses. Their talking about the abuse and the mental anguish I put on Michelle. They call me a She-Devil heartless and ruthless. They know me so well. They even bring in the fact that I come from a distorted childhood.

I love it the way they think they're going to catch me. I'll present myself to them butt naked, my victim's blood dripping off my body let them see what insanity really looks like.

I step out of my room and eat go into the dining area. I change up my tone. My long wool skirt and black shirt my green eyes covered with dark brown contacts. I walk in and Ms. Joanne and Papa Paul are looking at the news. The news is talking about all of the adults coming forward about the Deacon and Pastor. The Deacon fathered seven children including Michelle. The boys where men either in jail telling their story from jail cells and mental institutions. Some is planning to sue for monetary gain. This shit was sickening I thought by killing them the past would finally rest in peace. I was wrong.

"Good morning, Mrs. Joanne and Papa Paul."

"Morning." They both say. The news is talking about fat girl vigilante."

I pour some oatmeal in the bowl and pretend to say grace. It's been my ritual every morning for four weeks. The news is trying to figure out the serial killer on the loose. Papa Paul said,

"Someone had to mess that woman up as a child, look a Pastor and Deacon who molested her. She is the victim and though I don't agree with her tactics she's hurting and hurt will lead to out of control actions." Mama Joanne sips her juice and answers,

"Papa, what they did to all them children ain't right and the fact that these parents didn't believe them is what got me all worked up. If

INSANITY AT ITS FINEST!

one person would have believed her. I don't think she would have went out and did all those killings. They need to get her help she needs. I mean these hypocrites took her in the shed, which to this day is still up and standing and did ungodly things after church services. Then for years went on God's throne and spoke his goodness. I'm disgusted Papa."

While they conversed finally people saw different, saw how I became what I became because of someone else's action. Understood the logic no matter how ugly the outcome was. I stood up and hug Papa Paul and Mrs. Joanne. I felt the closest to them like the parents I needed. They welcome me with open arms at their motel. I helped her to lose weight by putting her on regimen of walking thirty minutes a day and weight training. She's lost seventeen pounds so far. She's eating healthier and choosing to live again. I never in my life saw real love between a man and a woman the way I see it with Joanne and Papa Paul.

Joanne and Papa hugged, they kissed and cuddled. They still make love as old as they are. Love so authentic it's undeniable. When I think of my own husband that's what I desire from him. The longevity that no man could ever take that away. Maybe that only rang true for white folks not us black folks. Maybe for those who stay true to God's principles? Deep in thought Papa Paul walks in and startles me. He sits at the table and folds his hand, his glasses touching his nose. I sit in the empty chair across from him. His voice is low,

"I know who you are Patricia Sargent." My eyes widen and I answer, "That's not my name. I don't know what you're talk..." He cuts me off and holds my hands. He begins to say the Lord's Prayer.

"I know who you were the first day you walk in the store. They have been advertising your face for the past few months and I never forget a face. I felt compelled to help you because Mama Joanne and I have a daughter her name is Charlene. Hmm, she was and still is the apple of my eye, the only child I got. One day something changed her life. A man who came here at the hotel took my little girl in the backwoods and did god-awful things to her. She came from the woods never the same. I'm a god -fearing man but that anger

INSANITY AT ITS FINEST!

brewed in me something awful. Stole my sleep, stole the good in me.
I could not find it in my heart to forgive him for taking her
innocence. I needed him dead so I could sleep at night. So I took my
deer rifle and at night I'd drive through each bar in every town.
When I found him I lodged a bullet in the back of his head."
"How did you get away with it?"
"They thought it was in self-defense and I got probation."
"I went home after thinking now I can sleep. By that time my little
girl turn to drugs and she too was gone. We tried all those remedies
the doctors told us to do. Our only child out somewhere in the cruel
world. I search and search soon as I find her bring her home She
turned around steal from me and then late at night she gone. I
learned that one person can do one thing and it will set off a chain of
events. Just like that Pastor and the Deacon did to you." I look at
him and my eyes can't grow cold. I trusted Papa Joe and I never trust
anyone.
"Why didn't you turn me in? I could have killed both of you!" He
lights his cigar.
"I trusted the man upstairs and I also believe that you are tired of
killing. Am I right? I understand your anger, you're hurt and pain."
"I have no clue what to do. I have nothing my daughter is through
with me."
"Patricia what are your plans?"
"I have none."
"You need to make peace with your child but most of all with God.
She needs to know you love her. You do love your child don't you?"
"Yes I do. I can't make peace with a God that allows children to be
hurt like me. He's always hated me."
Papa Joe holds my hand and he lets me have my moment where I
realize that I should have never turn from my child. How would I
explain that to her? I was in fear of something for a long time and
that was the truth. I fear truth but hated lies. I fear lies because they
are able to destroy the truth.
"I do love my daughter. She will never forgive me. So are you going
to call the cops? Papas Joe raises his right hand and said,
"Here's my hand to God and you have my honor that I will not call
the police. You can hide out here but eventually they will find you." I
wipe my tears and stand up.
INSANITY AT ITS FINEST!

"I know Papa Paul. I would never endanger you and Mrs. Joanne. This is not going to be pretty and I know it. I'll leave."

"You sure because you're more than..." I cut him off this time.

"I know and I appreciate you but I have to take care of one more thing."

I watch him get up and he is the first man in a long time I allow to hug me. He hugs me tight how I deserve to be hugged.

"I'll be gone by night fall."

He looks back at me and closes the door.

Bishop

FOR THE BABY SAKE

She is sleeping when I enter the room the sound of the monitor
beeping. I walk to the window and I look down at ECMC parking
lot. I look at the paper on the tray and it's Richard. I study the
handwriting and throw back on there and the officer who on guard
taps my shoulder.
"Yes."
"The doctor's want to speak with you outside?' I follow him in the
room and two doctors are standing there with the ids on.
"Detective Jones have a seat?"
"No, I rather stand. What's up?" The tall doctor who dressed in a
long sleeve Grey shirt and black slacks his hair slick back.
"My name is Dr. Evans and Michelle is my patient. For the past three
days Michelle hasn't eaten and has not spoken to anyone. She isn't
doing well and for the safety of the baby I need her to eat. I was
thinking you could help her. She's been crying and we have no clue
what's going on. We've ordered for a psychologist to come and speak
with her.
 I understand you wanted to review her medical records. Being that
you have no warrant or a court order I can't discuss her medical
history. I can only discuss with you the injuries she sustained while
she was attacked because it is then that it does not violate HIPAA
laws.'
"Did someone visit her? Is the baby okay?"
"Yes. The baby is fine. The nurse said she was on the phone and
after that she was crying non-stop and then refuse to eat.
"I'll talk with her, Thanks." I get up and walk back into her room, I
know the only thing that could upset her is that her mother
contacted her. She is awaked and her dinner tray is here. I look at her
diner tray and she hasn't touched it. Her eyes are red and swollen, her
hair uncombed, she hasn't shower. I look at her and remember the

INSANITY AT ITS FINEST!

state her Aunt was in. She sniffles and wipes the tear. I sit next to her, take her hand in mine.

"What's wrong Baby?" She closes her eyes and looks out the window. No words come out her mouth but the sadness wash over me. I ask again,

"Talk to me. We've always talk. I'm here, please baby come on." Her eyes grow cold and she snatches her hand from.

"You don't give a damn about me, Bishop. I'm your suspect. I'm your key witness nothing else. You want me to talk? What the fuck you want me to tell you Detective Bishop. That my father is the man who raped my mother and that the man I thought was my daddy is my brother. That I'm pregnant by the detective who will put my mother away for the rest of her life, that I keep falling in love with sorry ass niggers like you. Is that enough information?" I try to absorb all that has been told me. I am for the first time speechless. I try to touch her and she pushes me away. She is right this is twisted, this is distorted picture the truth is feeding me.

"I know you hate me and that's your choice. I need you to eat for our baby. Our child needs you. I need you, I know you don't believe me but I need you." She rolls her eyes at me. . I lift up her the thing covering her food and it's a piece of chicken breast, mashed potatoes, peas, milk, peaches and a slice of lemon cake. I take the fork and lift up some mashed potatoes hold her chin and she opens her mouth. I feed it to her. I continue until she is has eaten most of the food.

"Thank you I can't begin to understand what you are going through. I'm here for you, our baby. I believe you. I believe you didn't murder anyone."

 I want to ask her had her mother told her where she was at. It was the wrong time and I didn't want to push her over the edge. She looks away from me. Her tears fall once again, her voice soft but filled with anger and disappointment

"Bishop stop pretending you care about me and our baby. I'm a suspect do your job and treat me like one. Don't come in here playing with my emotions, you've done a great job doing that. Right now I can't handle anymore lies. I can't do it. I love you Bishop I fell in love that night you dance with me in the parking lot of Rite Aid. I don't want you to pretend anymore, please."

She pushes the table away and she pulls the cover over her head. I remove the cover turn her face to see my heart through my eyes.

"I do care about you. I love you but I have a job to do. I need the truth from you. Your mother has taken a lot of lives. I want to help you but you're making it hella hard." She removes the cover from over her head and replies,

"Get Out Bishop! You don't love our baby or me and unless you're here to arrest me. I want you to leave. Get the fuck out of here!" She throw the tray at me and the milk splatters all over the wall." The nurse rushes in and tries to calm Michelle down. The nurse looks at me.

"I'm sorry sir you need to leave. Michelle, just relax you are going to upset the baby. I need you to take a deep breath and calm down love. It's okay." She's hyperventilating when I leave.

I walk out and need a cigarette. The black nurse walks over to me and taps me on the shoulder.

"What?"

"Meet me at Tim Horton's in ten minutes I have some information for you."

"All right!"

My mind plays back to the scene and I saw a side of her I never expected. I'll admit I've played her and how dare I expect her not to be angry. The heavy set black nurse sits across from me.

"Her mother 's been contacting her." I look around and leans forward."

"She told you all this? Where you there when her mother called?"

"Yes, I was taking her vitals. I heard the whole conversation. She told me she had to push you away because her mother would kill you."

"She told you that?"

"Yes, she told me that. She also afraid her mother's going to take her baby away." She gets up. I watch her walk away and now I'm baffled. I call Hernandez,

"Hey look I need you to meet here at ECMC. Can you do that for me?"

"Yeah, I can. I'll be there in fifteen. You're in Timmy Ho's?'

INSANITY AT ITS FINEST!

"Yeah." I order a large coffee and blueberry bagel with cream cheese. I sit and my mind is stuck on Michelle and her scene. I check my text messages and bite my bagel.

Hernandez walks in and sits down.

"You want coffee?"

"No I'm good, Bishop what's up?"

"Michelle killed Markel and Black Ice?"

"Black Ice the drug dealer. How you figure?"

"Richard was working for Black Ice and at the time he was smoking up the profits. One of the dudes said that Black Ice that night was going to murder?'

"The handwriting is not the same. All of the writing was written in print. The killings of Markel and" I pull out my phone and I show him the pictures of both of them.

"The ones at Markel and Black Ice match and is in Script. The other ones are in print."

"Do we know its Michelle handwriting?" I take another bite of my bagel.

"No not exactly before I could get a copy of her handwriting she kicked me out."

"Why?" I take a gulp of my coffee and raise my eyebrow.

"Man, listen she started talking about I didn't care and that her mother called telling her that her father was the Deacon who raped her mother." I wait for Hernandez to show a smile but he doesn't instead he said,

"She has been contacting Michelle. I dump her calls and she contacted her three times. The longest call being the longest was seven minutes and forty-five seconds." I rub my hand through my beard.

"Do we have a location as to where she may be?"

"No, the cell site she call from is a congested network of Sprint. It picks up two signals an analog and a digital one off a Pennsylvania tower. We couldn't pinpoint it because it also picks up Pittsburgh, Watertown and Binghamton."

"Damn!" Hernandez sucks his teeth and he clears his throat.

INSANITY AT ITS FINEST!

"Bishop, Captain is about to pull you off the case. I agree with him because you are too emotionally involved with this case. You can't separate the two of her being your lover and her being a suspect. I'm being honest my friend.'

"I've separated the two and I know my fucking job, Hernandez!"

"Not lately, Bishop! We know who did this and we're still running around like two amateur detectives without facts. This fucking chica is playing us. She is a murderer and you're playing yourself. You are in risk of losing your job. Is she worth it, Bishop?" Our stares are cold and it could chill even the warmest heart.

I stand up and he softens his face,

"Amigo, sit down please!" I sit back down and I put my face in my hands.

 The confusion lurking around. If I'm honest with myself I am overwhelmed and stressed out I have allowed myself to be in a spot that I haven't a clue how to get out of. This predicament is crazy to me, I need to regroup and reorganize. Every one's inside my head.

"Look Hernandez the one thing I don't want to do is work against you. I'm stressed the fuck out with this. You and I have worked on this case for over two years and it's never been instilled in me to quit. I've never been a quitter. So I'm going to see this case through because I want her in jail."

Hernandez shook my hand and without words we came to a mutual agreement of what we needed to do.

"Let's turn out the lights out and let that roach crawl out. So we can stomp that bitch"

INSANITY AT ITS FINEST!

Michelle
Therapy

"Michelle, what do you like about yourself? Mrs. Randall asked. My hands rubbing my protruding belly. I look at the full-length mirror she has in front of me. I stare at my body and for the first time when looking at myself I can smile.

"I like my stomach because my unborn child is inside of me." She writes it down and crosses her legs. She is a plus size woman with a neat Halle Berry cut; she has a pretty face with freckles.

"Besides being pregnant what is it that you see inside of yourself?" I close my eyes and search for the answer but can't seem to find it. "Can I skip the question?"

"No, I would like you to answer it, if it's the only question you answer today. "Her eyes are on me; she taps her pencil on her paper and then rips it off. She continues,

"What I love about myself Michelle is my body. I love my body and the way it feels the fullness .I love that I'm kind, sensitive and brilliant. Now your turn." I look at the mirror.

"I like my natural green eyes because it brings mystery to me. Like what a cocoa brown woman doing with those pretty eyes. I guess what I admire is I love being in love. No matter how much it hurt me I still want that feeling over and over again." She smiles and writes it down.

I am being analyze but at the same time the more I come here the more it helps me out.

"Can I talk to you about something, Mrs. Randall?" She nods her head.

"My mother is a killer and every day I live in fear that I want love so bad that I'll become her. Men have hurt me including Bishop, I don't want to hurt anyone." Her look turns serious and she sits up straight. She clasps her hands together.

"Do you feel that way now? Like hurting someone?"

"No, but after I lost the baby. It was like I couldn't erase the thought. It was bad that he abused me but he took the opportunity for

INSANITY AT ITS FINEST!

someone to love me." I take a sip of my water and I look away. Mrs. Randall writes on her pad.

"Are you angry with Bishop?"

"I don't know. I love him; he gave me a feeling he really cared that he had fallen in love with me. He was different. I 'm disappointed in him."

She writes something else. I look at the time and we have ten minutes left. I eat a cracker with cheese and apple stacked on top, my new craving.

"Michelle, did you kill Markel King?" I smile at her and take another bite of my cracker with cheese and apples, rub my finger together to remove the crumbs. The question she has asks for the past eight and a half months.

"You ask that question every time I come here? Why?" She takes a deep breath and she looks me in the eye.

"You seem to want to tell me something but you hold back, I cannot divulge anything you've done in the past."

"I'm not a killer. Markel told me I wasn't worthy of anything and he took his foot and repeatedly kicked me in the stomach. I lost my first child. Mrs. Randall I think your question shouldn't even be a thought as to whether I murdered him. Our time is up Mrs. Randall you have good day."

I walk out the room and without looking back. The patient -client confidentiality act was secure and every visit I pay for is in cash so there was no insurance agents who can track what I tell. The truth is that I will not allow anyone to take the only opportunity to be loved. My unborn child will love me because I plan on pouring every ounce into him. My son is the only chance I have at being loved unconditionally.

Bishop has played an active role in my pregnancy he hasn't missed a doctor's appointment and even participated in Lamaze classes. I have distant myself emotionally from him and he notices it. He still holds the door open for me. He is the most caring man I know. If he is trying to charm the truth out of me it isn't going to work. He holds my hand, he does those three o'clock in the morning runs for Hagen Daaz strawberry ice cream and pound cake. He rubs my back and feet. Shayla said he couldn't fake being a good man. I want to believe,

INSANITY AT ITS FINEST!

I want to open up but he played me once and I refuse to be a fool again. It's nice to be treated like a lady instead of some man's whore. My decision is that everyone that I have come close to has pretended to love me. I'm learning that in order to love my child I have to love myself. These sessions have gotten me closer to understanding my make-up as a woman understands. I understand why I killed Markel he took the opportunity away for me to love to care for someone and they will love me. I even understand my mother's motives she needed to cleanse her soul from the pain she carried around and still does. She can't love me because she can't love herself.

The thought of motherhood has given me a different outlook on life. I learn that I needed to let go of all that has hurt me. Even the situation with Bishop I had to let go. I also learn the whole process of letting go takes time. I want to forgive but I have also had to forgive myself for what I did as well. I feel a sharp pain shoot through my belly. I have a couple more weeks before going into labor. I take a few deep breaths as I am driving. The pain has subsided. I realized the whole time I had my phone off. I turn it on and realize I had ten messages. I try to dial but after about ten minutes another sharp pain causes me to drop it. I take deep breaths in and out. I keep saying I can't be in labor now. I'm five minutes from Bishop House. I have a doctor's appointment at four.

When I pull into his driveway I see Bishop's white truck sitting there. I can feel the pressure of the baby head weighing down my crotch. It feels weird but I'm okay. He steps out and he is alone. He knocks on the window and I face him. My face is frown up and I can smell his signature cologne. I roll down the window and he looks at me.

"What Bishop?" He bends down and his face is close to mine.

"You missed your appointment today. Just checking up on you"

"My appointment was at four today." I feel a sharp pain in my stomach and I winch. I take a deep breath and blow out air. The gush of fluid runs down my legs. I look down and a rush of feelings invades me.

"No, it was at eleven. I've been blowing up your phone all day long?"

"Bishop, please not now." I lay my head on the steering wheel as the pain once again hits a tear and me drop.

"You're in pain aren't you?" I shake my head and sit up.

"Bishop, leave me alone. I'm okay?" I lie

"I won't leave you alone. You are carrying your unborn child. You need to answer your phone when I call."

"Ah... Okay, Okay! Just go so I um, shit, it hurts." He opens the door and see the fluid on the floor." He moves me over and gets in the seat. He rushes me to the hospital and seems to be hitting every bump.

"Stop hitting every bump. Bishop Oh my god! Oh my God! Another one." I scream.

"It's okay where three minutes away." He gets on his cell and alerts the hospital I am coming. He pulls into the entrance of the ambulance and jumps out. He alerts the nurse and they rush me in to labor and delivery.

The pain is ripping through my body. I can think is please let my son be okay The smell and the pinch of the needle in my arm and seeing tubes of blood filling up makes me queasy. My clothes being taken off by Bishop and being slip in a gown. My legs being put in the stir-ups, the pain is becoming more violent. I screaming, "Please take this baby out of me. Bishop, please get me something for the pain."

Bishop holding my hand and every one telling me I'm doing well. I feel dehydrated. Bishop is rubbing my hair and holding my hand. He is nervous but so supportive. The doctor denies me pain medication because I'm fully dilated.

"Baby just take deep breaths. It's almost over." In agony, sweat drenching my body and my hair is all over my face. My lips dry and cracked. He feeds me ice chips. I push through the pain.

"Is he coming Bishop? Is he coming I ask the nurse." She looks at me and said,

"Almost dear. Almost you're doing well. I need you to push whenever you feel a contraction." Bishop takes a wet cloth and wipes off the sweat off my forehead. He kisses away my tears.

"I see his head Michelle, You're almost there." I pant and breathe, "I'm scared, Bishop!"

I feel another contraction and on the count of three I push and I hear his cry. His sweet cry. My son is here. They place him on my

INSANITY AT ITS FINEST!

stomach and the flood of love overwhelms me. Bishop cuts the cord and all that he has put me through is forgiven because he gave me someone to love. He was there by my side. He touches our son hands and I see something I've never seen before and that's him crying tears of joy. I hear him say,

"Thank you Michelle for this gift of life." He bends down and kisses me. I realize God has finally a reason to feel joy in my heart.
The doctor said,

"You have a beautiful baby boy. The tears flood my eyes and I touch his fingers and Bishop touches his. The nurse cleans him up, weigh him and put him on the Apgar scale. His cries are sweet music to my ears. If no one ever loves me again I know for sure my son will. I know for sure that I have his love. As they give me three stitches. My son weighs 7lbs and 13 oz.

"Look at him, Bishop isn't he beautiful?" He wipes his eyes p. Bishop is near him and I see his admiration of his first born son. The doctor places him in his daddy's arm and Bishop kisses him. He plays with his hands when he walks over to me he puts him in my arms.

"Thank you Bishop!" He kisses me on my forehead. Michelle

"No, thank you for my son."

"I would like to name our son with your permission Bishop Michael Ezekiel Jones Jr." He smiled and he kisses his forehead and then my lips.

"Michelle that sounds beautiful. The nurse takes the bracelet and wraps it around his wrist. She smiles,

"This is your access band it gives you the right to stay all night if you like. This band will match yours, the baby and Mom. Also we give you guys a steak dinner with all the trimmings and desert."

I attached BJ to my breasts and he suckled on. I look down at him and he was mine. Tears of happiness filled and when I look at Bishop he had that same wave of emotion. I look at him and he looks just like Bishop. I wonder whose eyes he will inherit Bishop or mine. I hear Bishop cell phone ring. He looks at it and excuses himself.

A few minutes later he comes back in, his facial expression changed. It was more serious and stern. He is still dressed in the paper gown. "Can I hold him one more time please?"

"He's your son of course." He takes him in his arms and he just stares at him and He holds his little fingers in his hand and then kisses them. The warmth that I feel seeing the man I love holing our son. I hear him say,

"Hi little man, I'm your dad. I'm so happy your here. I've waited to meet you for nine months. I promise to be a good dad to you the way your grandfather was to me. You're opening your eyes to see me? Huh?" He admires him a few more minutes and rocks him."

"Michelle, Can you sign those papers for me? You were ready to deliver and you couldn't do it then." I sign the papers for billing and care for our son. He puts him back in my arms and kisses me on the cheek.

"I have to go back to work, I'll be back tonight. I'll take those forms out for you. You did a wonderful job."

INSANITY AT ITS FINEST!

Patricia

INSANITY LET LOOSE

"Where is my daughter, Shayla?" I'm lying on top of her naked and the gun is pointed to her face.

"I don't know?" she yells. I push the gun to her forehead and I sit there gyrate on her chest.

"I think you know better than to raise your voice at me. You snitch on me to the Police along with your cousin. I befriended you, help you burn some of the blubber off and you betray me. You're going to tell me or I'll find one of children and set them on fire. Of course after I kill you. I really don't want to shed no real blood on you and your children. These bullets are for a specific person.

"Where my child?" Shayla has to think of her children she knows what Patricia is capable of. She swallows the salty taste of vomit down and yells,

"The hospital she just had a baby boy this afternoon. She's at Women's and Children's." I smack her face and say,

"Good girl, Shayla. See you just saved your children's life. She had my grandson two days before my birthday. How sweet?"

I look at Shayla and I pull the trigger and lodge a bullet through her brains. I never respected a snitch. Her blood splatter all over me. Damn, I think just when her life was coming together I snub her out. I turn on the shower water and let it register that I am a grandmother. I step out and dry off. Her house is clean and the towels freshly washed. I look over at the blood spilling from her temple. She would interrupt my plans if I had let her live. I wanted to stop Bishop from taking my child away from me. He'd take her and now that she had his child she'd run off with him. I won't allow it. The only way to stop him is to take their baby. I look over at Shayla and I close her eyes. I have a plan. I pick up her phone and call her ex-husband.

INSANITY AT ITS FINEST!

"Hi, how are you today and the children? I hope all is well and life is treating you kindly."

"I'm well. Who are you?"

"I just shot your ex-wife in the head you'll find her dead body at her home. You can thank me now."

I hang up the phone. I close her door and run down the stairs. I get in my car and drive off. I put on a brown curly wig. I pop in my hazel contacts and put on freshly bought hospital scrubs. I look just like the woman who had been in my class. I studied her and she made that mistake of leaving her badge. I attached it to my shirt. I walk in the hospital and hope this badge still works. I walk to the elevator and I swipe it through. I greet the security guard and he greets me back. I take the elevator to the third floor where the nursery and patient's rooms are.

The nurse said, "You must be the temporary Nurse from ECMC."

I answer, "Yes, I am how you are tonight?"

"I'm overwhelmed and overworked three of the nurses called in sick and none of the floaters were available. Thank God you came." I smile at her.

"You're welcome. Actually this is just extra cash planning a vacation to the Bahamas."

She hands me a cart and tells me the rooms I have. I have Michelle's. There I go into her room first and she is asleep. I leave the cart and grab the sleeping baby. Out the back door, I remove the alarm by zapping his ankle bracelet. I go down the back stairs and into the parking lot. I sit him in my lap and for the first time look at his face and he looks like his Daddy.

This is perfect this will bring Bishop to me, he'll want to save his son. I pull off and know that the news will be flooded with the search of a missing baby of the daughter whose mother is a serial killer. I stop at Walgreen's and purchase formula, diapers, wipes, clothes and a few blankets.

I drive right next down the street to Hotel Lenox and pull the car seat out. I go to my room and I examine my grandson. He had all of his fingers and toes. My grandson is a handsome boy. I kiss his forehead and check his diaper. I change him and put on the fresh sleeper I bought him. I cuddle him in my arms and hold him tight

INSANITY AT ITS FINEST!

and realize this little boy is a part of me. I lay him down on the bed. I wash his bottles and add the formula in them.

I turn on the news and just like I thought the news of the baby being missing has spread like wildfire. The news reporter said,

"The daughter of Fat Girl Vigilante's newborn son has been kidnapped from Health and healing hospital. The authorities are in an uproar over how the woman got in and identification was not verified. The mother is distraught and it is speculated that it may be her mother who kidnap her son and shot the nurse. The fat girl vigilante suspect Patricia Sargent has been on the run for ten months and has been suspected of killing Markel King Community activist and real estate tycoon, as well as Officer William aka Big Willie Johnson. She is also suspected in over seven other murders, which has occurred in the Buffalo area. The Police is asking that if you know of anything or has seen her please call the authorities. Do not I mean do not approach the suspect she is armed and dangerous

I have their attention and now let the games begin.
I dial Bishop's number and he answers,
"Hi Bishop! How are you on this fine evening? Myself well I'm doing just dandy. "I laugh.
"I want my fucking son. I swear if anything happens I will murder your ass."
"Now, now Bishop my grandson is fine and you don't make the rules to this game. I do. You want your son come get him." I hang up the phone.
Right now half of Buffalo Police Department will be on my ass and it is just the way I want it. It's about to be a hoe down in the Queen City. This is where I end the saga and reign as the beast who paralyzed a city. I learned a lot while away and realize that my daughter killed Markel King. She was just like me but hidden behind walls of Ms. Do Good. She had the heart to kill and by me taking her son she will attempt to do me in. It was in her nature. She inherited venom in her blood and once she had her first taste of killing she can never stop. Now I have to kill her, her man and my own grandson. I snuggle him close to my chest, he has soft curls. He is light skin God did something right by not letting him being cursed with dark skin.

INSANITY AT ITS FINEST!

The worst case scenario they take me down. I die like a warrior. The sound of his cries startles me I pick him up and his eyes are open. I warm the bottle and feed him, burp him and change him. I cuddle him and I look for our facial features. His eyes a sky blue. Bishop genes dominate of ours.

I dress him in a blue layette, and cover his small head with a hat. I rub my hands through his silky hair and his hand grabs my finger and his eyes are piercing through me. My goodness I love him already. His scent of Johnson baby lotion rubbed into his skin. I secure him in his car seat that has enough explosives to kill a block of people.

My cell rings and its Michelle. I let it ring four times and then answer, "Hello snickerdoodle! Good to hear from you I've missed you."

"Mama, bring me my son back. He has nothing to do with this? Don't hurt him, please. You hate me fine don't do anything" She's sobbing.

"Why would I hurt him? He apart of me and besides Michelle I want to kill all three of you together. You know how I do. I love a show," She yells,

"You psychotic Bitch! I have done nothing to you. Give me my baby back; please Mama I'll do whatever you want. Please just give me back my son!' I chuckle at her pleads.

"That the second time you've said that to me in a few months, 'doing whatever I want you to do.' Well, you want your son alive and well. You want me to save his life okay. I want you and your baby daddy to meet me downtown in front of M&T Bank at exactly four o'clock. I want the media there and I want the Mayor and wait Pastor Cosell of TRUE Holy BAPTIST CHURCH." I hang up and don't want to hear her damn crying. I begin to sing,

"Hush little baby don't you cry nana going to kill her another officer. Set him on fire and watch him burn. Sorry baby boy got to be your dad."

INSANITY AT ITS FINEST!

Bishop

CATCH A CRAZY BITCH!

The charge nurse on duty, the hospital director and staff of labor and delivery sits at the table. My chief, his boss, F.B.I, Missing and Exploited Children. I walk around them and he asks, "Why the fuck is my son missing?" The nurse face is red and full of tears, she pulling the tissue apart in pieces and begins mumbling,
"I'm... I'm.... sorry. I thought she was a temp coming over to help. We were short staff and I just worked a double shift she look like the picture on her Id." I throw my fingers up to stop her from speaking.
"Did you identify her? Did you even think to look at her badge?" She looks at the frown faces and the other officers around the room.
"No. I just assume because and I did she look like her. I am..." I slam my fist on the table and scream,
"You fucking jeopardize every woman and child in this hospital on an assumption. How fucking careless of you to not follow hospital procedure. If anything happens to my child I'll see to it you are in prison for life. Where you working with her? Huh? You was working with her wasn't you?" I scream.
"I never saw her in my life. Sir, I'm sorry! I'm so sorry! I'm so sorry." I hear the captain call me,
"Bishop, let's go! We'll handle this!" I storm out and slam the door.
"You got to get hold of yourself, Bishop? As of right now you're on leave and you're off this case."
"This isn't about this case it's about my son being in the care of maniac who may do Gods know what to him. This is personal, Captain. You can't take me away from being a father and saving my son's life" I walk away and he runs behind me.
"Don't do something you'll regret later. We have every man on this, Bishop. Don't lose your badge and honor over this, you're in deep, son." I put my hand on my hip and stare at him. The redness of crying and lack of sleep is evident.

INSANITY AT ITS FINEST!

"I don't want nothing to happen to my son. If it was your child would you let it ride or would you give this badge up to save your son's life. It's more to life for me than being a cop." I wait for his answer.

"I thought so!" I walk to Michelle's room and she is fully dressed. "What are you doing?" Her green eyes cold and red.

"My mother wants us to meet her at M& T Bank on Church Avenue. I'm going to get my baby. Bishop you can write it down and record it because if she does anything to my son. I will kill her, and that is a promise. I don't give a fuck who hears me. She has ruin my life for the last time." Michelle gets up and the nurse hands her the release forms she pushes them aside.

"Fuck your papers, you guys couldn't protect my son. Now you want to follow procedure and policies!" I follow her.

"What time does she want us to meet her?"

"Three o'clock. She wants the press and everyone there. I want her gone Bishop!" She lays her head on my shoulder and cries. The tears burn as they roll down my face. I hold her tight and the loud sobs cut through my throat. The salt and vinegar taste in my mouth surfaces. In between sobs,

"I promise you Michelle I will risk my life for our son. I will die for him and we will get our son back."

The press is line up outside of the hospital as we leave. The whole media world is watching for the main event, the clock said 2:05pm. The reporters have their microphones in our faces.

"Ms. Sargent how do you feel now that your mother has kidnapped your son?" Michelle stopped dead in her tracks and she points her finger in the reporter.

"How would you feel if your one day old son was kidnapped? How dare you ask such and insensitive question?" I help her get into Hernandez car. I get in the back seat.

Another reporter asked,

"Will you sue the hospital for their negligence?" The very thought had me overwhelmed. Hernandez starts briefing Bishop on the Hostage retrieval plan

INSANITY AT ITS FINEST!

Tamyara Brown

"We've called SWAT, Emergency services, three ambulances and SWAT (STAR) team will be put into place will be covered; an entry team prepared to rush the facility. All traffic; metro rail service and bus service to the downtown area has been suspended. We've cancel greyhound, railways bus service in and out of Buffalo. The whole depot is covered with Police. The SWAT team will be equipped with state of the art listening devices, various kinds of visual scopes, body shields and patience. Michelle I know this is difficult to ask but I need you to remain calm. Bishop, this isn't the time to lose your head. This is your son involved and believes me I'm with you when I say this crazy bitch has cross the line. I'm concern about the baby safety.

I put on my bulletproof vest and load my both of my guns I say nothing and Michelle is still crying. The scene seems so surreal and if anyone told me this shit was happening to them I tell them that they are lying. The radio dispatches in a woman has sat a new born baby car seat which looks like explosives around it. She is naked. She has a gun pointed to the infant's head.

We pull up on Church Street and the whole area is block off in a ten-block radius. The hostage negotiator meets us and he explains he will try and bargain with her first.

No transportation can get in or out of the area. People are asked to stay where they are in the building, the downtown area is on lockdown. The officers tell people to go inside the mall and are locked in

I walk on the side and when I look up there are two sharp shooters on the top of the bank and the mall. Pastor Croswell's is surrounded by police and his personal security team and does not look scare. He walks up to Michelle and I he greets us.

"Detective Bishop and Michelle. I want to first say that I'll do whatever in my will to help diffuse the situation. I would like to pray with you. I know this is an intense time and overwhelm but prayer changes everything even in this situation." He reaches for our hand and he begins his prayer. We say Amen.

INSANITY AT ITS FINEST!

Patricia

LET THE SHOW BEGIN!

The news cameras are surrounding me, people wondering if I will kill an infant in broad daylight. The world is watching me and it's my time to put on the greatest show on earth. The hostage negotiator calls my name.

"Patricia, My name is Lamont Johnston and I am a here to help you. I don't want this to end ugly, okay. I know you're in a lot of trouble but right now what is that you want Patricia?" I keep the gun pointed to the baby's head.

"I want justice." Lamont shakes his head and inhales.

"Justice for what?'

"Everything Lamont people have taken away from me. Can you give me back virginity that was taken away from me by the Pastor and Deacon of New Deaconess church? Can you wake my father from the dead and tell him I wasn't lying? Huh? Can you tell me why my own flesh and blood would lead me to the back of a shed with my best friend and allow them to brutally molest us on my birthday? That how they said Happy Birthday to me, No cakes, no gifts or a party. "The tears drop and the baby stirs. Lamont looks at me standing on the Church Street platform.

"I can't answer that! I'll be honest with you, Patricia. What I do know is your endangering a baby for something other individuals have done to you. Is that fair?" I scream and push the gun toward the baby mouth he makes sucking motions towards it.

"Don't ask me a stupid fucking question about fair. Life is unfair, people on this earth is unfair. Don't you dare fucking ask me about fair? Let me talk to Pastor Croswell, Now. I look over at the short, small frame man with a bald head. The lion head ring on his pinky finger, cross around his neck.

"Step back or I'll blow off your dick?" He backs away and clears his throat. He has on his collar today and jeans.

"Talk to me Patricia. I'm listening."

INSANITY AT ITS FINEST!

"Why do you believe in God?" I ask. He looks at me and with ease answers,

"God is love! He gave his only begotten son so we could live on this earth." I applaud him and he tries to reach for the baby.

"That car seat has enough explosive to kill a hundred people. Don't be dumb Pastor, please. Don't be a motherfucking hero and have your new bride become a widow."

He said, "I'm sorry those men took your innocence. God does love you, he loves all his children even when you have sinned."

"God love is death, destruction of innocent children. Every minute a child is molested, teased, bullied and you preach about your damn God. You live on the Canal side in a fucking condo. You drive a Mercedes Benz and have never suffered a day in your life. You hung out with the good Pastor and Deacon didn't you?

He walks away and I can tell that for a moment I hit a nerve. The negotiator again calls my name.

"Patricia, you're angry and what happen to you is wrong and you made them pay by taking their lives. We messed up and we let them get away with this for years and as an officer of the Buffalo Police Department. On our behalf we apologize. Now just work with us, please. He's your grandson. Please hand him to the mother."

"I can't because if I do that bastard will take her away from me."

"Patricia you're making this harder on yourself. Look up Patricia those sharp shooters are ready to take you out. Those officers over there are angry because you kill a fellow officer and friend." I laugh at him and put the gun closer to the baby.

"None of you motherfuckers scare me. If they kill me I kill my grandson. In the end I'll be dead and so will he. Don't try scare tactics they've never worked, Okay Officer Lamont. I don't have nothing do you hear me? Nothing to live for anymore. My daughter hates me, my sister set me up to be molested and my parents died hating my guts. Men of God raped me over and over again. Hate is a part of me, Lamont!"

I look over and I see Bishop strip off his bulletproof vest. I see him hand his gun over to another officer. He begins to walk over but the officer holds him back. I hear him say,

"Stop playing games with her. I want my son away from this bitch unharmed. Don't tell me to calm down. I will die for my son." They grab him and put him in the back of the Emergency Service van.
Michelle then walks over to me, her hair wild and all over the place. She walks slowly but stand feet apart from me.
Our green eyes lock and for the first time I confirm that she murder Markel.
"Mama please give me back my son. I'm if you're going to kill me do it now. I'm not leaving this area until my baby is safe." She moves two steps closer.
"You want to kill me because I took your daddy and killed Markel. I fucked him and then I set him on fire. I kill everything you love just like I am going to kill your baby."
Michelle tears stream down.
"Please don't kill my baby. I'm begging you don't take him away from me."
"Chile, you look just like Deacon. He took everything out of me. I was a good girl.
Hernandez and Bishop Walks towards her. Bishop looks at Michelle and she extends her arms out to him. She holds her head down and cries some more. He takes her into his arms he holds her tight. Hernandez escorts her off.
"Patricia, it's hot, the baby hasn't eaten. What is it that you want?" She looks over at Michelle and Bishop.
"I killed Markel King and every person you found dead. She knows of every crime I did but she never helped me do any of them. You free her and I won't kill her son. I killed Michael Sargent her brother right in front of her eyes. I killed Camilla Wright in Rochester, NY. I massacred the deacon and the Pastor. I killed Big Willie, I also killed Goldie's daughter right at her hotel. I was the one who cut off her breasts and burned her alive. I killed the old man and also if you dumb ass cops check and see you'll find Shayla dead too just a day ago. If I must so say so I did a damn good thing for your community. She did what I told her to do or I would have killed her too. There your statements because the news is recording. I'll turn myself in and this whole ordeal is over. Buffalo will get airplay. You'll look like a hero and thus and far I'll be off the streets of the Queen City. My daughter you get her the help she deserves.
INSANITY AT ITS FINEST!

Tamyara Brown

INSANITY AT ITS FINEST!

Bishop
Faith over Fear

The captain has commanded for them to take a shot. The sniper on the top of the Main Street mall is anxious to shoot. He has an infant at home and the feeling and thought of what if fuel him even more to kill her. The sharp shooter has an infra-red dot on her head. My emotion is on high and I keep thinking she hasn't changed his diaper, he's been the hot son and she hasn't fed and I hear his cries. The thought of the fact he is hungry and unsafe in the hands of psychotic bitch.

Here I am his father and I'm stuck in this truck because of the thought of losing my badge and my captain saying I may insight a massacre. The little girl I shot in L.A., I tried to save her, resuscitate life into her lifeless soul. I remember her blood drenching my clothes and bulletproof vest and cradling her in my arms carrying her out. It could happen to my son, karma paying me back for taking her life. Miyama said my son soul was that of that little girl. Her name was Monica Simons she died at five years old, a baby living around sin and drugs. The house was being raided, guns drawn and Canine and his crew blasting from the 4trey5 gang. He had something over his shoulder. I should've yell drop it but my mind flutter with the thought of taking him down for the count. He ran out from behind the wall and the battle was his or my life. I had my finger on the trigger and he shot three times the bullet grazing my cheek. I return fire and with two shots I killed Canine and Monica. He dropped to the floor and there laid a beautiful innocent little girl. The little girl I killed.

That could happen to my son I keep thinking. One wrong shot and his life taken within a second I can't live with the fact of another child dying in my arms because of me. Patricia takes his little body to block a shot. I radio in, "Hold your fire. Hold your fire!"

The sharp shooter yells, "You're not my superior your captain is. Your fucking baby is out there."

The captain climbs in the back of the van," You don't shout orders Bishop."

INSANITY AT ITS FINEST!

"Look she is not stupid, she's outwitted every one of us! You think she won't use my child as a human shield. Huh? Let me go out there and get my son. I'm willing to die for him but I won't have him taken away from me by a plan she has already formulated in her mind."
The captain rubs his hand over his face and sighs heavily and radios to the sniper not to fire
"Bishop, do you understand that you are putting your life on the line? I just hope this doesn't blow up in our face." I look at Michelle and my partner Hernandez.
"This job is full of risks and right now my son is worth the risk of my life." I hug Michelle and whisper in her ear,
"I promise to save his life even if mine is lost. If I die Michelle I want you to know that I do love you." I walk out the door and I hear Michelle say,
"I love you too!"
I walk slowly out the back of the truck and remember the quote my Nana said to me before I went on the beat," No weapon formed against me shall prosper." I am with only those words as my protection.
No gun, no bullet proof vest, no badge around my neck. My heart is pounding so loud. The reporters are chatting away; the cameras focused on me. The brotherhood and bond Hernandez share he is behind me with his vest on and gun drawn to shoot once the singled is given.

"We're partners and Amigo we're going to save your son." Michelle walks behind me.
"Bishop, I want to be with you. This is our son, please." It seems I step out of my body and I am watching my every move. I walk towards Patricia and I stand approximately two feet away from her. I see nothing that is surrounding me. I want my son. I speak,
"I'm going to tell you what I'm about to do. Listen carefully to me. I'm taking my son from you and handing him to his mother. Whatever after I take my son is on you?" She picks up my son and kisses his forehead; she takes the gun and put it towards his mouth.

INSANITY AT ITS FINEST!

"Bishop, you tried to take my daughter away from me, made her tell you of my crimes, you know she is naive, weak and powerless. So you courted her, gave her some good sex and made her feel beautiful. Threw around I love you words a few times. You figure out she craved love. She lacks that from me. I am going to kill you if you come closer." I walk closer her threat not acknowledge.

"Do it, Bitch! I know your game too. You put fear in people and I'm not scare of you. Go ahead and do it Bitch. Come on shoot me." I take a step toward her and the rest of the SWAT crew has their guns drawn. I walk in front of her she's perspiring and the gun still pointed towards my son. I stare at her and extend my arms. She screams,

"Move Bishop I'll kill him right here." I lick my lips, my heart though pumping Kool Aid and sugar though I show no fear; I speak no fear because I will not lose my son's life. She searches my face for fear, looked inside my soul and it was hidden behind something she couldn't see through.

"You can't kill your own grandson, you love him already. Hmm, hmm you see all those other lives you took you had hate for them. You would have killed him by now. I know your pattern. My baby you can't hate he's done nothing to you. That's why you haven't killed Michelle, you love her." Her mouth gapes open, another tear falls from her eye and her pattern broken with truth. She looks at him and my son smiles. She removes the gun and I take him from her. I cradle him in my arms and kiss him on his forehead. I turn from Patricia my heart beating out of my chest. My son tucked in my arms.

I say out loud, "No weapon formed against me shall prosper." I walk five steps and the when I turn around Michelle is behind her mother, her look wild and bewildered. Michelle has the gun pointed to her mother's head, I hear the Hernandez yell, "Michelle, Your baby's safe don't do this. Don't kill her, please."

Her hand is trembling, her lips quiver and she screams,

"Michelle can't kill you but I can, Bitch. You try to hurt my son and now I am about to put every bullet in your skull. "

Patricia has the gun pointed to her chin and Michelle has the gun to her mother's head. The officers' rush to grab Michelle and tackle her to the floor, Michelle's strength allows her to break away she points

INSANITY AT ITS FINEST!

to the gun to her mother fire off a shot but misses. I'm can't believe what transpiring before my eyes I yell,

"Michelle, don't do this. Put the gun down. Our son is safe. Come on baby it's over, please trust me" With all the confusion no one is paying attention to Patricia. She sits while all of this unfolds, not moving or trying to break free. The officers avert their attention back to Patricia. They restrained Michelle. She is kicking and screaming. The officers go for Patricia and she begins to sing, "Happy Birthday to me. Happy Birthday to me. Take a bullet to my brain and still beat the Police."

Immediately after the song ends, the sound of the gun goes off and Patricia has taken her own life. The Police are five seconds too late as blood splatters all over Michelle and the officers. Patricia's nose lands in front of my feet; she slumps to the floor. Patricia ends her own reign of terror on the Queen City.

The reporters who normally can handle anything gasped and a camera man at the actual death of the FAT Girl Vigilante. Her blood paints the tracks. The people staring are in shock, some scream and cry out. Pastor Croswell falls to his knees and begins to pray. I hold my son close and kiss him. I protect him from what has just been the craziest ending. It was her plan all along. To end her life the way she had ended so many others on her birthday.

Michelle screams and cries. I kiss my son over and over again. My tears are drenching his face. He soaking wet, I sit in the back of the ambulance and change him. They transport him to Sisters Hospital. I feed him and kiss him. His eyes wide open and clueless to today's events the EMT takes his vitals and mine.

He says, "What you did today was the bravest shit I ever seen in my life."

"He's my son." I put him on my shoulder and burp him as if I have been doing this all my life. He inserts a needle in his tiny hand to help hydrate him since he's been in the hot sun for hours. My mind flashes back to Patricia taking a Bullet to her face and blowing it to pieces. I think of Michelle who witness another parent dead. My cell rings,

INSANITY AT ITS FINEST!

"Is the little and big guy good?" Hernandez accent thick.

"Yes, he's fine they gave him some fluids to hydrate him. I'm good! What about Michelle?" Hernandez takes a sigh and he said,

"They admitted her to ECMC for Psychiatric evaluation. Captain said she is on suicide watch. She wants to see the baby. She keeps saying she isn't Michelle she's Sarge."

"Sarge?"

"Yeah man, Michelle seeing that shit has taken her over the edge. Bishop, I've seen a lot of horrific shit in my life but I don't think I'll ever sing Happy Birthday in English or Spanish again. The media is hailing you a hero. You're all over the news even on Telemundo. That my man was some brave shit to walk up to her and take your son out her arms and then turn your back."

"My father would have done the same exact same thing for me."

"Speaking of your father he and your mother are flying in. They should be in tonight. You got calls from Good Morning America, Nancy Grace, and Oprah. Amigo, you are about to be famous."

"I'm going to decline those interviews. They build you up and then shoot you down. I'm about my son and Michelle." Look let me check on her. I call you later."

"Okay, Amigo! If you need me call me."

I needed to see Michelle, hug her and let her know the baby was okay. "I walk upstairs and the administrative assistant recognizes me. "I found what you did today to be so brave and beautiful. You give me faith that there is good black fathers around." I smile and say, "Thank you and I appreciate that. I'm here to see Michelle Sargent." The nurse has sadness in her eyes.

"They have restrained her and hit with some Ativan to calm her down. She's asking to see the baby. Is he alright if you don't mind me asking?"

"He's doing well?" She buzzes me in and directs me to the room. I knock on the door, Michelle is tied to the bed and she turns her head to me.

"Bishop, why did she do that to me again? Is BJ okay? I want to see him please." I kiss her and hug her.

INSANITY AT ITS FINEST!

"I don't know, Honey! He's fine and after he finishes his IV I promise to bring him to you. I know this is hard for you everything you have been through but who's Sarge?" She looks at me and shakes her head and her words are slurring

"I don't know. I just want to hold my baby, please. I can't even breast feed they gave me all these medicines." She closes her eyes.

"I'm sorry baby. I am! I love you Michelle." I look at the door and I see Richard looking in. I watch her sleep.

I close the door and there Richard and I meet again. He holds on to the mop.

"I respect what you did out there for your son. Little man is okay, right? Michelle too?" I lean against the wall and look at him.

"My son is good. Michelle I'm worry about. Did they actually show on TV Patricia shooting herself in the face?" He lets the mop lean against the wall and greets the pretty nurse walking by.

"Yeah, Real talk it was some gruesome shit. It happened so fast and to top it off that she sung Happy Birthday to herself and then Boom. Her face pieces flying all over the place"

"I need you to answer a question Richard? He raises his eyebrows and look at me."

"Okay!" he leans against the wall with me.

"Who's Sarge? Richard's eyes widen.

"I don't know." He speaks softly.

"This is not the time to stay Mum. Who is Sarge? We need to help her" He looks in on her and she still sleeps. He scratches his head and looks at me.

"It is her sister."

"Michelle has a sister."

"Richard, the truth I need to help her. Stop bullshitting me, please."

"Black Ice tried to rape her. I don't know what happen she changed."

"Did she kill Black Ice?"

He slings the mop across the floor and slides to the floor.

"She don't need to be in jail. She needs help. She picked up the machete cut off his head and dick. She needs help all the shit her

Mama put her through, me, life and you. She doesn't need to go to jail."

"I know."

He walks away and I touch the back of my pocket. I pulled the pink journal I took from Michelle's room. I open it and then close it. I don't want to know the truth but I have to know. I squeeze the book in my hand and I pull it open. I read several pages and the answer to the question.

November 15, 2008

Last night Sarge killed Markel. I don't know why she keeps making me do bad things.

I close the book and lower my head. A tear drops because I am plagued with arresting the woman I love. I took the stairs and went into my son's room. I pick him up and realize that he would never see his mommy. I get him dressed the hospital said he could go home. I would have to break that promise to Michelle tonight. I needed to take my son home and meet my parents. I needed to figure out how I could her; they're no easy solution and answer to this. The hospital clerk gives me a brand new car seat. I put him in it.

I needed to sleep and I thought with Patricia being gone the story had ended. It has just begun.

Michelle

A Month later

Being in this hospital I have had time to think. I wish so many people could take a break from life for just a small moment. I wish people could have the opportunity to reboot and figure out what the hell has gone wrong and the most important how to fix it. Yet, in this world they won't allow that to happen everyone is in a rush to fix lifelong problems in a day. When in reality it may take years to get back to normal if that the place you are seeking.

I have held my son in my arms and that is my normal that I need to get to, being a good mother. I talk to the psychologists who analyzes me and they have come with the fact that I am dealing with PTSD. Their definition of what's going on inside, because wanting to be loved is never a disability. It's what God has put on this earth for us to have. I have been exercising because I don't want to be

INSANITY AT ITS FINEST!

overweight again, that is my fear. I'm not trying to be neither Tyra Banks nor Beyoncé Knowles; I'm just trying to be me.

Being overweight is the one thing I do thank my mother for instilling in me to eat and live healthy. I wish that while she was injecting the truth in me she had told me she could love me at any weight. I'm still losing weight but this time I know it's the one stigma I never want to carry. I hated myself more when I was that size I was and wish I could of love myself no matter what size I was. I hope to get out of here and teach women to love themselves at any size. To be fit and still look good it is my goal.

What I learn is being a certain weight will not determine whether or not you have a good husband. Any one at any size can have their heartbroken. But when it comes to real genuine love his eyes have no view of your weight because a good man will look in your heart and not your outer frame.

Who am I? Is the question that is lurking in my mind? Society takes pictures of who we are as a woman and if you give something enough exposure and put it in a person's mind this is beauty, this is how a family looks, this is what perfection is. You too will do anything to achieve that notion. A picture of what someone else feels and thinks you should be.

My mother was a drummer who March to her own beat and she created a beat for what my life should sound like and look like while playing the drums. She took lives because in her mind two men who had issues took away her innocence and her daddy., My auntie who was jealous turned against her own flesh and blood all because she wanted her daddy to herself. Parents who couldn't look beyond the fact that that two people who were dignitaries could never use their power to sexually assault children because maybe just maybe her father would feel inadequate as a man.

Every little girl and boy needs a daddy. I needed mine and my mother needed hers. Men who procreate with women and choose not be a father has a lot of boys and girls who have missing chapters to their story. They have women like me craving for that daddy love from the wrong people and individuals.

Our daddies or whoever takes that role is the first man we fall in love with. If that opportunity is taken away. The image is presented in the wrong light we will choose the man who emotionally beats and abuses us. If we watch our mother trying to convince a man to love us we will emulate that lifestyle with our own men. I did it! Or the other reaction is some will build a brick wall so tall that any man out who is trying to love with the fear one day she will wake up without him there.

A few people can change the way a person's life is. I ask myself would my mother have killed all of those people if my grandfather believe her and got the required help she needed. The answer is not clear because she decided to end her life right in front of me. Daughters need to hear from their Mommies she is beautiful and loved. That though she is flawed she is her fabulous daughter and she loves her no matter what.

"What's good my G?" His thick voice startled me, thick afro, full beard, flannel shirt, and converses. He picks his hair and slouches in the chair.

"Do I know you?"

"No, but you will. Your mother killed my daughter. What I should be doing is shoving this magnum in your pussy and blowing a hole in it but I feel for you."

I begin to scream and he runs behind me and covers my mouth.

"Shut up and listen to me."

She removes her hand and I bite my lip.

"I believe in life for a life. I birth my baby out my pussy."

I scratch my head, look her up and down. She has muscles, a full beard, her legs wide open and her hand grabbing her crotch.

"But you're a man. I'm confused." I stutter.

"Now I am but twenty-five years ago I was a woman. Your mother and I hooked up. She didn't know at first but once she found out."

"So if you're not going to kill me what do you want from me?"

He rubs his beard, spread his legs open and licks his lips.

"Look my G, in a minute they about to throw you under the jail. You won't see your baby. I can help you become free."

"Bishop wouldn't never let that happen."

"You are not that dumb to believe because he dicked you down, made a baby and all that good phony shit he not gone put the silver
INSANITY AT ITS FINEST!

bracelets on you. Come on now you are smarter than the average boo boo the fool."

"He loves me too much."

She pretends to play the violin and picks her hair."

"I will know when shit hits the fan, I will rescue you and train you to gut a nigger for his kidneys, eyes, heart, pancreas, lungs and hands, feet whatever the black market wants I get."

"I'm not a killer."

"My G, you are a killer we all are. Some are just afraid to act on it. If you step on a bug, spider or a roach you have the instinct to kill. You murdered and decapitated a dude than killed your ex-boyfriend. Let's not play innocent. "

"What do you want from me?"

"I'm in the business of illegal organ harvesting. I get paid a 100,000 for a kidney, 250,000 for a heart, and 180,000 for a pancreas. You want to get into this business because as long as Cancer, diabetes, renal failure and heart disease is around we will get paid."

"I don't want to."

"Pretty Mama you don't have a choice and you are damn fine. Your man is going to lock you up because he has a job to do. Old boy Richard snitched you out. Look, I'm out but think about my offer."

She stands, picks her hair and walks towards the door.

They haven't arrested me yet for killing Markel and Black Ice maybe they will keep me in this mental health facility for years until I am fixed and repair enough to deal with the outside world. Richard told on me I thought he loved me. I've talked to the media and told of my horrific events hoping this will keep me free of a prison term. I told them the truth and the world feels quite sadden for me and even my mother.

Bishop will be coming with BJ today and my god he looks just like him. He is beautiful in more ways than I can imagine. I've met Bishop Parents who are like the most perfect and normal family structure I've ever seen. I envy that it's what I desired that relationship Bishop shares with his parents. He has been a saint in allowing me to spend as much time with him. He talks to me and sometimes we play cards. I don't think he loves me like he uses to.

INSANITY AT ITS FINEST!

Or maybe being a full -time father even with his mom and dad helping burns him out.

He takes his role as a father serious, he told me he was going to therapy because he realized he too had been dealing with issues. I believe I am one of them. I looked out the window and the sun is bright, I let it shine on my face. I've been cooped up and until just recently they took me out of restraints. I wanted to hold my son and when I see him he is the constant reminder of what love is and how beautiful it can be.

The nurse aide walks in and check on me, "Michelle if you're hungry they have lunch ready." I nod my head and answer,

"No, thank you I'm not hungry." She closes the door and I lay down and I realize I have no living relatives. That the only person I have in my life is my son. I look at his picture and I kiss it.

Mrs. Randall knocks and then walks in. She has been coming on a regular of three times a week. She asks me the same question over and over again, "how am I dealing with the death of my mother." My answer to her is, "Day by Day." She wants me to cry hard and have the sniffles over a woman whom emotionally and physically beat me. The woman who killed my father and took her own life in front of me has left me with nothing but my son. How the hell do I feel now that she is gone? I want to tell her I'm elated and filled with joy she will no longer torture me or the Buffalo area. I want to get away from Buffalo, NY and never come back. Erase my pass and create a better future for my son and myself.

She snaps her fingers and calls my name.

"Michelle, are you okay?'

"Yes just in thought. I no longer have to chase love anymore Mrs. Randall from my mother or some guy."

"BJ he loves me and when I hold him close to my chest he is so content."

"What about yourself? Are you loving yourself?" I walk back to the window and look out of it, look at my son's pictures.

"I am learning first to handle situations, look at life through my eyes and no one else. Self-love for me is trying to form my own opinions, my own likes and dislikes. I don't love the things I did. I don't admire the fact in some sense what my mother said is true. So I'm taking baby steps in my life." She scribbles down what I said.

INSANITY AT ITS FINEST!

"Did you kill Black Ice and Markel?"

"Yes. I don't want to live the lie anymore." She writes some more.

"Are you afraid that they will send you to jail? I mean you admitted to murdering two men?" I look at her and realize she knows something more than she is telling me.

"Are they pressing charges on me for their murders? Taking me away from my son?"

"I don't know Michelle. It was just a general question." She is trying to calm me down and for the moment I do.

"I don't want to miss raising my son or living without every day. That would...." "She sits up and ask,

"What would it do?"

"Nothing. Nothing at all but makes me love my son harder. My life has been full of disruptions and mishaps. My life is an open hellhole. I'm cursed and you know it too. It's not your job Mrs. Randall to say I have the worst luck in the world. Or that my mother, my father and I have crap out in this life." I snicker because the look on her face tells me that I have spoken the truth, what I was saying she was thinking.

"I don't think that way of you or your family." She rolls her eyes because I have frustrated her by digging into her thoughts. She dislikes that about me because I ask her questioned about her life, her family and her make-up.

"So let's talk about, Sarge?" I mumble under my breath calling her out her name.

"I don't want to talk about her?" I turn my back towards her and she digs deeper into the subject.

"Does she still talk to you? Does she make you think thoughts of hurting people maybe, maybe Bishop? He did betray you and hurt you?"

"I said Mrs. Randall I don't want to talk about her. Please leave now." I see the nurse aide who's looking and she can hear everything, which works to my advantage. She doesn't leave and begins taunting me.

"Michelle or wait is it Sarge I'm dealing with?'

INSANITY AT ITS FINEST!

"Please Mrs. Randall get the fuck out of my room now. I'm pleading with you to leave." The charge nurse and the psychologist comes in."
"Mrs. Randall what the hell are you doing? When the patient ask you to leave. You meet me in my office."
"She attacked me." The nurse aide chimed in and said,
"Oh no she didn't. She kept asking her about Sarge and Michelle said politely she didn't want to talk about her. Then Mrs. Randall kept asking her about that lady and she never attack her. I was standing there the whole time to give her meds."
Mrs. Randall storms out and doesn't look back. What was it she wanted from me? I look and the Bishop is standing at the door. His badge hanging around his neck and Hernandez beside him. I knew what was happening. I was being arrested for the murder of Markel King and Black Ice.
"Michelle can we talk?" I continue looking out the window and fold my arms. He was coming to tell me I would no longer see my son. Goldie, was right he would betray me again. I knew this day was coming sooner or later. My son face flashes before me and all I can think is he will grow up without his mother. My chances of real love are gone.
"Talk Bishop." He stands close to me and wipes my tears. He kisses them as they roll down my face and I know this is his way of saying that I'm going to prison.
"This is the hardest arrest I have ever had to do. I love you and please believe me when I say I fought for your freedom. Told them everything I knew about what your mother did but the fact remains you committed two murders. "
The tears fall harder because while I was in here they were preparing me to be away from my child. They did this for a month, had Nancy Grace, every media venue and me talking to Good Morning AMERICA. The cameras are fading, the media hype is gone and now I am going to jail.
"Bishop, please don't take me away from our son. I'm his mother please, please don't do this to me. He is all I have, I have no one but him." Bishop wipes his eyes and when I look over at Hernandez and the two other officers are trying to hold back the tears.
Bishop clears his throat and he kisses both of my hands. I extend my arms and my fate is I won't raise my son. I drop my head because I
INSANITY AT ITS FINEST!

would rather my mother had killed me then to deal with betrayal and lost all over again. He handcuffs me and he begins to read me my rights.

"You ... have the right to remain silent.... Anything you say or do.... Will be use against you in the court of law. You have a right to an attorney and if. And if...you can't afford one. Fuck me! One will be appointed to you." Hernandez takes me out of the room. I see Bishop break down and fall to his knees.

I walk with my head in shame, what I see are so many people feeling sorry for me. So many people crying for me but no one here helping me to stay of jail. I see Bishop's mother holding BJ, Bishop takes him from her arms and he walks over towards me. I kiss him and my tears wet his face.

"Mommy loves you B.J. Bishop please doesn't let my baby forget about me, please. Promise me that if nothing else." They assist me in getting in the car and I hear Bishop say,

"I promise."

A woman with her hair pulled into a tight ponytail, another woman with a short haircut and slim both dressed in uniform. She pushes my head down and drives off.

"Goldie sent us for you. My name is Meredith."

"My name is Melissa and we are now M& M murderers the Broads that snub low lives for money, hearts and kidneys."

"We all have the same shit happening some nigger betrayed us, somebody broke our heart and we all on the run. We have nothing to lose but our lives."

She was right it was nothing left and right at this moment I will never be able to hold my son a free woman. The only way I get my son back is join them. I will kill Bishop he planned this whole thing from the time of conception to take my baby. He has to die.

"Michelle, look in the trunk."

I cover my mouth and gasp. Richard's chest split open, M & M spilling out of his gut.

Mellissa claps her hand, raises the bloody fish hook.

"It is rules to being a part of us. Lesson 1, never let a snitch get away with running their mouth and betrayal of the sisterhood means death.

INSANITY AT ITS FINEST!

Lesson two, our brand is gut and stuff a motherfucker. We target inmates, correctional officers and child molesters. Lastly, always have M&M's handy they are good for stuffing a dead body and they taste so damn good. Whether you want to or not you are with us. Goldie pays well. We save the lives by giving their organs to those dying. Are you down? Sarge wanted to take over and I give her permission. "Gut them and stuff them. M & M sisters in effect."

INSANITY AT ITS FINEST!

Author's Note

Words hurt and beware of the soul you shatter with them.
–Tamyara Brown

God, you know the trials and tribulations I went through and yet, you saw fit give me grace and mercy. To bless my son Ruben with a new Kidney seven days before the book release. My heart is overjoyed and I love you.

To my lovely children Tallissa, Alisha, Alexis, Alice, Ruben and Isaiah. You are the wind beneath my wings.
My Grandchildren Jeveon, Jai, Trayvon & Raymere.
I love you so much

INSANITY AT ITS FINEST!

Thank you to those who have supported me in this journey. Beautiful souls encouraged me and pushed me to be my best. Your love and support is amazing. I decided to do something different. It is so many of you who make me a better person. So many have impacted my life and changed me for the better. I ask that we all stop judging other women because of the color of her skin. We have to stop belittling and breaking down one another.

Mary B. Morrison said, **"No matter how well you cook, clean, how well you sex him or how small or big you are. He will never see your worth unless you do."**

Love and weight will never have a waist size.

Today, I ask that you support these great organizations who go and above to enhance the lives of women.

INSANITY AT ITS FINEST!

Tamyara Brown

AUTHOR!

I Write To Clear My Mind.
Release My Sadness. Let go
of the Madness growing
inside of me. I write Most of
All to save my life and
others. Writing gives me
permission to write what I
fear saying.

www.tamluvs2write.com

Tamluvsto Write
Writing my way
into your hearts & minds

INSANITY AT ITS FINEST!

Our Curls INC

CANCER CAN'T TAKE OUR CURLS

A non profit organzation designed to provide free beauty, emotional & spiritual needs of women of color dealing with cancer

You Are.........

strong
Courageous

www. Ourcurlsinc.org

A Non-profit Organization designed to provide free wigs, emotional & spiritual needs for women of color

INSANITY AT ITS FINEST!

Tamyara Brown

Lanasha Rose Foundation empowers our youth to know their self-worth, self-discipline and living the best life possible.

Lanasha Rose

Foundation

www.imaniwisdom.com

Author, Blogger, Playwright & Poet

Pink Noire Publications

INSANITY AT ITS FINEST!

Tamyara Brown

Thank You, Mom

You've always gone above and
beyond. Working two jobs and raising
us and grandbabies. I want to thank
you for always giving all of us the best
of you. Especially Me. Your love
touches so many. I love you forever
and a day.
Dawn

THE WITNESS PROJECT®

LADIES! NO EXCUSES MAKE YOUR APPOINTMENT FOR YOUR YEARLY MAMMOGRAM!

If you need HELP scheduling a mammogram call the Witness Project 7168453383. Transportation services are available

INSANITY AT ITS FINEST!

Tamyara Brown

W A V E Buffalo, Inc

INSANITY AT ITS FINEST!

INSANITY AT ITS FINEST!

Wonderfully Created Works

Believing in me has nothing to do with those who don't believe in me, it's a self-love responsibility.
Mekha Nizum

@mekha.nizum   @msmekha

@1derfulmsmekha   Msmekhanizum

www.unequexpressions.com

J. SHANEE BYERS

INSANITY AT ITS FINEST!

BONUS SHORT STORY 1
Love, Lust & Lotto

By Tamyara Brown

The three L's will fuck you over all the time Love, Lust, and Lotto. Love is the fuckery these dumb broads believe in when they me   : so-called soul mate. They have the grand wedding, the honeymoon, buy the house, the car, the babies and the dog. Sounds like the perfect marriage and the best love story, right? Love blurs your commonsense because "your husband is perfect." Love puts on blinders because in reality you have dreamt of this man all your life. He pays the bills, mows the lawn and family vacations. He is educated and in your eyes his shit don't stink. So when he comes home late, or has business trips more frequently or sends you on vacation with your girls while he works ever so hard. You close your eyes to other possibilities of the inevitable he may have another chick on the side.

The sudden nights he doesn't make love to you anymore because he is tired. The whispers in the dark on the phone and finally when lust by the name of Becky shows up at your door with her belly sticking out letting you know Mister done share the magic

INSANITY AT ITS FINEST!

stick with another trick. Now for other broads they cry, they go and file for a divorce that is protocol. They break things, curse him out, and hire lawyers to get half of the money and possessions. Now in the new age smart men realize marriage is a business. So some of these broads sign on the dotted line because love said so. So not only are they blind now he has dumb you down to a basic bitch.

Now ladies don't go getting your damn panties in a bunch. Some of you know I am talking about your ass. Some of you are living the so- called perfect life and maybe just maybe you do have a Mister who is perfect. Yet, for the rest like me we have a person that has done us wrong and that is my situation. Love for me shut down my common sense but it didn't shut down my sight.

I love playing lotto scratching off those numbers. It is because with lotto it all about spending a dollar and in the process hoping it will make your dream come true. With lotto the odds are win or lose no in between. I lose more than I win with lotto and on this particular day I so happen to catch my love, Simona holding hands with the next man. I knew all along she was fucking with this dude and she was scratching me out of her life. She gets in the car I buy her and pulls off. I pick up another ticket and the numbers ironically reveal the month and date of her birthday. The phone rings and she sings,

"Hi love muffin. I missed you today." I pick my Afro,

INSANITY AT ITS FINEST!

put a toothpick in my mouth gnawing away the hurt I feel.

"Really, so Bae what did you do today?" I scratch off another number revealing a coin meaning I instantly win fifty dollars.

"I went to work and after that I made a run to the mall for a quick bite to eat." I scratch another and this time it is not a winner. My heart is pounding, my pressure is rising, and I snap the toothpick in half with my teeth.

"Did you go with anyone, Bae?" I rub my temples and close my eyes.

"No, just me, myself and I. Hurry home love muffin I bought this sexy outfit just for you."

"I'll be there in about fifteen minutes doing a lotto ticket run and a special dessert just for you."

I don't take kindly to being cheated on, I never have. I gave up on men after I strangled my husband to death twenty –years ago. He hit me and I killed him while he slept. The woman I described in the beginning is I, Goldie. I thought I was the shit to have a man who took care of home. Love, lust and lotto taught me all three are an illusion, a brief moment of satisfaction that clouds your judgement. Killing him released the real me a woman who is a lesbian, who loves to rock converses, flannel shirts, khaki pants and play lotto. I am also kill people for hire. I don't need to win millions my bank account is loaded with money. Back in the day I use to wear make-up, heels and dresses. I was a fake and a fraud being something I am not. I free myself the day I took his life.

I walk into the store buy twenty more lotto tickets, Liquid Drano and lighter fluid. I drive home and a tear is released. I don't cry and when I do it is dangerous. I realize as hard as I try to be a man I am still a woman. I pull up and her car is in the driveway. The cherry red Mercedes Benz I bought her for Christmas. I step out and grab the bags she opens the door greeting me with a hug and a kiss. I must admit she is fine ass woman. Her deep dark complexion, her full lips and African-Goddess braids dangling past her shoulder. My Nubian queen body is curvaceous, a fat ass that shakes when she walks, her tree trunk shaped legs and the fact she is bow-legged is the reason I lost my commonsense.

"Bae, I'm going to fix us a drink. You're usual with a special twist." I open the bottle and pour the Drano in a goblet. It sizzles and I sit in my seat. I pick my Afro and bite my bottom lip.

"I saw you with him today. And Bae please don't lie." She stutters, "I ... It... not... what you think, love muffin." I pull out the ticket and begin scratching loose change. The object is to get over a $1.00 and you win the prize in the box.

"If I get over a dollar I will let you live. Now if I get anything less you are going to die. I am going to make you drink that glass of Drano and then I am going to torture you until I am sleepy. You better hope Luck

INSANITY AT ITS FINEST!

be a lady tonight. Now know that the only reason I am giving you this chance is because I love you. Now it is clear you didn't love me enough because you allow lust to put you in this fucked up position. Stop shaking and start praying." She bites her nails and I scratch off one box at a time it is six in all. The first box reveals fifty cents, the second a penny, the third reveals a dime, the fourth reveals a penny, and the fifth reveals a nickel. She scratches off the final number and then the phone rings. She looks at the phone, she looks at Simona and then the number. Simona shaking, she urinates and falls kissing my thighs. The phone doesn't stop and she picks up the phone.

"Mommy, I need help. Please come help me." I throw the lotto ticket at her, push her to the floor, and kick her in the face. I pull out my gun and shoot her three times in the chest.

Like I said before those three L's will fuck you over all the time. Now it was time to save my daughter she needs me.

Death's Foot on My Shadow.

I stop at 7- eleven and I knew the moment I step out of the car and saw the dead pigeon lying on the ground the grim reaper was coming for me. I am not talking about the murder I just committed but karma was reeling her ugly head. Life is an echo and for my

sins they would eventually catch up to me. I walk in
and the second sign was all of my tickets I usually
purchase at the Lotto machine where gone. I bought
six tickets and none of them where a winner. Death
was hunt she was hungry for life and my time was up.
I'd lost love, I'd lost lotto and this scared me because
losing for me signified the end. I walk out the door
the man dressed in overalls covered in dirt, his hand
extended and he slurred each word, "hunt, can I
please have some change for food. Thank you hunty."
I dug into my pockets and handed him forty dollars.
He smile and the single tooth was dangling.

"Hunty, The Lord will bless even the wicked so she
will go out and do his will. Thank you." He handed
me a cross and limped away.
My cell flashed and his voice announce, "Teleka Mia
is safe."
"Thank you, William. I'm five minutes away."
I step into my truck and flying over my head was
black crows. It was hundreds of them flying in a
circular motion, the sound of their caws where angry
and white poop covered my truck. Death was
knocking on my door. The bitch was trying to get me.
I pulled off and several of the crows followed me. I
parked behind William Matter's Mercedes Benz. I
took several deep breaths and picked my Afro.
I went into the side entrance and William was sitting
in his leather lounge chair. His hair now had speaks of

INSANITY AT ITS FINEST!

gray, he'd cut off his Afro and now sported a fade, he grew a full beard and on his finger was a wedding band. I looked at the picture of him and his wife. He had changed but still the same William.

"William Matters what it do Bro ham?"
"Goldie, I'm blessed and highly favored."

William hated seeing me I was a reminder of his past life. A reminder that he is a dangerous man. He had taken many of lives for me back in the day. He turned over a new leaf to serve his community and The Lord. He wanted to redeem his life by doing well for others. In his eyes I could see that he still enjoy the adrenaline of ending a life.

"Where did you find her this time?"
He folded his hands on his belly and answered,

"In Niagara Falls back in the spot we normally find her. She is fed and cleaned up."
"I owe you one, William." He sat up and looked me in the eyes
"You owe me nothing. Iron sharpens Iron."
I looked over at the picture of his wife.
"Does she know?"
"There are no secrets in my marriage." He picked up the picture of her and kissed it.
"Would she ever snitch?"

INSANITY AT ITS FINEST!

"My wife would never utter a word. She is loyal to me and I can trust her with my life and secrets."
"You really love her?"
"Yes, she is the best part of me. Let me take you to your daughter."

William never went into detail about the woman he was married to. He open the door and his wife sat next to her. She was heavyset, her hair was braided and pulled into a ponytail. She sat the bowl down and William walked over and kissed her forehead.

"We'll give you some time alone." He took his wife by the hand and they walk out the room. Teleka eyes where sunken in, her cheeks where bruised, her once beautiful skin was now a grayish colored. She was only nineteen but life, drugs and sadness aged her.

"Mommy, I need help. I need help." She repeated over and over again.
"Let me help you then."
"Mommy, I want some candy to make it go away. To make the pain go away, please."

She shivered, she scratches her skin until it bleeds. The girl with everything gave it up for drugs and the streets. She lived in a beautiful home, lived with the best of everything money could afford. Love over the top but I never got the why would she fall in love with

INSANITY AT ITS FINEST!

drugs. It began when she was fourteen when she came home and I saw my little girl was dying inside. Her heart wasn't pure, her anger was so deep she began cutting off her hair and her wrists.

"No. What can I do to fix you baby?" She lay her head on my lap put her thumb in her mouth and she began to talk.

"Mommy remember Bishop Gerald Goode?"

"Yes." Anger began to fill up in me and my left eye twitch.

"William, told me to stay away from him. He told me he was dangerous. I didn't listen I just fell in love with him at fourteen. He started me on candy and then he gave me his venom. He gave me his sickness and then he stopped loving me. He stopped loving me like daddy stopped loving you."

Tears drenched my face, anger cause hives to break out on my skin. Living in this lie serving his church and his Idolized God. He was sticking his dick in my baby. He was raping my baby.

"He molested you."

She sucked on her thumb and pulled at her ear. She

wanted to pull him out of his grave and piss in his face.

"Did William know his father was doing this to you?"

"No, he didn't. He was his victim and so was his wife. Mommy, I need candy to forget."

She shook and vomited in my lap. I cleaned her up and I could see her rib cage. I could see the sores on her back and her hair falling out in my lap. She was dead already, her heart pumping but her soul was dead.
"Mommy, I love you so much. I want to get better. I need your help, please."
"I love you too and I promise to get you help." She sucked on her thumb and pulled at her ear. I kiss her forehead. She was my princess still. She was snoring and finally fell asleep. I stood and pulled out my magnum. 357 because William better speak fast.

I snatched the door open and walk towards William. He stood and didn't flinch. Tasiyana opened her mouth to scream and he covered it with his hand.

"Go to my office and close the door. It is just business." His hazel eyes turned orange. His lips twisted up and he watched his wife walk into the office and close the door.

INSANITY AT ITS FINEST!

"Did you fucking know your father raped my daughter?"
She studied his eyes because William almost always spoke the truth. He was not a liar even if it meant his death.

"No, I did not know. I warned her along with other children to stay away from him."

Her chest was heaving in and out. My gun still pointing to his face and he never blinked. I sniffle turn my head and swallow back my tears. He was dead and nothing more could be done but to save my daughter.

"She needs you and none of us can change the past. She is sick. I have a spot for her at Melrose clinic in Florida. They have a unit dedicated to H.I.V and drug addiction I will cover the cost."

"I don't know how to fix her, Yo!"

"No one can fix her but your daughter. She has a lot of hurt inside of her. The way I did but the Good Lord will."

"Don't throw your God in my face. God has nothing to do with bringing her back to healthy."

INSANITY AT ITS FINEST!

He has everything to do with saving souls. Don't use his name in vain your angry with him for no reason. The enemy is..."

I raise my hand and walk close towards him. He pulls out his gun and I sneer at him.

"Don't start preaching to me about redemption. I've seen you carve open a man face and dissect each of their body parts like a frog. I watched you Pastor Matters enjoy every murder you've committed. It's an urge that will never die. I don't give a fuck how much praying, or doing good or ministering souls the fact remains just like me you are a murderer."

His eyes water and he looked at the gun in his hands. He ran his fingers against the gun. He nodded and then he closed his eyes. He shuttered and released a sigh. He put the gun in his holster.

"He is a redeemer. I believe in my God. I just want to help Teleka. We both want to help her."

I heard the shatter of glass, the sound of shots as William and I ran to the room. William pulled out his gun and kicked open the door. Teleka's frail body was riddle with bullets as I drop to the floor. Sitting on the edge of her bed was a black crow who did a series of

INSANITY AT ITS FINEST!

long caws. I ran to her body cradle her into my arms and became fixated on the Initials FGV carved into her forehead. I disappointed her again. Left her side and my baby is gone. I glance at the windows and several crows appear all on the window sill. I gasp and the old man I gave the forty dollars was cover in blood. Death scent filled the air of her soul rotting, her mouth gaped open. I push on her chest trying to revive her. The grim reaper had collected her soul and claimed her as his. I rocked her into my breasts. I sung to her favorite lullaby as she empty her bladder on me. As she made her last bowel movement. The sirens, the police and the crows lined up singing death's lyrics.

I took several deep breath, my body numb but I could see her being put in a black body bag. I could hear them describing her wounds, her HIV status as they were dressed in full armor. William cradle his wife face into his chest as she cried. At least she knew I loved her. The detective walks towards me and he said,

"Any enemies?"
"Plenty of them."

I walked out the room and out the door. The black crow was resting on my truck. Death was chasing me, it was closer than I could imagine. It wanted my soul

INSANITY AT ITS FINEST!

because I rolled with Hell's Angels. I was evil and deadly. I was alone. I lost life and the pain was eating my entire soul. I couldn't cry as I followed the coroner's truck. I ran red lights because I didn't keep her safe in life. I fail her in life but in death I would find her killer.

I walked into the hallway of where I could hear the sounds of voices of the deceased. The walls where a dreary gray, the dingy white tiles squeaks with each step and the slamming of the doors of each drawer. She was lying on a table, her skin was the color of clay, her eyes wide open, dried tears and her face still stained with blood. It was my only child in a room of other dead people. The coroner bit into two jelly donuts while it oozed down his chin. My eyes became fixated on the bullet wound in her forehead, the initials FGV on her cheek. I grabbed my mouth, my chest pounding and my throat feeling clogged with salt water. FGV played the game the way I taught her. My baby was my pride and joy. I reach my hand to close her eyes and the man with the silver hair and jelly stain slapped my hand. He bit into the donut dripping the purple goo on her face. I snatched him by the collar and busted him in the face
"Have some damn respect for the dead. She is my daughter now clean her off right now.
I was trying to save her. I was trying and I failed her in life. I promise in her death I would find her killer.

INSANITY AT ITS FINEST!

FGV had motive I stopped loving her. She was the one I turned out and yet I could not see love in her eyes. I hated the way she abused her daughter every second she had. That broad was wicked. Her revenge was her signature to get me to notice I had scorned her.

I walk out of the building and the man I gave forty dollars to the man covered in black crows. He opened his mouth and began cawing a loud. His eyes turn black and disappear. One by one the birds disappear.

"Death's coming to get you."

I never feared a human being in my life but I feared her. She was a woman who lacked love. I feared that she loved me enough to kill. Love is more deadly than hate because it has a thin line. She had been deny by many men and then me. She attempted by sending flowers, candy, lotto tickets and converses. I return her love with no reasoning why. She took the only thing that would get a response out of me.

She took my princess and my instinct is to attack and kill. She wanted me to chase her because for so many years I had deny her my love and friendship. She needed to be the one who took my life. Love, Lust and Lotto go hand and hand. Tricia wanted me to

INSANITY AT ITS FINEST!

love her because I satisfy her lust and winning my love was the luck of the draw. This broad is psychotic and I was insane we were a concoction of that drink liquid cocaine with specks of gold. It was the type of lust that felt good but toxic to the body

I trembled at the fact of ever eating her yoni. I should have fear her the moment I saw have an orgasm over a dead body. Did this broad cum while my daughter was taking her last breath? I thought.

I could hear my daughter voice saying, "I love you so much Mommy. I need help." I was avoiding my tears. I was avoiding fucking pain cause that wench FGV took life away. She murder my baby. I was supposed to be mourning her death but instead I was ravage with anger. I am driving in a frenzy, black crows following me and I want to kill. I stop at a red light and there he was that man again. I pulled out my gun and shot him in the face three times.

"Death is chasing me but death caught your ass." I yell out the window and pull off.
It was no time for tears. Tears were for broads who show there weakness. I am in the business of death and revenge. Life is fucking echo and revenge is a girl's best friend. It was resting in my soul to kill this broad slowly. To torture her until I am sleepy. She won for a moment but I will win for a lifetime."

INSANITY AT ITS FINEST!

BONUS SHORT STORY #2

"Cash stay your head in the books and don't ever let pussy steal your power or dishonor family. Let no woman break this family apart." -Supreme

A woman was made for a man. She is his rib and the right woman can build a man up, help him to rule nations and she can also break down a man, rip apart his soul and steal his Kingdom. Onika Sin is a she - devil and angel in disguise. The way she is charming, sexual, deceiving and yet she slowly poisons your soul with the kiss of her lips. Sitting on top of my father's billboard is black crows. Successful entrepreneur, full time gangster and my father. Hundreds of them cover the naked tree. A group of crows are called a murder and for the past seven days seven people who I consider friends have died. The latest victim was only ten years old and my half - brother. He died because of me. He died because I allowed pussy to dishonor our family and a woman to tear our family apart. My secret hovers over my head like the crows flying in circles. I am marked for death and I am in love. Only a man crazy in love and lust would take foolish risks. Dead bodies, sirens, limbs, found in the Fort of Ferry and all because he wants his wife back. Supreme has fallen fool for Onika just I had. I know who the

INSANITY AT ITS FINEST!

murderer is but I have to honor the code of never snitching. Death before dishonor has always been what my father has instilled in us. I am guilty of every dead body. I am a murderer though I have never shot the bullet and my secret and my truth makes me an accessory to murder. I was never at the scene of the crime but easily my actions could get me tried, convicted and executed by the hands of my father. The scent of Gigi's restaurant signature candy yams and collards greens fills the air. The smell of Avenue's pizza, a Mercedes Benz pulling into Mandela's gas station playing, "no flex zone." The city surveillance by video cameras, the police station at the corner and yet no one has seen no crime committed.

All he wants is for his woman to come home. He can't and never will accept defeat. He will never digest the fact another man took from him. Gunshots rings in the air and a few minutes later the sound of sirens echo in the air. I want to spill my guts but the wrath of my father would mean death. No questions ask as to why. He is thirsty for revenge, blood on his hands mean nothing because venom pumps through his blood.

Money, my twin on the other hand is thirsty to be my father's successor. He about the life of crime and ruling with an iron fist. I study the law and Money finds a way to break it. He is crazy because he has no remorse and he doesn't fear death. He also knows my

INSANITY AT ITS FINEST!

truth and I will never reveal.

Money

I am the fucking King and I plan to rule my father's dynasty."

Today I had the opportunity to kill my father in cold blood. Instead I bitched up and let him take out my little brother. Our guns was pointed at one another's temples my sweat dripped on the tip of his barrel, heavy breaths and on the ground is my half-brother Terrance. His fragile body covered in bullet holes, blood dripping from his forehead. His blood on my Jordan's. My father killed his own son over fifty dollars and to send a message to his mother to come home.

" Money don't play Russian roulette with your life. I have no problem burying two sons in one day. Be smart drop the gun. "I pressed it against his skull and I applied pressure to the trigger. Supreme chest rose and the gold Jesus piece sparkled. My heart banged on my chest, I felt the weight of Terrence arm on my foot.

"He was a fucking kid Dad and you went too far. You kill your own son how insane are you?

He ran his tongue across his teeth and his nostrils flared. "He stole from me and I despise a thief. I raised him better and the little shit had the nerve to

INSANITY AT ITS FINEST!

tell me to suck his dick. I have permission to take him out of this world and to your answer your question there is now answer to the amount of insanity I have raging inside of me. Son, when a man steals something is the deepest violation."

I looked down and the scent of his death enters my nostrils and I feel the salty taste in my throat. I swallow it down. I watch his lifeless body jerk, see piss run down his leg and the smell of shit. As his last tear ran down his tear I realize every man cried his last tear. Maybe his tear was the pain of his father taking away his life or worst his older brother not preventing his demise.

I hold the trigger and I know in an instance that my life could be ended by the man who gave me his sperm to create me. He puts the gun down and his waist. He instructed his workers to dispose of the body. They move swiftly the same routine wrap of wrapping the lifeless body in plastic, lighter fluid pour on him, vinegar, salt and thrown into the incinerator.

"You letting a trick like Onika break down your mental state. You let her bring your castle and your business to gravel. In your age you slipping and tripping on her secretions. That is not the Supreme I know."

"She'll come home, worried and confused. She'll need my help and the death of our son will weigh

INSANITY AT ITS FINEST!

heavily and she'll move back home."

He was sick beyond the reason why. He was a lunatic with two heaps of insanity. He was a man without a conscious but yet enters True Bethel as a servant of the Lord. Darius and the rest of the world is oblivious to who he is really is.

Hours have pass by and Cash is typing away at some paper for school. We both have the same face, deep dimples, chocolate complexion, same haircut, tattoos and built like athletes. Only our parents can tell us apart. We've done some devilish shit to teachers. Cash is about the books and I am about power, money and respect. Both of us hold one another's secret.

"Dad is losing it over Onika. "Cash cuts his eye at me and rubs the back of his neck.

"I know and he has to accept she is gone."

"Dumb ass when have you ever know Dad to accept defeat? Your dumb ass better stop her vjayjay juice will have your ass shredded and grinded into hamburger meat."

"You think he knows?"

"If he knew I wouldn't be having this conversation with you. Cash no pussy isn't worth it."

"She loves me."

"Yeah okay whatever. All Onika know is how to be whore, suck dick, and fuck men over. She don't love you and she damn sure ain't feeling Dad. All I know is if he finds out you two better move to another country.

Strange Fruit
By Tamyara Brown

*"She is sin in a beautiful body named, Onika. Her long legs spread wide open, her fruit fuzzy like a peach ana her clit is pierced. Her pussy drenched with a nectar so thick, creamy and the scent of her is the aphrodisiac I crave for. I am addicted to her strange fruit. My father is addicted to her love, her beauty and that is the problem. Both of us guilty of indulging at different times. What is it about all three of us that drives her to want two sons and a father?" I enter with quick, long and strong strokes she arches her back, tears fall from her eyes, she speaks in her native languages of Yoruba and Dagbani and like a possessed woman she bucks each time I go deep in her yoni. She loves it and I know in my heart of all hearts she wants me and only me. It is what I allow my heart to believe."-
Cash*

How did it begin?

INSANITY AT ITS FINEST!

Cash

"Cash go deep, baby." She purrs
I pull her to the edge of the bed, push my length into her mouth. She licks her lips, smiles then looks at me and then my father's picture. The scent of the room is of cinnamon and vanilla candles. The flicker of the flame illuminates the act of indiscretion and sin against my father and her husband.   I push deeper into her mouth, she holds my hips, knees bent, and leaning on her tippy toes and like a professional she takes all of me without gagging. I hold her head and move faster as her jaws collapse around my lingam. My knees buckle, I lean my head back and let out a loud grunt.

She slides me from her mouth and I push her down, she spreads her legs in a V formation and I enter her an inch at a time. She squeals, she curses, and she shakes as I pull her into me. I am so deep into her yoni she begins to speak in her native tongues of Yoruba and Dagbani. She pulls out her hair and I can't help but wonder if she is imagining all three of us making congress with her. If she would want us to celebrate in her yoni, bathe her in our sperm. Sick, I know but for some reason this derange notion makes me cum hard.

INSANITY AT ITS FINEST!

I fall on top of her and all the times I've performed this act I've never kissed her lips. I stroke her head. She is sin. She is my father's wife but slowly I begin to love her. I begin to think I can make her mines. I create fantasies of healing her heart that she will divorce him and marry mesh sits up and rushes to the shower. I hear the water running, my jisms is bagged up in a condom. As taught by my father I set it on fire and flush it down the toilet.

"He'll be home soon. I need to wash the sheets, shower and...."

I cut her off and snatch the curtain open. Her deep brown skin glistens and the sweet smell of strawberries. Her weave hangs on her shoulder, now forming ringlets of curls and her thick lips still coated with my cream.

"Play like I wasn't all up in your yoni . Who do really want?"

"I want you but I am your father's wife. I have to honor our marriage vows." She lathers with the loofah

INSANITY AT ITS FINEST!

and the soap runs down her yoni.

"You are afraid to leave him?" She looks up at me and clicks her tongue.

"Yes. He will kill us both. What we are doing is wrong and we must stop."

" It is never wrong when I am fucking you in his bed. You don't complain when you're drinking my jism. Stay with him and be unhappy." I storm out of the bathroom and stop in my tracks as I see my twin brother Money stood outside his room door and his arms folded. He snorts.

"On some real shit she playing both of you. Onika is a whore and I can't believe Mr. 4.0 college man is being suck into her game."

I am staring at the identical look of me. We are different but the same. I pull in air and look in the sky.

INSANITY AT ITS FINEST!

"It is deeper than sex. She doesn't want him she wants me."

Money chuckles and asks,

"Are you shitting me, Brah?" Are you like seriously falling in love with this T.h.o.t? What the fuck is in her Vjay jay juice that makes yawl so stupid? You smarter than that, kid."

"Why can't there be a chance she actually loves me?" I hold my hand to my heart and
Money raises his eyebrow and smacks his forehead.

"She is our father's wife. This bitch is setting you up for major failure if you think she is going to take a bullet for you. You must want to die doing stupid shit like you doing. She only loves one person and that is herself. I'm scared for you because when he does find out he is going to rip your guts out through your ribs."

Dripping wet she steps out and stands in front of Money. She glares at him and he frowns at her.

INSANITY AT ITS FINEST!

"You don't know shit about me, Money. Real talk keep my name out your mouth. I can't stand your ass."

He rubs his neck, moves it side to side. He walks close to her and puts his finger in her face. Cash jumps in between the both of them.
"I know you more than you think. What you are is a whore and a filthy one at that. Those dudes running a train on you over on Box Street. You tricking in the fall and letting..."
She click her tongue and smiles.
"And don't forget me sucking you off every third Saturday years ago. Are you mad or nah, Money it isn't my pussy juice on your dick.

Money and Chase stared at one another. Truth was delivered by express mail. I slid to the floor and money ran his hand over his face.
"So Onika you're loving the crew. Is this your shit screwing family members?" I shoot a look at Onika who lowers her head and sucks her teeth.
"Like I said she a whore." Money screams out.
She walks in the room and locks the door. I was in a triangle of deception and how do we untangle the web I weaved?

"Cash, brah it was way before you and Dad." He pleads

INSANITY AT ITS FINEST!

"When was you gone tell me?" I slam my fist into the wall. "Seriously you can't be tripping over this? What you are doing playing in the devil's den? Onika is going to serve your ass to Dad for dinner. Yo, I'm telling you to get your mind right. Dad is crazy on a laxative, brah. She isn't worth your life and you damn sure can't wife her and live in the B-low."

Money

"Sex is one of the roots of all evil. It will make you insane, lose your mind and religion. Make you break commandments it will start wars, tear down empires and make a King become a pawn. One trick is tearing a family apart. We all are in danger from eating the devil's shepherd pie spiced with strange fruit. Only one of us will come out alive and that is me."- Money

I met Onika while chilling with my boys in Perry projects. I was young and everyone told me about the Super head of the pjs and like the rest of the dudes I wanted her lips on my dick. I will admit she was fine and so we started kicking it. The thing is I watched her in action. I knew from the start she wasn't about nothing but the streets. She and I only had sex once but after that it was all about her lips to my microphone. I learned a long time ago to never share your sperm with a whore.

A year ago

INSANITY AT ITS FINEST!

"Money, I want to have your baby."

She sat in between my legs and slob glisten her lips. I ran my hand through her matted weave. The dirty bedroom she lived in had clothes all over the floor, plates with dried food and mold. I pushed her away and zipped up my pants she erased the good feeling and what blew my mind was she actually thought she qualified to carry my seed.

"Come on Ma, you know better than to say some dumb shit like that. I don't share sperm. My sperm is reserved for my future wife. Don't ever disrespect me thinking you fit the description of being the mother of my child. Fuck outta here and just for that you no longer have permission to suck my nuts." I chuckle and walk towards the door.

She was loving the crew gaming mofos for their money. She lost respect the moment my man Lincoln caught her screwing some random white dude. She jumps up, slips on her pants and her shoes. She kicks my leg and I grit my teeth to honor the code never put my hands on a woman. She attempts to slap me and I grab her wrists.
"Now you know in twenty seconds or less I will have some of my goon chicks beat you bloody. I'll watch your ass get stomp out while eating a bag of hot Cheetos and put it on World Star hip hop. Now do

INSANITY AT ITS FINEST!

you really want to go there and put your hands on me?"

She is breathing hard, her eyes are flooded with tears. I know in my heart someone stole her soul. Some creep did her dirty, put out in the streets and promised to love her and then break her heart. You don't just jump up and decide to become a whore some dude introduced her to that lifestyle. She experienced a horrible life and maybe I should care but I don't.

"You gone get yours, Money. Always playing me dirty and using me. I hate you and every man who exists." She screams.

"We all gotta die, boo. You came at me disrespectful talking shit about me making a baby with you. Don't you have a son your Mama raising and you want to bring another child in the world you can't raise? Get your life right and even then you wouldn't qualify to be the mother of my child. You know your position every third Saturday is to suck me off and in return for your services I get your hair did and buy you a steak sub. You mad at yourself for accepting the terms and conditions un befitting of even a Thot. Now get your ass gone and find some self-respect." I wave her off and she breaks down in tears. I throw the money on the table and sling the steak sub on the floor.Just like that I thought Onika was gone from my life until one day at dinner Dad brings her home

INSANITY AT ITS FINEST!

announcing their engagement. I am 100 percent sure her plan is to divide and conquer. Her plan is to tear our family to shreds by deceit. Isn't that how you ruin a family? Isn't it how you devalue a man? I peep game and Onika is stepping on the wrong shoes.

The Devil's Den
By Tamyara Brown

The last time I was in this den was in 2002. I closed this place off because I gave up the life of killing someone because of the change of the season and of course owing me my money. I would take off a body part, shred their faces and feed them to Rocco my Pitbull. The den is cold, dark, wet and smells like pig's shit. I take a deep breath and a single tear rolls down my face. Never in a million years could someone convince me that I would have to torture my son for sins against his father. I lean against the wall and take a deep breath before taking another step down the stairs. His mother's voice echoes in my ear "don't kill my son." I don't think I can honor request the disrespect and deceit is too deep. The wounds cause a child produce by seed, a mofo I fed, clothed and put through college. I will never let that slip and slide away. The crime of fucking my wife in my bed is death plain and simple. Love and hate don't mix. One overpowers the other. I light a cigar and blow out rings of smoke hoping it will evaporate my pain. I pull

INSANITY AT ITS FINEST!

the knife out of it sleeve the teeth of it is so sharp it cuts my finger. Blood is supposed to be thicker than water and family should equal loyalty. It is what I instilled in my sons over the years. Nothing or no one came above them. So it is eating at my flesh for him to screw her in my house but more than that my bed. That shit is something I can never wrap my head around.

I open the door and he is sitting on the floor. His eyes are swollen, he flinches as I sit in front of him. I wipe his tears with my bloody handkerchief and like a good father console his son walking the green mile of death.

"Why?"

He looks away and mumbles,

"Love."

"What?"

"I love her."

My face becomes hot, a salty taste in mouth and my teeth baring into my lips. I pick up the clump of dog shit and smash it in his face.

INSANITY AT ITS FINEST!

Tamyara Brown

"You still disrespecting me about my wife. You have the audacity to profess your love about my woman that college education made you lose all your common sense." I scream.

"She loves me it is why she left you." He laughs as the shit drips off his face.

"Jake hold his hand down on the fucking table. "

"You got it, Supreme." Jake grabs his hand and slams it on the table. Cash squirms but can't break Jake's strong hold on him.

My muscles begin quivering, I could feel my heart pounding in my ears. Tears sting my face because his words burn in my heart. No apology or apololie just straight 100 proof disrespect.

"Dad, I.... Don't....please.... Don't."

He smells like death, his blood smell like fresh

INSANITY AT ITS FINEST!

raspberries and urine. I slam the ridges of the blade down on his fingers. His thumb falls on the table and his pinky follows. His screams causes my heart to ache. His blood splatters on Onika's face she shrieks and slides to the floor. I take the knife and wipe it off on her shirt.

""Onika, you know it is your fault that I had to amputate my son's fingers. Betrayal cost him his a day of torture in the Devil's den. Was it worth it, honey? Cash, now I don't have my star bowler on the league and a damn shame too because I made good money off the team. All cause you want to slip your pole in my wife's hole. I want you to know son it hurts me more than you ever know to be put in this position of whether to let you suffer or take your life. Oh what a tangled web you weave when we put pussy over family loyalty."

He moaned as Doc sew up his numbs. His eyes rolled in the back of his head. He blurts out,

"I wasn't the only one."

"I'm sure you aren't the only one. Onika likes to fuck.

INSANITY AT ITS FINEST!

She likes to suck dick, but my issue is you, my flesh and blood dicking my wife down. You know that is some nasty shit to fuck the same woman as your father."

"Your wife is my woman. She is in love with me. Ahhhh..." Doc pierce his skin with the needle in and out, no pain relievers, and no relief for the slick lip son of my boasting about my wife's love for him. "

"Cash, You my boy have fucked yourself in the ass with six dildos and no lube. You betray me and what I can't wrap my head around is why. I could have gotten you any woman <u>you</u> wanted but you chose mine. You know how insane I am. Me, cutting your fingers off is just the beginning, my boy. I am far from finish but first I need an explanation. Stop crying, please. You didn't share one tear while fucking her in my bed how disrespectful. Now from the top and speak clearly I taught you to never mumble. Tell me why you would betray your father? Onika doll, be a dear wife and pour your husband a glass of Cîroc. Now that boy P.Diddy did that with this Vodka."

"Sheeeee..... Doesn't love you. Tell him the truth, baby. Puleese." He stuttered. I spit in his face and run

INSANITY AT ITS FINEST!

the knife across his head removing part of his Afro. "You don't know shit about love, boy. You don't have stinking clue what it feels like. I love you from the moment my seed spill in your mother's womb and produced you. I love you unconditionally and even at this waking moment my heart is in overflow of love for you." I place my hand on my head and one tear drops. I exhale and hit my chest. I cut my eye at Onika preparing my drink. I study her body language, the way her hands are shaking, the twitch of her left eye and the click of her tongue.

She grabs the bottle with a blue dot and pours it into the glass. She lights my cigar. She kisses me on the cheek. I love her dirty drawers, the sweet taste of her juices that flow from her punanni. Love and lust often confuses us McDaniel's men. Cash was smitten with his first sexual encounter. Poor boy lost in the illusion of lust. Maybe I too was trap in the list of Onika Sin.

"I love your father. I always have and I always will." She smirks blows me a kiss of death. She raises her eyebrow.

She hands me the drink. I look in the glass as it fizzes, the scent of it burns my nose.

INSANITY AT ITS FINEST!

Something in my core told me to not drink the Vodka. It look cloudy, it smell like lighter fluid and I say,

"Honey boo babe, have a drink?"

" I... I.... Don't drink Cîroc." She stutters and her lip trembles.

"Did you do the naughty, naughty thing and try to poison me?"

"No...my...love."

Deceit and betrayal was running in wolf packs trying to devour Supreme. I take the bottle and smash it over her head. She falls to the floor. I take the heel of my shoe and step on her face. Her eye pop out of her socket.

"Baby boo bear see what you made Supreme do. See

INSANITY AT ITS FINEST!

how crazy you made me. All I wanted to do was love you. All I desire to do was care for you. I love...."

The sound of the gun shots echo in the air. All of the air in my lungs escape through the wound in my throat. I stumbled three steps forward and the room is spinning. Doc is slumped over, Rocko is dead and Onika is barely alive. I slump to the floor and when I look up Money is standing over me.

I reach for him and he kicks my hand away. I hear music, I see a light and I struggle for life.

"I am my brother's keeper and you can rot in your devil's den. I told you sooner than later I be the King."

I hope you enjoyed the bonus short stories please be sure to stop by Website.

www.tamluvs2write.com

INSANITY AT ITS FINEST!

Tamyara Brown

Please Sign Up For My Email List

http://eepurl.com/buo-xH

Follow Me on Social Media

Facebook

Twitter

Instagram

INSANITY AT ITS FINEST!

INSANITY AT ITS FINEST!

www.ingramcontent.com/pod-product-compliance
Lightning Source LLC
Chambersburg PA
CBHW051941090426
42741CB00008B/1230